The Lavender Palette

David Martin

to Peter —
I hope you enjoy the book!

David

The Lavender Palette

GAY CULTURE AND THE ART OF WASHINGTON STATE

David F. Martin

CASCADIA ART MUSEUM

Contents

Foreword

Five years ago, when Cascadia Art Museum was just an idea, I reached out to my friend David Martin to ask if he would be interested in curating our exhibitions . . . on a volunteer basis. Even though I'd known David for thirty years, this was a big ask to curate five galleries for five shows per year for free.

David, of course, was passionate about our mission to celebrate the lives and work of Northwest regional artists. He was instrumental in my learning about these artists, especially those who remain largely unknown despite their undeniable talent. My excitement about these discoveries inspired me to gather a volunteer board and establish Cascadia Art Museum so that others could discover these hidden treasures and take pride in the rich artistic heritage of our region.

David moved to Seattle in 1986 with his partner, Dominic Zambito, and has since become the preeminent authority on artists who were living in Washington State from the mid-nineteenth through twentieth centuries. David and Dominic's gallery in the Capitol Hill neighborhood of Seattle was evidence of the relationships they had built with artists who had been neglected by local art and museum authorities, who chose to focus on European or Japanese art. Even Seattleites thought that little good came from this region; to find talent, stubborn curators thought they had to look overseas or to the East.

David found a dedicated group of collectors who were committed to ensuring that the legacies of these artists—and the works themselves—were not forgotten to history. He was *thrilled* that Cascadia Art Museum would present an art history that included the work of women and minority artists who made substantial contributions to the Northwest's cultural identity.

He agreed to volunteer as Cascadia's curator for the museum's first two years—with one condition. The museum would allow him to put on a show he's always wanted to do, the idea for which several other museums in the country had refused. David wanted to curate an exhibition presenting the work of gay and lesbian artists who lived in Washington State in the mid-nineteenth through twentieth centuries to illustrate their significant influence on what would become the artistic legacy for which the Pacific Northwest region is now known.

Maybe the idea of presenting an exhibition featuring solely gay and lesbian artists seemed too controversial for some museums and arts institutions—after all, the US Supreme Court only declared same-sex marriage legal in all fifty states in 2015, a very recent memory for many of us. However, our board members trusted David, so we agreed to support his idea for this show.

Fast-forward to 2020, and *The Lavender Palette: Gay Culture and the Art of Washington State* became the most visited show in Cascadia Art Museum's history. In essence, the show was emblematic of David's life's work: building relationships with artists and their families, meticulously researching their history, and conversing with them for countless hours. This book is the product of David's effort spent learning about the triumphs and tragedies experienced by these artists. It will become evident to the reader how much care David has put into the research that fills these pages. *The Lavender Palette* is truly a labor of love.

David is no longer a volunteer, but still serves as the museum's curator. We will remember this important show fondly, and we are proud to present *The Lavender Palette* catalog to commemorate the exhibition and to add to the historical literature of our region so that the significant legacy of these artists will be celebrated for generations to come.

Lindsey Echelbarger
Board President

Donors to the Publication

Special thanks to The Helen Johnston Foundation for their sponsorship of *The Lavender Palette*.

Sharon Archer & Don Eklund
Ashford Creek Gallery/Museum
Linda and Peter Capell
Paul Carlson & Shawn-Marie Hanson
James Carraway
David L. Chapman
Michael Cunningham
John & Penn Curran
Diane Divelbess and Grethe
    Cammermeyer
Sue Dixon
Wayne T. Dodge, MD & Lawrence
    Kreisman
Virginia Dunthorne
Lindsey & Carolyn Echelbarger
Douglas Foster & Leo Dunbar
Glenn Fox
Donald Hall
Kenny Harsch & Yuri Miyata
Lucy Hart
Randy & Jan Holbrook

Greg Kucera
Stephen Lacy
Flora Ling & Paul Sturm
Julie Long
Peter Mack
Ed Marquand
Margaret Minnick
Barbara Pomeroy
Norma Prichard
Herb & Lucy Pruzan
Garratt Richardson
Nancy Rothwell
Rose-Marie & Bill Seawall
Thomas & Dorothy Sheehan
Milton & Sherry Smrstik
Michael Stewart
Mel & Leena Sturman
Grady West
Iyla Winterfeldt
Virginia Wright

Preface

David F. Martin

For the past thirty years, I have completed extensive research on women and minority artists of the Northwest. While I am proud of the substantial contributions my publications have made, both regionally and internationally, I have never before been given the opportunity to document the impact made by regional gay and lesbian artists in the early part of the twentieth century.

Being gay myself, I have long been concerned about the downplaying or ignoring of the sexual and emotional orientations of historic gay artists, which I have witnessed over the past several decades by both regional and national institutions. With this publication and exhibition, I felt that my own life experience might add some insight that would assist in a greater understanding by the general public.

I selected the title *The Lavender Palette: Gay Culture and the Art of Washington State* to cover two aspects of this project. The first was to amend the formerly pejorative use of the colors lavender and purple in association with homosexuality, as signs of weakness and frivolity. The second was to establish the effect these artists had in defining a regional aesthetic that still remains to this day. Washington State is arguably the only region in the country whose artistic identity stemmed originally and predominantly from the work of gay artists.

A particularly difficult problem in researching homosexual artists from the early twentieth century is that most of them had no children. After their deaths, the surviving relatives, if any, were often embarrassed about the artists' personal histories and destroyed the archival materials and the art that related to this aspect of their lives. Luckily, that has not always been the case in this state.

For this exhibition and publication, I have included only artists whose sexual and emotional orientations I was able to definitively document. In some cases, I knew them personally or know their families or close friends.

Some of the artists in this study are already well known and have been the subjects of multiple exhibitions and books. With this in mind, I did not concentrate on these bigger "name" artists and instead favored those lesser-known individuals who are worthy of rediscovery. I am also attempting to reveal a more human quality to those artists who have been summarily assigned into a "Northwest School" style of painting. The presentation of these artists as mystics has been completely overblown and is largely inaccurate, in my opinion. It is true that many of them shared interests in non-Western religions and philosophies, but I am positing that their sexual orientation had the most profound effect on their work and lives. Reading archival materials on the two best-known figures, Mark Tobey and Morris Graves, I realized that they struggled with unflattering human qualities such as jealousy, overinflated egos, greed, and selfishness, qualities that most of us grapple with throughout our lives. Rather than framing the artists represented here as mystics or visionaries, I chose to stress their human qualities that, in the end, make their lives and art more interesting and relatable.

Since this is a study of artists from an earlier period, I have refrained from using current terms and abbreviations in my essays and biographies. If you had called any of these artists "queer" in their lifetime, it would have been taken as a painful personal attack. I also found no evidence of any of these artists having any type of gender dysphoria that would define them by current terms such as transgender.

This project grew out of a lecture I gave at the Tacoma Art Museum in 2013. TAM has been in the vanguard of Northwest museums in including representation of LGBTQ+ artists.

Acknowledgments

There are several people I have to thank for making such substantial contributions to this project. The first is David L. Chapman, who wrote a wonderful essay covering his original documentation on regional male photography of this period. David and his husband, David Berryman, also took on the heroic task of locating and assembling the grid of mug shots of men who were arrested under the state's sodomy laws. These photographs are a chilling reminder of what most of these artists were born into.

A heartfelt thank-you and big hug to this book's designer, Phil Kovacevich, who is always a joy to work with and makes every one of our publications a work of art in its own right. Thank you to Nick Allison for his thoughtful editing, and to Carrie Wicks for her careful proofreading.

This project would not have happened without the support of our board and staff, who recognized the need for such an exhibition and accompanying publication. Their foresight made this the first documentation of its kind in the country and hopefully not the last. I owe a great deal of debt to founder and board director Lindsey Echelbarger and his wife, Carolyn; and to board members Stephen Clifton, Gary Faigin, Phil Grad, Hylton Hard, John Impert, Gwendolyn Johnson, Kristina Kulik, Julie Long, Susan Loreen, Marni Muir, Janette Turner, Ruthanne Weaver, and Richard V. West.

I thank our extraordinary executive director, Leigh Ann Gilmer, for her commitment to this project and her important contributions in so many ways. Thank you to our director of operations, Nate Hegerberg, whose patient problem-solving and creativity added so much to this exhibition and makes my life so much easier.

Several people were extraordinarily kind and patient with my endless inquiries. They include Sheila Farr, Jeffrey Ochsner, Maria Pascualy, Merch and Alice Pease, Paden and Norma Prichard, and these family members of the artists: Gretchen Harsch, Kenny Harsch, Peggy Hartzell, Deborah Healy, Layne Schneider, Steven and Brucie Schneider, Patsy Snyder, Thula Weisel, and Jonathan Wright. I'm also appreciative of assistance from artist family members John Butler, Arlis Flores, Patricia and Mike Green, Rhonda Healy, and Nathan Hinds.

I want to remember several close friends who would have been very proud of this publication and over the years shared many personal stories that contributed to my understanding of the lives of these artists or their own histories: Bud McBride and Richard Schneider, Mary Randlett, Robert M. Shields, Ramona Solberg, Lorene Spencer, Jan Thompson, and Virginia Weisel.

Other individuals who have been exceptionally helpful include Philip L. Brown; Jill Bullitt; Mikell Callahan; William Coniff; Ron Endlich; Edward Field; Dr. Alvin Friedman-Kien and Ryo Toyonaga; Ulrich and Stella Fritzsche; Tod Gangler and Abby Inpanbutr of Art & Soul Studio, Seattle; Rick Johnson of Ashford Creek Pottery and Museum, Ashford, Washington; Lawrence Kreisman and Wayne Dodge; Greg Kucera; Peter Mack; Ann Matsudaira; Michael McQuiston; Lawrence and Judi Mroczek; Michael and Danielle Mroczek; Jane Orleman; Jerry Paulukonis; Robert and Shaké Sarkis; Tom and Dorothy Sheehan; Adrien Sina, curator and performance-art historian, Paris; Terry Sparks; Mel and Leena Sturman; Thomas Reynolds Gallery, San Francisco; and Dr. Robert Wilkus and John Shadoff.

Many thanks to these professional colleagues:

Heather Horn Johnson, Gallery Manager, CWU
     Sarah Spurgeon Gallery
Carlos Pelley, Library and Archives
     Paraprofessional, Archives & Special
     Collections, James E. Brooks Library
Central Washington University, Ellensburg, WA

Jeffrey Karl Ochsner, Professor and Senior Advisor
     for Policy and Procedures
College of Built Environments, University of
     Washington, Seattle

Bridget Nowlin, Visual Arts Librarian
Cornish College of the Arts, Seattle

Susan Grinols, Director of Photo Services and
     Imaging
De Young Museum / Legion of Honor, Fine Arts
     Museums of San Francisco

Thomas Hamm, Professor of History and Director
     of Special Collections
Earlham College, Richmond, IN

Josephine Yaba Camarillo, Library Director
Regina Tipton-Llamas, Reference Supervisor and
     Local Historian
Ellensburg Public Library, Ellensburg, WA

Cory Gooch, Head of Collections
Nives Mestrovic, Assistant Registrar
Frye Art Museum, Seattle

Pauline Sugino, Registrar
Honolulu Museum of Art, Honolulu

Danielle Knapp, McCosh Curator
Jordan Schnitzer Museum of Art, University of
     Oregon, Eugene

Elizabeth Arbaugh, Director
Jan Parker
Mason County Historical Society, Shelton, WA

Robert Yarber
Morris Graves Foundation, Fortuna, CA

Kristin Halunen, Registrar
Museum of History & Industry, Seattle

Andrea Ko, Associate Registrar
Newark Museum

Alexander Till, Assistant Registrar
Pennsylvania Academy of the Fine Arts,
     Philadelphia

Shaun Dingwerth, Executive Director
Lance Crow, Education Director
Richmond Art Museum, Richmond, IN

Ashley Mead, Assistant Registrar—Rights and
     Reproductions
Seattle Art Museum

Jade D'Addario, Digital Projects Librarian, Special
Collections
The Seattle Public Library, Seattle

Riche Sorensen, Rights and Reproductions
Coordinator
Stephanie Stebich, Margaret and Terry Stent
Director, Renwick Gallery
Smithsonian American Art Museum,
Washington, DC

Craig Schiffert, Rights and Reproductions
Coordinator
Smithsonian Archives of American Art,
Washington, DC

Stacey Sherman, Media Specialist
Tara Laver, Archivist
The Spencer Art Reference Library at the Nelson-
Atkins Museum of Art, Kansas City, MO

Margaret Bullock, Interim Chief Curator, Curator of
Collections and Special Exhibitions
Rock Hushka, Director of Northwest Special
Projects
Tacoma Art Museum, Tacoma, WA

Beverly Choltco-Devlin, Manager, Main Library
Spencer Bowman, Archivist/Librarian
Tacoma Public Library, Tacoma, WA

David McCartney, CA, University Archivist,
Department of Special Collections and
University Archives
The University of Iowa Libraries, Iowa City

Lauren Goss, MLIS, Reference and Research
Services Archivist
Randy Sullivan
University of Oregon Libraries, University of
Oregon, Eugene

Nicolette Bromberg, Visual Materials Curator
Susan Fitch, MLIS, Visual Materials
Rebecca Baker, Invoice Clerk / Reproduction and
Publishing Services Coordinator
Kristin Kinsey, Digital and Visual Materials
Specialist
University of Washington Libraries Special
Collections, Seattle

Lynette Miller, Head of Collections
Eileen Price, Reference Archivist
Washington State Historical Society, Tacoma, WA

Micky Wolfson, Lea Nickless, Larry Wiggins, Frank
Luca, Jon Mogul, Amy Silverman, and Kim
Bergen
Wolfsonian–Florida International University,
Miami Beach

Michael M. Siebol, Curator of Collections
Yakima Valley Museum, Yakima, WA

David Whaples, Visual Resources Coordinator
Yale University Art Gallery, New Haven

Finally, as always, many thanks to my life partner of forty years, Dominic Zambito, for his constant support and assistance, and without whom I would have never been able to research and complete this or all my other projects. *Ti amo.*

The Lavender Palette

David F. Martin

*Giving my life to the study of what makes men and women, I cannot but feel
that it is not half so sad for a boy to be even killed in college as it is for the
influence in college in any way to trend toward a type of 'dude' or 'sissy,' young
men who are hardly worth killing.*

THOMAS F. KANE
President of the University of Washington, 1905[1]

When President Kane of the University of Washington wrote these words published in the *Seattle Daily Times*, they were not the first disparaging remarks aimed
against homosexuals to appear in the local press. There were regularly printed
attacks targeting gays, designed to instill fear in the general public as well as dimin-
ishing the self-worth of anyone who held those inclinations. Just a few months
earlier, under the headline "Prof. Padelford Declares That Lady Teachers Are
Too Gushing and Lack Necessary Degree of Sanity," the anonymous writer of the
article couldn't resist taking a swipe at the UW professor Padelford, declaring that
"he is rather effeminate looking himself."[2]

President Kane's diatribe was written only ten years after Oscar Wilde had
been arrested and charged with twenty-five counts of gross indecency, reflecting the
fact that homosexuality was illegal in England at that time. His nearly three-year
sentence to hard labor in prison took its toll on the brilliant writer, and he died
three years after his release at the age of forty-five as an exile in France. The United
States' sodomy laws, aimed at nonprocreative sexual activities even between con-
senting adults, were particularly threatening to homosexuals, as the government
tried to control their natural instincts.

This anti-homosexual crusade was not restricted to Washington State; it was
part of an initial "Lavender Scare" that swept across the world like a purple plague
at the turn of the twentieth century and would rear its ugly head again during the
McCarthy era of post–World War II America.

During this unenlightened period, female teachers, both gay and straight,
were especially suspect and were often blamed for causing any perceived threats to
traditional gender roles, especially where males were concerned. In a 1908 *Seattle
Daily Times* article, the writer quotes an unnamed "education expert" speaking at
a convention in Des Moines, Iowa, and insists that the person's statements would
be equally true in Seattle: "The cause of 'woman's rights' has gone so far that poor

man doesn't have a chance and he applies his remarks to the conditions of our public schools. These, he says, are becoming 'effeminized.' He says that the teachers were all women and what few principals of schools are men are becoming 'sissies.' A training which can make a 'sissy' out of a man who is supposed to be an example to our growing boys, is not exactly calculated to make very stalwart men out of their pupils. We don't care to have our boys made into little women any more than we care to have our girls made into brazen imitations of sissified men."

As early as 1897, articles appeared in the *Times* reinforcing standard gender roles and the potential trouble that could come from straying outside what was expected and acceptable: "The woman who rides a bicycle must, first of all, be mannish—not alone in costume and in the attitude she assumes on her wheel, but in desire and feeling. And the woman who is mannish has ceased to be womanly. Nature flouts the effeminate man, but he is a better thing than the mannish woman! He does less harm."[3]

That same year, a Seattle resident left for San Francisco to expand her musical training and would become a twentieth-century symbol of homosexual independence

—even if she did have to leave the country to do so. Alice B. Toklas (1877–1967) was the daughter of Ferdinand Toklas, a partner in the Seattle clothing store Toklas, Singerman & Co., whose financial success allowed his daughter to pursue a career in music and the arts.

Alice had been well known in Seattle as a piano instructor and concert artist and attended the University of Washington. When she traveled to Paris in 1907, she met writer Gertrude Stein (1874–1946). They fell in love and together became internationally known cultural figures for the remainder of their lives, never denying their relationship and often displaying their gender nonconformity.[4]

In 1903 the *Seattle Daily Times*, to keep up the barrage of hatred against homosexuals and to legitimize their bias by quoting a higher authority, printed a single small column with the following succinct statement for all their readers to see: "Worse and

Fig. 1. A 1903 Toklas, Singerman & Co. store advertisement in the *Seattle Daily Times*, November 11, 1903, page 9 Courtesy of The Seattle Public Library

Fig. 2. This illustration in the *Seattle Daily Times* on November 18, 1906, instructed readers in how to read personality characteristics by observing individual hand gestures. "In figure 6 we have the 'Miss Nancy' who walks with a mincing gait, with left arm held between the chest and abdomen, hand devitalized and held loosely, the right hand often brought to the face, held loosely, flourishing in the air or swayed gently as he walks. The upper body is held erect and steady as if supported by corsets. This person is affable, polite and agreeable, and full of tact, but hypersensitive and 'finicky,' and very effeminate in action, often painfully so, besides caring more for the appearance of dress than for the strength of masculinity, and often worthless through the aberration of discarded imagination and affections." Courtesy of The Seattle Public Library

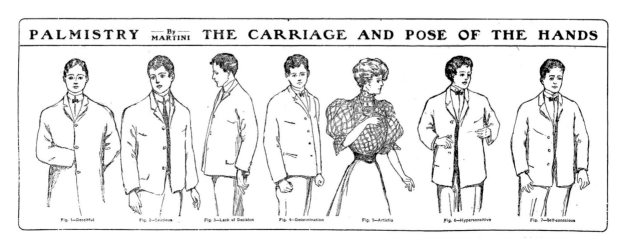

PALMISTRY By MARTINI THE CARRIAGE AND POSE OF THE HANDS

Fig. 1—Deceitful   Fig. 2—Cautious   Fig. 3—Lack of Decision   Fig. 4—Determination   Fig. 5—Artistic   Fig. 6—Hypersensitive   Fig. 7—Self-conscious

Fig. 3. "How we Westerners despise a sissy—But it's different in the Orient." This news photograph depicts a leading *onnagata*, Ichikawa Danjūrō X, Japan's leading actor, as "Lady of Kasuga." Over it was the heading "Gentlemen Actresses Who Delight Japan" in a featured article in the *Seattle Daily Times,* September 25, 1910. Courtesy of The Seattle Public Library

Fig. 4. Strauss Peyton Studios *Portrait of Julian Eltinge,* 1913 Gelatin silver print 10 x 8 in. Private collection

More of It—If there is anything more pitiful than an effeminate man it is a masculine woman —New York Press."

Affluent homosexuals like Toklas were able to maintain successful and productive lives. She and Stein moved to Paris, where gay people were accepted and even celebrated, especially in the arts. But for gay people in Washington State, especially in rural areas, it was a different story. If you were not independently wealthy, you lived in constant fear of exposure. There were numerous looming threats, such as losing your job and income, expulsion from your family and friends, being arrested or, worse, being the victim of violence and murder, neither of which was uncommon. This drove many gay people into secret lives, having unfulfilling relationships with the opposite sex, and being trapped in "lavender marriages" to appease their families and societal demands.

Although homosexuals, especially effeminate men, couldn't be tolerated in everyday life, they were allowed to entertain the general public. Northwest audiences welcomed with open arms female impersonators such as Julian Eltinge (1881–1941), who first performed in Seattle in 1909. That same year, the city was attracting national attention through the Alaska-Yukon-Pacific Exposition (AYPE). Perhaps the local public was becoming more sophisticated because of the fair; or, conceivably, a female impersonator supplied another human oddity to observe, as was the case with the fair's Philippine Igorot Village, whose residents were basically confined in a human zoo for spectators to gawk at as savage primitives.

In any case, female impersonators were now becoming part of the local cultural scene. Eltinge was a hit and performed in the region over the next two decades. He was soon followed by others. At that time, performers like Eltinge were considered artists and, hard as it is to believe, masters of illusion. It is likely that their homosexuality was never even considered by some of their fans. These proto–drag queens would often make up stories for the press about wives or girlfriends, or they stressed their masculine athletic abilities to mitigate their feminine behavior and to make straight audiences less uncomfortable.

As Seattle grew, so did the city's cultural opportunities. Art institutions began forming, including Nellie Cornish's legendary school, which was established by 1914. Besides music, Cornish had a deep interest in promoting modern dance in the region. The great ballerina Anna Pavlova had appeared several times in Seattle since 1910, as had Ruth St. Denis and her closeted gay husband, Ted Shawn.

On November 5, 1916, the *Seattle Sunday Times* posted a very interesting and somewhat enlightened (for the time) feature article titled "Are American Men Ashamed to Be Graceful?," written by three of the leading male dancers of the period: Andreas Pavley, Ted Shawn, and Vaslav Nijinsky. All three men were gay or bisexual, and Pavley and Nijinsky led tragic lives.

Nijinsky, who suffered from mental illness, was trapped in the middle of a vicious emotional battle between his wife, Romola, and his lover, the dance impresario Serge Diaghilev. His career came to an abrupt end after initial displays of genius, and he spent the majority of his life in a psychiatric institution. Pavley, a member of Pavlova's troupe, succumbed to threats and blackmail and ended his life in 1932 by jumping out of his sixteenth-story hotel window.[5] In January 1917, just two months after this article was published, Nijinsky performed with the Ballet Russe at Seattle's Moore Theatre. The program included *Le Spectre de la Rose*, *Scheherazade*, and *Les Sylphides*. By the end of the year, his brilliant career had ended.

In Washington State, the dramatic arts were just starting to develop at this time as well. Seattle-born actor and director Guthrie McClintic (1893–1961) started his impressive career here in the teens, guided by his Lincoln High School teacher Rose Glass. His close friend Harold Harshman was an actor as well as a writer, and they collaborated on local productions. They befriended the Annie Moran Crow family of Seattle and Orcas Island, who became benefactors.

The Crow sisters, Etta, Norah, and Jean, were well-known local classical musicians in the early twentieth century. They formed a string trio at the turn of the century, and for a few years their piano accompanist was Nellie Cornish. Louise

Fig. 5. *Seattle Sunday Times* article, November 5, 1916
Courtesy of The Seattle Public Library

Fig. 6. From left: artist Louise Crow, actor Harold Harshman, musician Jean Crow, and actor Guthrie McClintic, at the Moran estate, Orcas Island, circa 1915
Private collection

Fig. 7. Guthrie McClintic
in drag at the Moran
estate, Orcas Island,
circa 1915
Private collection

Fig. 8. Harold Harshman
with Guthrie McClintic in
drag at the Moran estate,
Orcas Island, circa 1915
Private collection

Crow became one of Seattle's most successful early artists and was an instructor at
the Cornish School during the 1920s and early '30s. The family had open-minded
attitudes toward homosexuality because Jean was a lesbian; later in life she ran the
family's Rosario Resort, sporting a man's haircut and masculine attire.

McClintic eventually left for the East Coast and became a giant of the New
York theater. He had two lavender marriages, first with actress Estelle Winwood
and later with the "First Lady of the Theater," Katharine Cornell, who was also a
lesbian. McClintic went on to be one of the greatest and most successful producer-
directors in the history of American theater, his aesthetic having been shaped in
his hometown of Seattle.[6]

The visual arts in Washington State had been on a steady rise since the AYPE
in 1909. J. Edgar Forkner (1867–1945), a watercolor specialist from Indiana, visited
relatives in the Northwest and held his first Seattle exhibition in 1910, while he was
living in Chicago. Within two years, he moved permanently to Seattle and established himself as a leading painter and teacher whose influence lasted for decades.
Forkner specialized in sensitive, atmospheric watercolor landscapes and floral still
lifes, as well as marine subjects painted on the local docks. He turned to oil painting in the early 1920s. Forkner was Seattle's most prominent art instructor outside
the university systems. His shy, effeminate personality often made him the target of
bullying, although his position as one of the city's most capable artists earned him
the respect of everyone in the arts community.[7]

One supportive friend was the handsome young (and gay) artist Orre Nelson
Nobles (1894–1967), who made this diary entry on June 21, 1917, insinuating
Forkner's romantic interest in him: "Visited the Fine Arts Society rooms and there
met Mr. Edgar Forkner. We chinned and chatted and gossiped about the exhibition
and the artists. Of course I should visit him, et cetera and take an apartment in
Chicago with him, etc."

Female impersonators continued to be popular in the Northwest during the
1920s. Besides Julian Eltinge, another popular performer was the internationally

known Karyl Norman (George Francis Peduzzi, 1897–1947), who made many successful appearances in Seattle. Several of these performers—like Norman, who billed himself as the "Creole Fashion Plate" even though he was from Baltimore—appeared on the cover of the leading cultural magazine of the region, the *Town Crier*, illustrating their local popularity.

While drag performers attracted the masses, more serious and innovative artistic performances were being conducted at the school of Nellie Centennial Cornish, or "Miss Aunt Nellie," as she was called because of her materteral attitude toward her students and faculty. Cornish's own sexual orientation is unknown. She was never romantically linked to anyone and never married, preferring the company of gay and lesbian performers and friends.

Cornish sought out the best teachers she could find, as nothing was too good for her students. Her first department head for music and associate director of the school was pianist Franz Boyd Wells (1877–1929). A gay man from New York and Chicago with an outstanding musical career, he became one of the guiding forces in the formation of the school's curriculum. On his recommendation, Nellie hired his niece, Mary Ann Wells (1894–1971), who would become a major figure in Seattle's dance history. She founded Cornish's Dance Department in 1916 and remained there for seven years until the school's dire financial situation caused her to open her own studio, which operated until 1958.

Nellie Cornish had known a young drama student, George Brown, who had left Seattle to seek his fame and fortune in New York's Greenwich Village after attending her school. Following several unsuccessful attempts to establish a career, he returned to Seattle in 1921, bringing with him his friend Mark Tobey (1890–1976), whose career was also faltering. Tobey had very little experience when Cornish took a chance on him, giving him a teaching job at the school in the children's art department. The attractive and charismatic young man fared better as an actor at first and starred in several of the school's productions while assisting with stage and costume designs.[8]

Fig. 9a. J. Edgar Forkner, circa 1900, cropped from a larger image of artists from the Richmond Group Esther Griffin White Collection, Friends Collection, Earlham College Archives, Richmond, IN

Fig. 9b. J. Edgar Forkner (1867–1945) *Land and Water*, undated Oil on canvas 20 x 24 in. Collection of Richmond Art Museum, Richmond, VA, gift of the Hoosier Salon, Richmond Art Museum sixtieth-anniversary gift, 1958

Fig. 9c. Sheet music for
"Midnight Rose," as sung
by Karyl Norman, the
"Creole Fashion Plate,"
1923
Private collection
Karyl Norman was the
stage name of George
Francis Peduzzi, a leading
female impersonator
who appeared regularly
in Seattle in the 1920s.
Notice the inset photo of
Peduzzi with a cigarette in
a masculine pose to offset
his female persona.

Fig. 10. The *Town Crier*,
September 9, 1922, with
cover girl Karyl Norman.
Courtesy of The Seattle
Public Library

Fig. 11. The *Town Crier*,
September 15, 1923, with
cover girl Julian Eltinge
Courtesy of The Seattle
Public Library

Fig. 12. The *Town Crier*,
July 30, 1921; special
edition dedicated entirely
to the Cornish School
Courtesy of The Seattle
Public Library

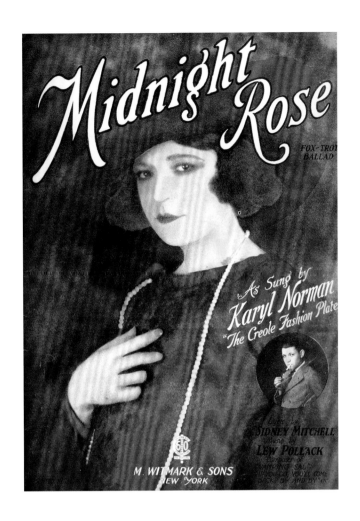

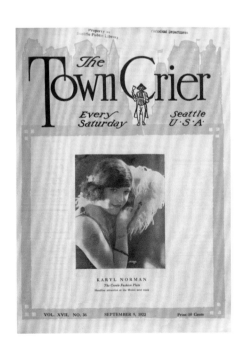

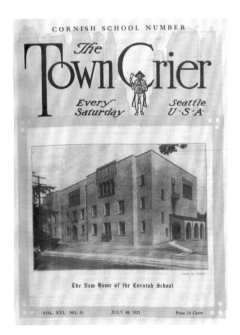

Fig. 13. Mark Tobey
(1890–1976)
Costume sketch for
unknown Cornish produc-
tion, circa 1922
Black crayon on paper
14½ x 10¼ in.
Courtesy of the archives
of the Cornish College of
the Arts Library, gift of the
Burton and Florence Bean
James Estate

Fig. 14. Mark Tobey
(1890–1976)
Costume sketch for
unknown Cornish produc-
tion, circa 1922
Black crayon on paper
14½ x 10¼ in.
Courtesy of the archives
of the Cornish College of
the Arts Library, gift of the
Burton and Florence Bean
James Estate

Fig. 15. Wayne Albee
(1882–1937)
Mark Tobey acting in the
Cornish production of
John Galsworthy's Joy,
circa 1924
Gelatin silver print
Courtesy of the archives
of the Cornish College of
the Arts Library, gift of the
Burton and Florence Bean
James Estate

In 1928 another brilliant young gay man moved to Seattle, this time from San Francisco. Lionel L. Pries (1897–1968) arrived to join a former classmate in developing an architectural firm. Besides establishing his architectural career, he accepted a position at the University of Washington's Department of Architecture, where he would become one of the most influential instructors over the next several decades.

Pries's talents were not restricted to architecture. He was one of the region's finest watercolorists as well. In 1931–32 he served as director of the Art Institute of Seattle, where he established friendships and relationships with some of the leading painters of the region. He would continue to exhibit his paintings in the Northwest Annuals when the art institute merged with the new Seattle Art Museum in 1933.

Pries played an important role in the careers of several of his students who became prominent architects. These included Paul H. Kirk, Victor Steinbrueck (who later assisted in the design of the city's iconic Space Needle), and Minoru Yamasaki, who designed the World Trade Center towers in New York in 1964.

Pries's reputation as a leading force in the region's cultural community was rewarded in 1946 when the Seattle Art Museum honored him with a solo

Fig. 16. Mark Tobey
(1890–1976)
Stage scene, 1930
Lithograph on paper
13½ x 16¼ in.
Seattle Art Museum,
gift of the Marshall and
Helen Hatch Collection,
in honor of the seventy-
fifth anniversary of the
museum
2009.52.73
Photograph by Elizabeth
Mann

(bottom left)
Fig. 17. Mark Tobey
(1890–1976)
Paul McCoole, 1929
Conté crayon on paper
24 x 18⅜ in. (sight)
Seattle Art Museum,
bequest of Mrs. Thomas D.
Stimson, 63.105
Photograph by Paul
Macapia

(bottom right)
Fig. 18. Mark Tobey (top)
with artist Olaf Anderson,
painting a mural panel
for the Seattle Fine Arts
Mardi Gras ball, *Seattle
Post-Intelligencer* article,
February 13, 1928
Seattle Fine Arts Society
scrapbook, courtesy of
The Seattle Public Library

exhibition of his watercolors. By midcentury, Pries had left his substantial imprint on modern architecture in the Northwest. He incorporated Native American design elements into some of his projects, influenced by his friendships with Delbert McBride and University of Washington anthropologist Erna Gunther.

In 1958 the country was back in the throes of the "Lavender Scare," led by the federal government and fueled by despicable figures such as J. Edgar Hoover and Roy Cohn (both of whom were gay themselves) and Senator Joseph McCarthy, whose parallel smear campaign of the anti-Communist "Red Scare" also ruined the lives of thousands of American citizens. That year Pries became a victim of the witch hunt. He was arrested in a vice sting while visiting Los Angeles, and upon his return to Seattle, lost his position at the university. The school apparently hadn't progressed very far since Professor Kane's vituperative remarks some fifty years earlier.

Pries's stature descended from pillar of the community to persona non grata, even among some of his former friends and faculty members. Many of the gay faculty in the art department went deep into the closet for fear of losing their livelihoods. Luckily, Pries had a few devoted students who didn't judge their professor and sympathized with his situation. They hired him as a drafter, and as demeaning as this was, it at least gave him an income after losing all the benefits he would have accrued from the university had he not been arrested.

Fig. 19. Lionel H. Pries, 1929–30
From *Washington Alumnus*, December 1931; University of Washington Libraries, Special Collections, UW14755

In 2007, Pries's reputation was finally reinstated through the efforts of several local historians, especially Professor Jeffrey Karl Ochsner, whose superb book *Lionel H. Pries, Architect, Artist, Educator: From Arts and Crafts to Modern Architecture* offered a welcomed mea culpa on behalf of the university, and to the institution's credit, illustrated the progress made in the fifty years after Pries was dismissed.[9]

Although he was not an architect, Orre Nobles designed and created one of the most interesting regional buildings of the 1920s, Olympus Manor, located in the idyllic setting of Hood Canal, on Washington State's Kitsap Peninsula.

The multitalented Nobles had attended Pratt Institute in Brooklyn in the early 1920s and, while there, began designing the manor after his parents had purchased a large tract of land to develop along the water. Nobles and his family created an artistic oasis there, which attracted creative individuals in all disciplines of the arts. By 1924 it had become a gathering place for musicians, visual artists, theater folks, and progressive individuals seeking a respite from mainstream society. Once the manor was established, Nobles became an art instructor at Seattle's

Fig. 24. Lionel H. Pries
(1897–1968)
Keystone Bunker, Mukilteo,
circa 1935
Watercolor on paper
16 x 21 in.
Private collection

Fig. 25. Lionel H. Pries
(1897–1968)
Untitled (La Push,
Washington), c. 1940
Watercolor on paper
16½ x 20¾ in.
Private collection

Fig. 25a. Lionel H. Pries
(1897–1968)
Dining-room table that
Pries decorated with ink
and pigments to simulate
wood inlay, 1943
44½ x 89½ in.
University of Washington
Libraries Special
Collections, gift of Sandra
Lynn Perkins and Jeffrey
Karl Ochsner
Photograph by Kaz
Tsuruta, 2005

The table bears a quote
from John Ruskin: "That
virtue of originality that
men so strain after is not
newness as they vainly
think; It is only genuine-
ness; It all depends on this
single glorious faculty of
getting to the spring of
things and working out
from it."

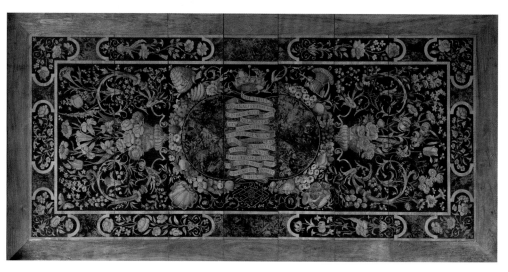

Ballard High School and on weekends ran the programs at Olympus Manor, often engaging his students in the process.

From an early age, Nobles was an adventurous spirit and followed his wanderlust wherever he was able to forge a path. He did not, however, have the resources to travel to Paris like his financially secure friends Mac Harshberger and Thomas Handforth of Tacoma, to indulge in that city's extraordinary cultural and artistic institutions. While Nobles was still in college, Harshberger and Handforth followed the advice of Seattle artist John Davidson Butler, the leading painter in Seattle since the previous decade. Butler had moved to France following service in World War I and encouraged his young acolytes to follow suit. Butler, even before leaving for Europe, had been highly influenced by the English illustrator Aubrey Beardsley, and Butler's drawings were often seen in regional publications. Both Handforth and Harshberger adapted the Beardsley style as filtered through Butler.

In Paris the two younger men were free to express their interest in homoerotic imagery. Harshberger created an extremely daring series of erotic watercolors in Paris (see pages 158–59) while simultaneously painting decorative watercolors of beautiful women wearing haute couture designs (see fig. 39). Handforth created highly acclaimed figurative and landscape etchings but also privately produced drawings of male erotica. Harshberger and Handforth's erotic and sexual imagery was likely derived not from personal experience but from the pornographic art photography of Wilhelm von Gloeden and Guglielmo Plüschow (see fig. 40).

Harshberger, who had a life partner named Holland Robinson, did not have the same restless spirit (and libido) as Handforth and Nobles. As early as 1917, Nobles traveled to various ports, including some in China, working on a tramp steamer. He was likely struck with the free (or at least indifferent) attitudes toward homosexuality in China and areas of North Africa at the time.

Published materials on homosexuality were practically nonexistent until the 1885 translation of *One Thousand and One Nights* (often called *The Arabian Nights*) by British explorer and writer Sir Richard Burton (1821–1890). His "Terminal Essay" in volume 10 of the collection asserted that male homosexuality was prevalent in an area of the southern latitudes and he equated same-sex intimacy and pederasty within the same rubric. His "Sotadic Zone" theory postulated that homosexuality was based on geography, economics, and climate rather than being a variation in human sexual expression.

Nonetheless, when his writings reached the Western world, they began drawing homosexuals, especially artistic and scholarly ones, to his ascribed areas.[10]

Nobles returned to China in 1927 and again in 1929, this time bringing along with him a handsome young Seattle friend named John Dean. The nature of their relationship has not been established but appears likely to have been an intimate one.

On this trip, Nobles was able to use his artistic talents to his advantage when he was hired by the Fette-Li Company as master designer for their rug manufacturing business. A Washington State artist was now making an imprint on international design (see figs. 41–44). By the summer of 1931, Thomas Handforth arrived in China, sponsored by a Guggenheim Fellowship. He met up with Nobles and Dean in Peking, and they traveled and worked together. In a June 7, 1931, letter from Handforth to his mother, he stated, "As always happens, everywhere I go I at once fell under the protection of welcoming friends . . . and most surprising of all, your old friend Orre Nobles who has been living here for the past eleven

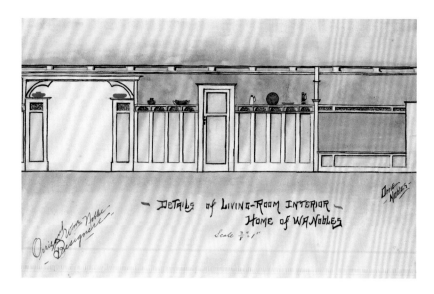

Fig. 30. Orre Nobles in the music room at Olympus Manor, circa 1925
Turner Photo, University of Washington Libraries, Special Collections, Orre Nobles Photograph Collection, UW 22254z

Fig. 31. Invitation for the Music Hall opening at Olympus Manor, circa 1922
Block print with hand coloring
University of Washington Libraries, Special Collections, Erna Tilley Papers, UW 40135

Fig. 32. Olympus Manor "Yuletide Greetings," circa 1922
Block print with hand coloring
University of Washington Libraries, Special Collections, Erna Tilley Papers, UW 40136

Fig. 33. Olympus Manor greeting card, circa 1922
Block print with hand coloring
University of Washington Libraries, Special Collections, Erna Tilley Papers, UW 40134

Fig. 34. Olympus Manor advertising card, circa 1925
Collection of the Mason County Historical Society, Shelton, Washington

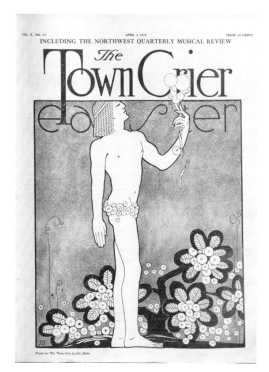

(top left)
Fig. 35. Orre Nobles
conducting a drawing
session at Olympus
Manor, circa 1925
University of Washington
Libraries, Special
Collections, Orre Nobles
Photograph Collection,
UW 23399z

(top right)
Fig. 36. Orre Nobles at
the entrance to Olympus
Manor, ca. 1925
Private collection

(bottom left)
Fig. 37. The *Town Crier*
Easter edition with cover
by John Butler, April 3,
1915
Courtesy of The Seattle
Public Library

(bottom right)
Fig. 38. Mac Harshberger
(1901–1975)
Untitled, circa 1922
Ink on paper
14 x 11¼ in.
Collection of John Impert

Fig. 39. Mac Harshberger
(1901–1975)
Couture fashion design,
Paris, March 10, 1923
Graphite and watercolor
on paper
19 x 13¼ in. (sheet size)
Thomas Reynolds Gallery,
San Francisco

Fig. 40. Thomas
Handforth (1897–1948)
Untitled, circa 1921
Graphite on paper
9 x 11¼ in.
Private collection
Former collection of James
Baldwin

months—(he has a house with another chap from Seattle) and has been doing rug designs for one of the best rug concerns here. He has also been buying up all sorts of curios, having jewelry made, and going on all sorts of exploring expeditions into Mongolia, etc. He is shipping all his treasures to Seattle where he himself is going soon to sell them for a fortune—yesterday we went out to the edge of the Western Hills spending hours exploring the enormous pleasure grounds of the Dowager's Summer Palace."

While the United States was mired in an economic depression, these resourceful young men from Washington State were generating successful businesses that allowed them to continue their travels and work without financial stress. Their sexuality, which initiated the need for travel, actually became an asset and not a hindrance, providing important social contacts and involving no wives or children to be responsible for. Nobles began planning a series of cruises to various ports based out of Seattle. His ebullient personality and firsthand knowledge of the destinations made him a popular guide. He would continue his "odyssies" until 1937, allowing him to travel along with his wealthy clientele while maintaining his teaching responsibilities at Seattle's Ballard High School. Handforth also continued to work in China, developing a new technique with lithography and disseminating his prints throughout the world (see fig. 55). The two men would remain friends for the rest of their lives.

Back in Washington State, while the Depression was wreaking havoc on the local economy, many visual artists were fortunate to have President Roosevelt's New Deal programs, such as the Works Progress Administration (WPA), to allow them to survive and continue their work. The initial phase of the program, called PWAP (Public Works of Art Project), began in late 1933, rescuing several talented artists from abandoning their artistic pursuits.

The Cornish School, which was still functioning, also provided work for local and national visiting instructors. One of them, dancer Martha Graham, gave classes at Cornish in 1933. She had been performing in Seattle and elsewhere

(top left)
Fig. 41. Orre Nelson
Nobles (1894–1967)
The Great Wall, China,
1927
Private collection

(top right)
Fig. 42. Orre Nobles
in front of the Fette-Li
Company, Peking, 1930
Collection of the Mason
County Historical Society,
Shelton, WA

(center left)
Fig. 43. Orre Nobles's
business card as designer
for the Fette-Li Company,
1930
Martin-Zambito Archive

(center right)
Fig. 43a. Orre Nobles (left)
and John Dean in China,
1930
Collection of the Mason
County Historical Society,
Shelton, WA

(bottom)
Fig. 44. Orre Nelson
Nobles (1894–1967)
Rug designed for the
Fette-Li Company, Peking,
circa 1930
Northwest landscape motif
10 x 8 feet
Collection of Tom and
Dorothy Sheehan

Fig. 45. From left: Père Conrad, Orre Nobles, and Thomas Handforth at the Catholic mission in Jehol, China, 1931
Laurence Sickman Papers, Nelson-Atkins Museum of Art Archives, Kansas City, Missouri, MSS 001

Fig. 46. Thomas Handforth (left) and Orre Nobles at the dowager's summer palace, Peking, 1931
Laurence Sickman Papers, Nelson-Atkins Museum of Art Archives, Kansas City, Missouri, MSS 001, NAMAA

Fig. 47. Thomas Handforth (far left) and Orre Nobles (far right) aboard a riverboat on a four-day journey that originated in Jehol, China, summer 1931
Laurence Sickman Papers, Nelson-Atkins Museum of Art Archives, Kansas City, Missouri, MSS 001, NAMAA

in Washington State since 1920 and was well known for her innovative choreography. Through the school she met Mark Tobey, with whom she formed a lifelong friendship. He created a series of nude studies of the dancers in her class at Cornish using simple gestural lines in the manner of Jean Cocteau and other European artists connected with dance (see fig. 58). In 1937, Graham gave a successful performance at Seattle's Moore Theatre. It was attended by several local artists, including Malcolm Roberts, who produced several dance-related images, obviously inspired by Graham, for his hand-colored lithographs under the auspices of the WPA (see fig. 59).[11]

That same year, another local artist associated with the WPA in Washington State, Edmond James Fitzgerald (1912–1989), created an interesting watercolor of two of his friends, artist Jule Kullberg and her life partner, Orlena Harsch, at their cabin on Whidbey Island (see fig. 60). The lesbian couple were close to the sensitive young man, who, although not gay, formed a lifelong bond with the women that continued through his twenty-six-year career in the US Navy, including his service during World War II. This watercolor depicts an extremely rare subject for a regional painting of the period.

Watercolor and water-based paints such as gouache and tempera were the mediums preferred by local artists, especially gay painters. Besides the aforementioned Edgar Forkner, another important watercolor instructor in Seattle during this period was Raymond Hill (1891–1980), who was originally from Massachusetts. He attended the Rhode Island School of Design, and his first paintings were exhibited in 1914 at the Providence Art Club when he was twenty-three. This was followed by participation in the Society of Independent Artists exhibitions in New York City a few years later. His first solo exhibition was at the Homestead Gallery of Provincetown, Massachusetts, in 1919, then a mecca for gay artists. Before

Fig. 48. Orre Nobles, China, 1931 (detail) Collection of the Mason County Historical Society, Shelton, WA

Fig. 49. Orre Nobles (standing, left), John Dean (foreground left with white bandanna and flower next to his ear), and Thomas Handforth (center foreground) with village residents, China, 1931 Collection of the Mason County Historical Society, Shelton, WA

Fig. 50. John Dean (left) and Orre Nobles posing by a touring car in China, 1931; the car's sign originally read "Central Asiatic Expedition" but was covered by Nobles's comical rearrangement Collection of the Mason County Historical Society, Shelton, WA

(opposite, top)
Fig. 51. Thomas Handforth sunbathing, China, summer 1932 Laurence Sickman Papers, Nelson-Atkins Museum of Art Archives, Kansas City, Missouri, MSS 001, NAMAA

"We (Laurence Sickman and I) worried about nothing, ran around the hill sides stark naked, sketched, bathed, slept like lizards on the hot smooth rocks, and read long evenings into (what do you guess?) Leonardo and the Italian Renaissance!"

Fig. 52. Thomas Handforth sunbathing, China, summer 1932 Laurence Sickman Papers, Nelson-Atkins Museum of Art Archives, Kansas City, Missouri, MSS 001, NAMAA

Fig. 53. Advertising card
for Orre Nobles Oriental
Odyssey Tour, circa 1935
Collection of the Mason
County Historical Society,
Shelton, WA

Fig. 54. Advertising card
for Orre Nobles Oriental
Odyssey Tour, 1936
Collection of Thomas H.
Wake

Fig. 55. Thomas Handforth
(1897–1948)
Child Actors Dancing, also
titled *Strolling Players*,
1933–34
Lithograph on paper, trial
proof, edition of two
14 x 13 in.
Translation of Chinese
text:
"Printed by the Minghua
bureau of lithography at
Xiheyan, Qianmen"
Translation provided by
Spencer Bowman
Collection of the Tacoma
Public Library

"Two young boys are giv
ing a street performance.
The one on the right is
dressed as a woman with
short stilts to simulate
bound feet." —Thomas
Handforth

Fig. 56. Frank Pixley, Orre
Nobles, and Thomas
Handforth, Union, WA,
1944
Scan from color slide
Collection of Peggy
Hartzell

Fig. 57. Irwin Caplan
(1919–2007)
Illustration for article
"The Feminine Touch"
*University of Washington
Columns*, October 1939,
pages 14–15
Ink on paper
8½ x 27½ in.
Private collection

Fig. 58. Mark Tobey
(1890–1976)
Sketch of a nude dancer
from Martha Graham's
classes at Cornish, 1933
Crayon and graphite on
paper
29¾ x 20 in.
University of Washington
Libraries Special
Collections, Mark Tobey
Papers, UW 40137

Fig. 59. Malcolm Roberts
(1913–1990)
May Dance, 1937
Lithograph with water-
color on paper
13⅝ x 10 in.
Works Progress
Administration
Allocation, 1943.504.037
David Owsley Museum of
Art, Ball State University,
Muncie, IN

Fig. 60. Edmond James
Fitzgerald (1912–1989)
*Jule and Orlena at Their
Whidbey Island Cabin*, 1937
Watercolor on paper
10½ x 14½ in.
Collection of Gretchen
Harsch

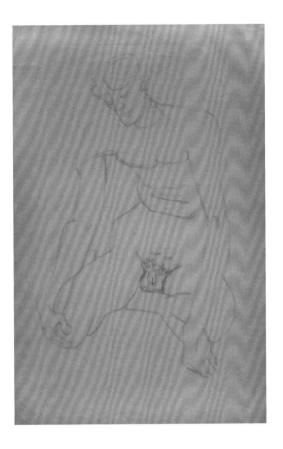

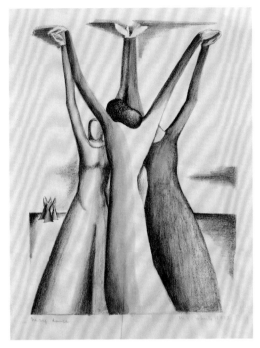

Fig. 61. Ray Hill (1891–1980)
Washed Up, circa 1935
Oil on canvas
19½ x 29½ in.
Collection of Lindsey and
Carolyn Echelbarger

moving to Seattle in 1927, he studied at New York University and the California School of Fine Arts, and spent time in Spain, France, Italy, and later Tahiti.

Beginning in 1927, Hill taught painting at the University of Washington's School of Art, where he befriended Lionel Pries. The two men became traveling companions and painting partners, sometimes producing watercolors that are almost indiscernible as to authorship. Whether they shared an intimate relationship is not known, but it is highly probable. Like most of his academic contemporaries at the university, Hill kept his personal life a secret. His sexuality and preference for nude sunbathing at Seattle's hidden gay beaches were known only to his closest friends.[12]

One of Hill's students at the UW in the late 1930s was a young painter and cartoonist named Irwin Caplan. Although he was not gay himself, Caplan had many gay friends, as well as a keen eye for satire and observation of human behavior. One of his illustrations for *Columns*, the university's humor magazine, depicts five men, ranging in appearance from the androgynous to the butch, on a stage with discerning and befuddled older men gawking in appreciation.

Caplan's lighthearted caricatures were likely not intentionally vicious from his own point of view, but several of his gay teachers would definitely not have approved. A few years later, Caplan also produced a watercolor of an imaginary street scene in Seattle in a magic realist style. The painting depicts the denizens of an anonymous neighborhood populated by society's outcasts: prostitutes and pimps, johns, handicapped people, and a trio of young gay men on bicycles cruising each other in a circular staring observation. The inclusion of gay cruising in a regional painting of that period is very rare, and although the implication of homosexuality as a lurid activity restricted to the bad part of town is problematic by today's standards, it nonetheless provides evidence of the existence of gays within the region's social structure.

Caplan was too young to participate in the WPA art programs in Washington State. However, another local young man on a similar career path was able to receive assistance since his slightly greater age made him eligible for public funding. Hans (or Hannes) Bok (a pseudonym for Wayne Francis Woodard, 1914–1964) was a precocious talent in Seattle and one of the youngest of the regional WPA

Fig. 62a. Ray Hill
(1891–1980)
Shore—Puget Sound, 1947
Watercolor on paper
15⅛ x 22 in.
Seattle Art Museum,
Eugene Fuller Memorial
Collection, 48.210

Fig. 62b. Irwin Caplan
(1919–2007)
Untitled, circa 1950
Watercolor on paper
20½ x 24½ in.
Private collection

Fig. 63. Hans Bok
(1914–1964)
Untitled (fisherman), circa
1940
Ink on paper
7½ x 6 in.
Private collection

Fig. 64. Hans Bok
(1914–1964)
Mandala, 1960
Block print on unryu paper
11¼ x 11¼ in.
Private collection

artists. Although active in Seattle only intermittently during the 1930s, he met and befriended some of the successful gay artists in the region, as well as sympathetic straight talents like artist Fay Chong, who remained a lifelong friend.

Bok, Thomas Handforth, and Richard Bennett were among several Northwest gay artists who gained fame as illustrators. However, Bok found his niche in science fiction, becoming one of the country's finest and most influential illustrators in that genre. He moved to New York for career opportunities, and although he became successful in his field, he could never lift himself out of poverty. He died of a heart attack at age forty-nine, purportedly the result of improper nutrition and starvation.[13]

Local artists not on the WPA found other ways of making a living. Several gay artists became art instructors, despite the persistent threat of being fired hanging over their heads. Sarah Spurgeon (1903–1985) had been active in Iowa and worked with gay artist Grant Wood before moving to Ellensburg, Washington, in 1939 to join the art faculty at Central Washington College (now University). After a brief leave of absence to work for Boeing Aircraft Company in Seattle, she became involved with Women Painters of Washington, where she befriended like-minded female art professionals and assisted in raising funds for the war effort through the organization's art auction in June 1945 at the Frederick & Nelson department store. When she returned to Ellensburg, she became a beloved instructor, influencing generations of students until her retirement in 1971. Before she died, Central Washington University honored her by naming their art exhibition space the Sarah Spurgeon Gallery.

In Seattle, gay men and women also provided art instruction outside the university systems. Jule Kullberg dedicated her life to teaching at the expense of pursuing a national career in fine arts. Although she painted and exhibited locally, her influence as a teacher was also substantial. Some of her students went on to become major figures in the region, including Fay Chong, Morris Graves, Leo

Fig. 65. *Finishing Touches*, 1955
Sarah Spurgeon depicted in 1954, working on her mural for the Gingko Petrified Forest Museum, Vantage, Washington
Courtesy of Archives and Special Collections, Central Washington University, Ellensburg, WA

Fig. 66. Jule Kullberg teaching, circa 1950
Collection of Gretchen Harsch

Kenney, Neil Meitzler, and Malcolm Roberts.[14] Kullberg never hid her relationship with her life partner, Orlena Harsch, so she naturally would have been a trusted figure among her gay students.

Leon Derbyshire (1896–1981) was another influential local teacher who was rightfully counted among the more prominent local artists in the early twentieth century. He began his studies locally under Fokko Tadama at the short-lived Seattle Art Students League and also worked as a window dresser for the Bon Marché department store. After serving in the army during World War I, he continued his art studies at the Pennsylvania Academy under Hugh Breckenridge and Daniel Garber and traveled to Europe in 1930 for further studies. By 1938 he was given a solo exhibition at the Seattle Art Museum, and in 1939 he traveled to Paris to study with André Lhote. Derbyshire was a quiet and reserved man who kept his homosexuality private except to close friends and lived all his life with his parents, caring for his widowed mother after the death of his father. Like Edgar Forkner, he suffered at the hands of bullies because of his reserved personality and mild-mannered demeanor.[15]

Without children to carry on his reputation and to preserve his work, Derbyshire has been relegated to a mostly forgotten footnote in regional art

history. Within a few years after his death in 1981, his surviving relatives sold off all his works through classified ads and a yard sale and destroyed his scrapbooks and the archive of his career, making an assessment of his life's work impossible.

During the first half of the twentieth century, many regional architects thrived under the guidance of instructors like Lionel Pries, and their reputations have been more sustainable because their discipline was more utilitarian than ephemeral, like that of visual artists. One of Pries's students, Robert Shields (1917–2012), became not only a successful architect but also a talented watercolorist, designer, and ceramic artist. In 1946, after serving in the US Navy during World War II, he joined forces with another gay architect, Roland Terry, as well as Bert Tucker. Together, the three men helped to establish a Northwest aesthetic in regional architecture, partially influenced by Pries's knowledge and collecting of Asian art and antiques.

Having been one of the early members of the Clay Club, which formed in Seattle in 1948, Shields actively promoted craft and ceramic arts. In 1955 he attended the Archie Bray Foundation in Helena, Montana, where he befriended Peter Voulkos and other key figures of the era. Shields's friendship (and romances) with visual artists of the period helped to shape and define his architectural and design production.[16]

While the University of Washington produced talented students such as Shields, the Cornish School continued to be a major force in Washington State's cultural identity. Its founder, Nellie Cornish, had left the school by 1939, but some of her accomplished instructors had remained. One field in which the school continued to excel in was dance. In 1946 a young man named Abdullah Jaffa Bey Khan enrolled in the school to enhance his private instruction with the department's founder, Mary Ann Wells, who had opened her own studio in 1923. The young man changed his name to Robert Joffrey and, along with his lover, Gerald Arpino, founded the Joffrey Ballet in 1956 after the couple had moved to New York in 1948. Joffrey and Arpino visited Seattle often to work with various Northwest productions and to present special classes at Cornish.[17]

Fig. 67. Josef Scaylea (1913–2014)
Leon Derbyshire in his studio
Seattle Times Color Rotogravure Pictorial section, January 11, 1953
Courtesy of The Seattle Public Library

Fig. 68. Leon Derbyshire (1896–1981)
Looking West on First Hill, circa 1938, finished 1974
Oil on canvas
30 x 36¼ in.
Collection of the Frye Art Museum, gift of Chester Nelson, 1990.001

While Joffrey was attending Cornish, one faculty member, Karen Irvin (1909–1999), was beginning to take local dance performance to another level. She had joined the school in 1945 after being a student there since the 1920s, with additional studies in New York. By the late 1930s, Irvin was a noted local performer and dance instructor, along with her lesbian accompanist Catherine Rogers, who remained a fixture at Cornish for several decades.

Around 1952, when Irvin became head of the dance department, she met Pamelia "Mea" Hartman (1930–1983), and they soon became lovers. In 1956 the two women, along with close friend and artist Malcolm Roberts, founded the Cornish Ballet. Irvin, Hartman, and Roberts guided the ballet into becoming the leading regional company of the time. Besides Irvin's choreography, the trio designed and built the stage sets, made the costumes, and even sold tickets. Irvin remained head of the department for twenty-seven years, during which time the ballet company continued to prosper.

Several of Irvin's students went on to distinguished national careers in professional companies. After developing a celebrated local reputation, her principal dancer, Terry Sparks, went to New York to study at the School of American Ballet under a Ford Foundation scholarship. A lesbian herself, Sparks weathered the social pressures imposed on young gay people during that era. In spite of this, she maintained an exemplary career as rehearsal director/ballet mistress for Twyla Tharp Dance in New York as well as for the Anna Wyman Dance Theatre in Canada. She was on the faculty for the Pacific Northwest Ballet, University of Washington, Cleveland Ballet, and several other companies. Her career came full circle when she returned to teach at Cornish in 1996 until her retirement in 2007.[18]

Another Cornish student, Del McBride (1920–1998), was changing the world of local craft by incorporating elements of his Native American heritage into a range of contemporary designs for artistic and utilitarian purposes. In 1950 he formed Klee

Fig. 74. Malcolm Roberts
(1913–1990)
Poster for Karen Irvin
dance concert, 1941
Screen print on cardboard
14 x 11 in.
Private collection

Fig. 75. Malcolm Roberts,
circa 1955
Courtesy of the Estate of
Karen Irvin

Fig. 76. Mea Hartman (on
couch) and Karen Irvin at
their home, circa 1955
Courtesy of the Estate of
Karen Irvin

Fig. 77. Karen Irvin at
Cornish, circa 1958
Scan from color slide
Courtesy of the Estate of
Karen Irvin

Fig. 83. Cornish Ballet
principal dancer Terry
Sparks, circa 1960
Courtesy of the Estate of
Karen Irvin

Fig. 84. Malcolm Roberts
(1913–1990)
Cornish Ballet program
for *L'etoile filante*, 1963
Martin-Zambito Archive

Fig. 85. Malcolm Roberts
(1913–1990)
Stage set design for the
Cornish Ballet production
of *L'etoile filante*, 1963
Watercolor, ink, and
gouache on paper
14 x 18 in.
University of Washington
Libraries, Special
Collections, Karen Irvin
Papers, UW 40140

Fig. 86. Cornish Ballet
production of *L'etoile
filante*, 1963
Costumes and sets
designed by Malcolm
Roberts
Scan from color slide
Courtesy of the Estate of
Karen Irvin

Wyk Studio with his cousin Oliver Tiedemann (1919–1986), a talented designer and painter. They were soon joined by Del's brother Albert "Bud" McBride (1927–2012) and Bud's life partner Richard Schneider (1928–2015). The studio was located in the Nisqually flats, north of Olympia. For over ten years, Klee Wyk Studio produced architectural and decorative tile murals, fabrics, hand-printed cards, and utilitarian objects that were among the finest regional midcentury designs utilizing Northwest Coast Native American motifs. The name Klee Wyk was an homage based on Canadian artist Emily Carr's memoir *Klee Wyck* of 1941.

For their designs, the four gay men traveled to the coast of British Columbia and southeastern Alaska, producing sketches and photographic studies. In 1959, Bud and Richard had formed their own business, Crow Valley Shop, at Eastsound on Orcas Island, while still working part-time for Klee Wyk until the studio disbanded in 1961.

The proprietors of Klee Wyk Studio formed a close friendship with ceramic artists Lorene and Ralph Spencer, whose studio was also south of Seattle. Although the Spencers were both gay, they maintained their marriage until Ralph's death in 1973. Afterward, Lorene and her life partner, Ruth Henry, had a close friendship with Bud and Richard, who sold Lorene's work along with their own Crow Valley pottery, as well as work by other talented artists, until their retirement in 1995.[19]

Along with Klee Wyk and Spencer Pottery, still another ceramic establishment formed, this time in nearby Bellevue, just ten miles east of Seattle, in 1958. The Kiln was owned and operated by a lesbian couple, Virginia Weisel and her life partner, Aurilla Doerner. The women had been together for nearly ten years before establishing their own business where Virginia, a seasoned ceramic artist, was in charge of production and "Rilla" provided the financial stability for their success. They offered classes through the studio and participated in all the region's finest crafts

Fig. 87. Malcolm Roberts (1913–1990)
Costume design for the Evil Magician character in the Cornish Ballet production of *L'etoile filante*, 1963
Watercolor, ink, and gouache with fabric swatches on paper
20 x 15 in.
University of Washington Libraries, Special Collections, Karen Irvin Papers, C-UW 40141

Fig. 88. Design for a Cornish Ballet production, 1957
Ink and gouache on paper
10 x 8 in.
Courtesy of the Estate of Karen Irvin

Fig. 89. Klee Wyk Studio artists, from left: Richard Schneider, Del McBride, and Oliver Tiedemann, 1957
Seattle Times press photo by Roy Scully
Martin-Zambito Archive

Fig. 90. Oliver Tiedemann (left) and Richard Schneider, 1958
Martin-Zambito Archive

Fig. 91. Del McBride and his brother Bud McBride, circa 1955
Scan of image provided by Richard Schneider in 2010
File altered with Photoshop
Martin-Zambito Archive

Fig. 92. Bud McBride and life partner Richard Schneider, circa 1955
Scan of image provided by Richard Schneider in 2010
Martin-Zambito Archive

Fig. 93. Klee Wyk Studio
Longhouse at Totem Bight
near Ketchikan, Alaska,
circa 1958
Ceramic charger with
underglaze painting
13¾ x 2 in.
Private collection

Fig. 94. Klee Wyk Studio
Raven totem pole, circa
1958
Ceramic charger with
underglaze painting
13⅜ x 2 in.
Private collection

Fig. 95. Klee Wyk Studio
Table, circa 1958
Inset ceramic tiles with
underglaze painting
22¼ x 22¼ x 14¾ in.
Private collection

Fig. 96. Klee Wyk Studio
Coffee table, circa 1958
Inset ceramic tiles with
underglaze painting
20¼ x 32¼ x 15 in.
Private collection

Fig. 97. Delbert J. McBride
(1920–1998)
*Portrait of Oliver
Tiedemann*, circa 1955
Oil on board
26 x 20 in.
Collection of the
Washington State
Historical Society

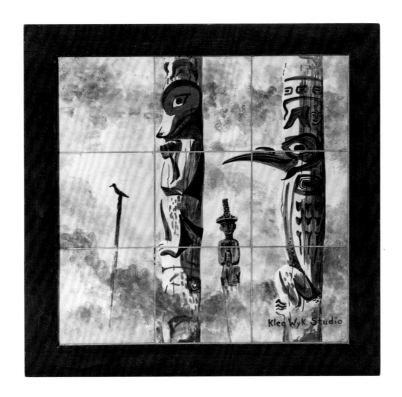

Fig. 98. Oliver Tiedemann
(1919–1986)
Untitled wall hanging,
1954
Ceramic tiles with under-
glaze painting
18 x 12 in.
Private collection

Fig. 99. Klee Wyk Studio
Untitled tile mural study,
circa 1958
Watercolor and graphite
on paper
6½ x 12½ in.
Private collection

Fig. 100. Klee Wyk Studio
Untitled tile mural study,
circa 1958
Watercolor and graphite
on paper
7 x 14 in.
Private collection

Fig. 101. Klee Wyk Studio
Christmas card, 1956
Block print on card stock
3 x 5 in.
Collection of Cascadia Art
Museum, Edmonds, WA

Fig. 102. Mary Randlett
(1924–2019)
Richard Schneider and
Bud McBride at their
home in Nisqually, WA,
2010
Courtesy of the Estate of
Mary Randlett

Fig. 103. Lorene and Ralph
Spencer, circa 1958
Scan from color slide
Martin-Zambito Archive

Fig. 104. Ralph Spencer,
circa 1958
Scan from color slide
Martin-Zambito Archive

Fig. 105. Spencer Pottery
studio, circa 1960
Scan from color slide
Martin-Zambito Archive

Fig. 106. Painted door inset
for Spencer Pottery, 1952
Signed "Reynolds"
Oil on burlap
74 x 23 in.
Private collection

Fig. 107. Spencer Pottery
advertising card, circa 1955
Martin-Zambito Archive

Handmade contemporary stoneware
by Ralph and Lorene Spencer

One-half mile east of U. S. Highway 99
on South 144th Street, Seattle.
Hours: Tuesday through Saturday, Noon to 6:00.

exhibitions. Virginia was known for her classically inspired modern stoneware and especially for her unique and innovative glazes.[20]

Washington State's cultural identity continued to benefit from the lives and works of these regional gay artists, but societal views were still in flux over homosexuality. With a lack of quality publications available to gay people at that time, numerous books appeared containing dangerous misinformation by purported experts. These included *The Homosexual* by Benjamin Morse, MD (pseudonym of Lawrence Block, who was not a medical doctor), published by Monarch Books in 1962; and *Everything You Always Wanted to Know about Sex: But Were Afraid to Ask* by David Reuben, MD, in 1969. Reuben's abhorrent, bizarre statements about homosexuality drove many gay people to despair.

Little hope was offered by the film industry, which reinforced negative stereotypes in movies such as 1961's *The Children's Hour*, 1967's *The Fox*, 1968's *The Killing of Sister George*, 1970's *The Boys in the Band*, and numerous others that portrayed a hopeless, unhappy existence for a gay audience.

Although society was basically indifferent to the harm spread through books and movies, gay people began taking control of their own destinies. Tolerance and credible information for homosexuals were advancing at a snail's pace, but by the 1960s, the efforts of pioneering organizations began to take shape. Inspired by Chicago's Society for Human Rights, founded by Henry Gerber (1892–1972) in 1924, events like the 1950 founding of the Mattachine Society in Los Angeles by several activists, including Harry Hay (1912–2002), were beginning to evince significant positive change.

Fig. 108. The Kiln ceramic studio, Bellevue, WA, circa 1958
Courtesy of the family of Virginia Weisel

Fig. 109. Virginia Weisel, circa 1958
Courtesy of the family of Virginia Weisel

Fig. 110. Newspaper clipping showing Virginia Weisel and her life partner, Aurilla Doerner, in their studio, 1959
Seattle Post-Intelligencer photo by Tom Brownell / Ken Harris
Courtesy of the family of Virginia Weisel

Fig. 111. Interior of the Kiln
ceramic studio, Bellevue,
WA, circa 1958
Courtesy of the family of
Virginia Weisel

Fig. 112. Virginia Weisel at
her wheel, circa 1965
Courtesy of the family of
Virginia Weisel

Fig. 113. Virginia Weisel
with her ceramics, circa
1964
Scan from color slide
Courtesy of the family of
Virginia Weisel

Fig. 114. Virginia Weisel
(1923–2017)
Bottle, circa 1960
6½ x 5½ in.
Collection of Thula Weisel

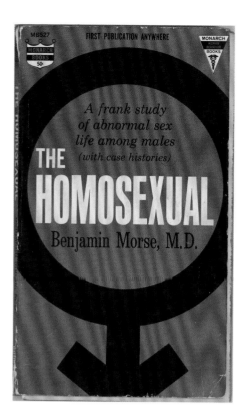
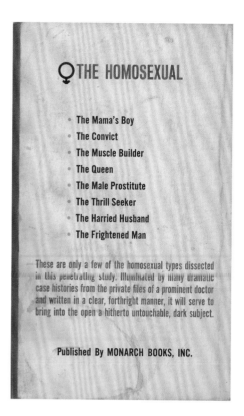

Several brave activists, such as Frank Kameny (1925–2011) and Barbara Gittings (1932–2007), led marches in cities—including one in Philadelphia in 1964, and a famous White House protest the following year in Washington, DC, where participants wore business suits and formal clothing to demonstrate their respectable places within society. Kameny, who had lost his government job as part of the Lavender Scare of the McCarthy era, became a guiding force in the gay-rights movement. In San Francisco, lesbian couple Del Martin (1921–2008) and Phyllis Lyon (b. 1924) founded the Daughters of Bilitis in 1955 as the first organization for lesbians.[21]

Seattle's first gay-rights organization was the Dorian Society, founded in 1966 by University of Washington professor Nicholas Heer and other local activists. That same year, an article featuring Dorian Society member Peter Wichern (1946–1996) appeared on the cover of the organization's magazine identifying him as a businessman and a homosexual. Although Wichern was portrayed as a conservative, upstanding local citizen, he was in reality a young man with strong convictions and not as sedate as the article implied. He eventually became more radical in his activism until his death from complications of AIDS in 1996.[22]

The Stonewall Riots in New York in 1969 marked a turning point: gay people were no longer tolerant of being harassed by police or other authority figures, who had traumatized them for decades. And this attitude was spreading to other cities throughout the country.

By the 1970s, several important early gay artists of Washington State had died, including Thomas Handforth, Mac Harshberger, Orre Nobles, and Mark Tobey. With the exception of Tobey, many of their reputations suffered because of lack of scholarship and shifting trends in the art world, causing their work to become lost to art history. Even those who continued to work and thrive did so mostly without emphasizing their personal lives and sexual orientation, whether by personal choice or through deliberate suppression by nongay historians and curators.

Fig. 117. Front of wrap-around cover of *Fruit of the Loon*, by Ricardo Armory (pseudonym of George Davies), 1968
Private collection

Fig. 118. Back of wrap-around cover of *Fruit of the Loon*, by Ricardo Armory (pseudonym of George Davies), 1968
Private collection

Fig. 119. *Seattle: The Pacific Northwest Magazine*, November 1967
Courtesy of The Seattle Public Library

With the current trend toward inclusiveness and equity in the art world, there are new opportunities for the rediscovery of marginalized artists, especially in a regional context. It is up to current institutions and historians to bring these talents to light and to recognize the significant contributions gay artists have made to American culture.

NOTES

1 "Kane Stands by Football," *Seattle Daily Times*, November 30, 1905, 2.

2 *Seattle Daily Times*, January 4, 1908, 6.

3 *Seattle Daily Times*, May 29, 1897, 12.

4 David F. Martin, *Invocation of Beauty: The Life and Photography of Soichi Sunami* (Seattle: Cascadia Art Museum, 2018), 18–20.

5 Arthur Corey, *Danse Macabre: The Life and Death of Andreas Pavley* (Dallas: Bridwell Library, Southern Methodist University, 1977).

6 Guthrie McClintic, *Me and Kit* (Boston and Toronto: Little, Brown & Company, 1955); https://prabook.com/web/katharine.cornell/3739217. In 1963, after McClintic's death, Katharine Cornell donated his archive to four institutions in Seattle: the City of Seattle, Seattle Center, the Seattle Public Library, and the University of Washington Drama School. The current location of any parts of the archive is unknown, and the material is not in the collections to which they were originally donated (*Seattle Daily Times*, February 19, 1963, 12).

7 Forkner's homosexuality, effeminate personality, and bullied existence were conveyed to me by two of his friends, Doris Jensen Carmin and Winifred Warhanik Clifton. Their mothers, Elizabeth Warhanik and Dorothy Dolph Jensen, two of the founders of Women Painters of Washington, were close friends and students of Forkner's. Jensen's husband, Lloyd, the region's most prominent frame maker, was repeatedly exasperated by Forkner's endearing nickname for him, "Baby."

8 Nellie C. Cornish, *Miss Aunt Nellie: The Autobiography of Nellie C. Cornish* (Seattle: University of Washington Press, 1964), 134–35.

9 Jeffrey Karl Ochsner, *Lionel H. Pries, Architect, Artist, Educator: From Arts and Crafts to Modern Architecture* (Seattle and London: University of Washington Press, 2007).

10 For a study of homosexuality and China, see D. E. Mungello, *Western Queers in China: Flight to the Land of Oz* (Lanham, MD: Rowman & Littlefield, 2012).

11 *Seattle Daily Times*, April 5, 1937, 13.

12 Information about Ray Hill's personal life was relayed to me on numerous occasions by his close friend and fellow UW professor Everett DuPen, who was not gay but was sympathetic to Hill's situation at the university. DuPen declined Hill's numerous invitations to accompany him to Seattle's gay nude beaches even though the prospect of free life models was tempting.

13 See https://en.wikipedia.org/wiki/Hannes_Bok.

14 *Seattle Daily Times*, June 2, 1956, 73.

15 Seattle Public Library, artist files, untitled article on Leon Derbyshire dated February 2, 1932; no author listed. Additional reminiscences about Derbyshire came from conversations with Doris Jensen Carmin and a Derbyshire student, artist Donald Peel. Carmin once conveyed to me that her parents, artist Dorothy Dolph Jensen and frame maker Lloyd Jensen, were close friends of Derbyshire's and assisted him after he was taunted and physically assaulted outside his studio in the late 1940s by a group of men who beat him because of their hatred of gay men.

16 Information derived from a clipping file provided to David Martin by Robert Shields.

17 Joffrey information derived from papers of Mary Ann Wells, provided by her estate and now housed in University of Washington Libraries, Special Collections.

18 Information derived from the Karen Irvin estate, now housed in University of Washington Libraries, Special Collections, and from an interview with dancer Terry Sparks, June 5, 2015.

19 Klee Wyk information derived from archives shared with David Martin by Bud McBride and Richard Schneider. Also see Maria Pascualy, "Delbert J. McBride, Native American Artist, Designer, Curator, Historian," *Columbia*, winter 2017–18, 13–19; and Maria Pascualy, "Klee Wyk: Artists on the Nisqually Flats," *Columbia*, winter 1998–99.

20 Weisel's glaze technique was described on page 38 of *Ceramics in the Pacific Northwest: A History* by LaMar Harrington (Seattle: University of Washington Press, 1979): "Glazes brushed on warm, bisque surfaces to build up a thick coat, kiln turned off when glaze began to flow off foot, multiple glaze firings for richer color." Additional information provided by the family of Virginia Weisel, which maintains her archive of clippings, photographs, and personal writings.

21 Sources include Wikipedia entries for Mattachine Society, Del Martin and Phyllis Lyon, and Frank Kameny: https://en.wikipedia.org/wiki/Mattachine_Society, https://en.wikipedia.org/wiki/Frank_Kameny, https://en.wikipedia.org/wiki/Del_Martin_and_Phyllis_Lyon.

22 Sources for this section derived from Gary Atkins, *Gay Seattle: Stories of Exile and Belonging* (Seattle: University of Washington Press, 2003); Chrystie Hill, "Queer History in Seattle, Part 1 to 1967," Historylink essay (https://www.historylink.org/File/4154); and Ruth Pettis and Angie McCarrell, "What Happened to the Gay Man from This 1967 *Seattle Magazine*?," KUOW archive site (http://archive.kuow.org/post/what-happened-gay-man-1967-seattle-magazine).

Shaping a Northwest Aesthetic

David F. Martin

The terminology describing any perceived school of art is usually based on shared characteristics denoting a style that is specific to a certain country or region. This is apparent when examining widely recognized groups such as the Ashcan School, the New York School, and the watercolorists known as the California School. In Washington State, before a shared aesthetic was acknowledged and promoted as the Northwest School, several young gay artists were creating the basis for the region's future artistic identity in the visual arts. Many of these artists were born during a time of severe sodomy laws in the state and an overall social hatred of and intolerance for homosexuals (see pp. 96–97).

In the Pacific Northwest, a unique regional expression began in the late 1930s when three gay artists—Mark Tobey, Morris Graves, and Guy Anderson—started developing a specific technique that included a subdued and minimal color palette; the use of mostly water-based mediums like watercolor, gouache, and tempera; subject matter that often had a focus on male figures; and an implied spiritual relationship to the region where it was created. Although not gay, a fourth artist associated with this style, Kenneth Callahan, is also identified with this group.

Laying the groundwork in Washington State before this aesthetic was established were Thomas Handforth (1897–1948), Orre Nelson Nobles (1894–1967), Mac Harshberger (1901–1975), and a few others, who achieved international recognition in the early decades of the twentieth century and provided a template for other artists to follow. Their development included international travel, the study of non-Western spiritual and religious philosophies, and an unquenchable thirst for knowledge. It may be that these characteristics were based in part on the imposition of repression, isolation, and an inability to conform to societal roles of the period. Early gay artists in the state, especially those in more rural areas, did not always have firsthand access to intellectual and cultural influences. This helped imagination and personal creativity flourish, and fostered in these artists a need to travel for experiences they weren't able to have at home.

~

In the early twentieth century, artistic representations of men in physically close contact or in nude groupings were rare in general, and were especially so in the Northwest. It was acceptable to depict men in military and athletic situations or even collegial horseplay, but not as expressions of eroticism and romance. If you were a gay man in the Northwest at the turn of the century, you had to locate or create other alternatives.

In the nineteenth century, English photographer Eadweard Muybridge had emigrated to the US, where he accepted various commissions on the West Coast and in Alaska. His multicamera technique led to the establishment of stop-action

Fig. 1. Eadweard Muybridge (1830–1904) *Animal Locomotion: An Electro-Photographic Investigation of Consecutive Phases of Animal Movements*, 1872–85 Plate 522, USC Digital Library, 2010

Fig. 2. Still from the
*Dickson Experimental Sound
Film*, 1894–95
Screenshot

film and motion pictures. His 1887 publication *Animal Locomotion: An Electro-
Photographic Investigation of Consecutive Phases of Animal Movements* offered numerous
images of naked men in close proximity to one another, and these images were
widely distributed. To the scientist and heterosexual man, it was science, but for
a gay man, it was fuel for the imagination. The Muybridge photographs eventually provided stimulus for international artists from Thomas Eakins and Marcel
Duchamp to Francis Bacon and David Hockney.

A few years after the publication of Muybridge's tome, the *Dickson
Experimental Sound Film* of 1894–95 became the first motion picture to use live
recorded sound, as developed by William Dickson and Thomas Edison. The
short film depicts two men dancing very closely to the music of a solo violinist.
Although the film was not intended to be a documentation of same-sex intimacy
(there were probably no women in the studio), the men are affectionately holding
each other and do not appear to be awkward (although their dancing skills leave
something to be desired). This short film has been co-opted in recent decades by
gay historians, not entirely unjustly. Images of female same-sex intimacy were
more common and acceptable at the time, as they could be observed as illustrations of the sensitive, nurturing aspects of women and didn't always necessarily
contain a sexual implication.

Mark Tobey, one of the earlier artists of significance in the Northwest, produced an unusual painting between 1922 and 1927 titled *Dancing Miners*. It depicts
two rough-looking miners dancing affectionately with each other. In this instance,
knowing the artist was homosexual, the implication could be that they are a couple. One man is taller and looks fondly down at his more diminutive partner, their
hands interlocked. It presents endearment rather than satire.

At about the same time, local artist Guy Anderson, who was in the beginning
stages of his career, won a prestigious Tiffany Foundation scholarship in 1929.
This allowed him to spend the summer at the Tiffany estate at Oyster Bay, on New
York's Long Island, which attracted a select group of young painters of promise

Fig. 3. Mark Tobey
(1890–1976)
Dancing Miners, 1922–27
Oil on canvas
67 x 39¼ in.
Seattle Art Museum,
Eugene Fuller Memorial
Collection 42.19

from across the nation. These included gay artists such as Luigi Lucioni and Paul Cadmus, who were there at the same time as Anderson, acting as advisors.[1] The scholarship did not offer instruction at the estate but provided art materials, lodging, and interaction with other artists, as well as access to excellent museums in nearby Manhattan.

When the Seattle Art Museum opened in 1933, its founder, Dr. Richard Fuller, continued the tradition set by its predecessor, the Seattle Fine Arts Society, in featuring an annual exhibition of Northwest artists. This practice began in 1914, and Fuller was an important member of that earlier organization as well. In the initial exhibit at the new museum, the first prize in oil was given to the precocious twenty-two-year-old Morris Graves, who had just returned to Seattle after attending high school in Texas. His winning painting, *Moor Swan*, displayed a unique but rudimentary talent not quite developed and almost as awkward as the bird he had depicted.

By this time, Graves had been a world traveler. After dropping out of high school, the tall and strikingly handsome young man traveled as an employee of the American Mail Line with his brother Russell during the period 1928–31. The brothers traveled to numerous Asian ports, during which time Graves became aware of the art and culture of Japan and China, influences that would have an effect on his work in the coming years.[2]

In 1932, Graves and Guy Anderson were both living with their parents in Edmonds, just north of Seattle, and the two became lovers.

Graves's self-portrait of 1933 is a striking and sophisticated painting with a debt to the German Expressionists. It is possible that Graves viewed the University of Washington's Henry Art Gallery exhibition of the Blue Rider group in 1927, featuring the work of Kandinsky, Feininger, Jawlensky, and Klee. The influence of German Expressionism on his early work is significant. Graves and other local artists would also have come under the influence of husband-and-wife painters Peter and Margaret Gove Camfferman, who settled on nearby Whidbey Island in 1915 and were among the state's earliest modernists. Margaret Camfferman owned a portrait of herself painted by her instructor Robert Henri in 1915, right before her arrival in Washington State. This was a rare painting in the region at that time, since the few local collections of that era contained little, if any, contemporary American art by artists of Henri's stature. There is no doubt that Graves saw this portrait, because the influence on his own self-portrait is apparent. They share a similar color palette and facial expression and, most obviously, the unnatural elongation of the neck.

In 1934, Graves and Anderson traveled to Los Angeles together, painting along the way. A photograph from this trip has survived and shows the young Anderson outdoors with a large painting of a male nude placed on an easel behind him. The photograph doesn't explain which of the two created the painting. At this early stage of their careers, the two young men's paintings shared a very similar approach and technique.

An extant watercolor from this period shows that the young couple were adventurous beyond just traveling together. They had a mutual friend, architect Lionel Pries, who was well connected in the community as the head of the Department of Architecture at the University of Washington as well as being involved with the Seattle Fine Arts Society. The three men apparently had a romantic tryst together, and the resulting two-sided artwork, a nude study of Graves by Anderson and one of Anderson by Graves, was a gift to Pries as a memento of their intimate night together.[3]

Two Graves paintings from this period with implied sexual subtext depict elongated figures in a rather cryptic situation. The painting titled *Morning* has been described, not by Graves, as the artist representing himself just after masturbating.[4] This observation is likely untrue due to the presence of a shadowy female figure in the background. A recently rediscovered companion painting depicts two male figures and two female figures in a similar bedroom. One couple lies in bed with the male figure looking longingly at the departing man while the sleeping woman next to him covers her face, perhaps in frustration, while the sitting female figure in the upper left quadrant is wistfully resigned.

~

In the 1930s, the Seattle Art Museum's generous founder, Dr. Richard Fuller—who, along with his mother, Margaret, provided the funds to build the museum— began hiring local artists to work for the museum during the difficult years of the Depression. The wealthy, intelligent, and handsome Fuller formed a close bond

Fig. 4. Morris Graves
(1910–2001)
Self-Portrait, 1933
Oil on canvas
25½ x 19¾ in.
Seattle Art Museum, gift
of Florence Weinstein
in memory of Max
Weinstein, 85.268
Photograph by Paul
Macapia

Fig. 5. Robert Henri
(1865–1929)
Portrait of Margaret Gove,
1915
Oil on canvas
24¼ x 20¼ in. (sight)
Seattle Art Museum,
gift of Mrs. Peter M.
Camfferman in memory
of her sister Miss Helen
Gove, 58.66

Fig. 6. Guy Anderson on a
trip to Los Angeles, 1934
Morris Graves Papers,
Coll. 326, Box 126, Folder
1–10, Special Collections
& University Archives,
University of Oregon
Libraries, Eugene

Fig. 7. Morris Graves,
not dated
Morris Graves Papers,
Coll. 326, Box 126, Folder
1–19, Special Collections
& University Archives,
University of Oregon
Libraries, Eugene

(bottom left)
Fig. 8. Guy Anderson
(1906–1998)
Nude study of Morris
Graves, 1933–35
Double-sided watercolor
painted on single sheet
19½ x 15½ in.
Collection of Heidi
Charleson

(bottom right)
Fig. 9. Morris Graves
(1910–2001)
Nude study of Guy
Anderson, 1933–35
Double-sided watercolor
painted on single sheet
19½ x 15½ in.
This watercolor was orig-
inally given to architect
Lionel Pries as a memento
of the three men sharing
an intimate encounter.

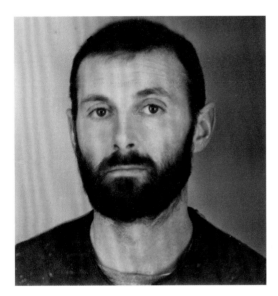

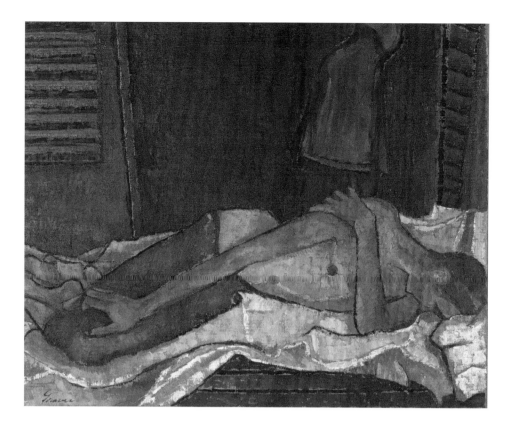

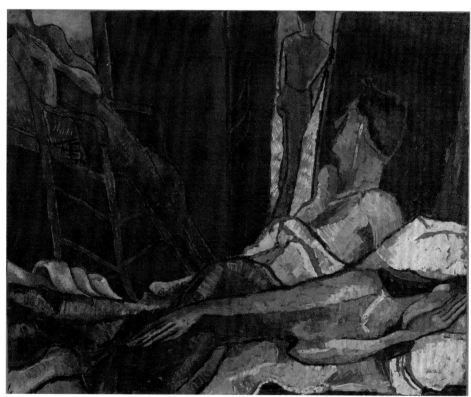

with the region's artists, especially the gay ones.[5] Graves and Anderson both worked for the museum in its early years, as did Kenneth Callahan, who would become its director and curator.

When the museum opened, the collections were predominantly made up of Asian antiquities collected by Fuller. The objects included ceramic and bronze urns, chalices, and other vessels that caught the eye of the young artists and soon began to appear as forms in their paintings. Artist Malcolm Roberts stated in a 1937 letter to Callahan, "Just ran into Morris Graves and Earl [Fields] on Broadway—Morris is working at the museum unpacking ceramics."[6] These vessels are ubiquitous in Northwest art of that period.

Mark Tobey had an interest in Asian art and especially in calligraphy. His friendship with Chinese artist Teng Baiye is well documented and is likely a source for his later abstractions. Tobey's travels brought him not only to New York but also to England, where he developed a close friendship with ceramic artist Bernard Leach, whose promotion of Japanese ceramics had a wide international influence. Most of these experiences did not immediately alter Tobey's art. He was still producing works that were in the style of American Scene Painting, and he often depicted workingmen and the unemployed, such as in the series of ink washes depicting the denizens of Seattle's Pike Place Market that were all drawn and painted on pages from a Japanese sketchbook, and in a major work of that period, *Skid Road Philosophers* of 1942.

In the mid-1930s, Tobey had experimented with the introduction of an abstract calligraphic style that would later be described as "white writing." He must have been somewhat apprehensive about his experimental abstract works, since he usually sent his more figurative works to national competitions. The most noted of these

was a tempera painting titled *Sunday Afternoon*, which was included in the *American Art Today* exhibition at the New York World's Fair in 1939–40.

Besides Dr. Richard Fuller, other wealthy patrons in the region supported local art and presented an air of culture to the up-and-coming artists. One of these, Kay Harshberger, whose brother was artist Mac Harshberger, encouraged younger gay artists with her style and exuberant personality. Morris Graves would later recall, "I remember beautiful and spirited Kay Harshberger with great pleasure. She lifted the quality of my life with her aesthetics, wit, style, and her alert, sensitive intelligence. And she had great sober and compassionate appreciation and encouragement for the few young people in the arts in Seattle during the Depression in the midthirties who could respond to her good heart and unpretentious—and for us a rare—sophisticated mind."[7]

There has been much speculation regarding the antecedents of Tobey's "white writing" style in the Northwest. The earliest to consider is Roi Partridge's drypoint *Early Morning, Notre Dame*, 1912, which would have been familiar to the public because Partridge received numerous exhibitions locally at that time. Partridge, one of Washington State's earliest internationally successful artists, created the image by scratching a series of webbed lines into an etching plate with varying degrees of density to resolve into an impressionist image of the iconic cathedral. Partridge, a Washington State native, and his wife, photographer Imogen Cunningham, had been greatly influenced by Asian art in their work before Tobey's arrival in Washington and before Graves was born.

Another probable influence was the gay artist Pavel Tchelitchew, who created several images—such as *The Thinker* of 1927—in which the figure (usually male) is contained in a series of weblike lines. The lines do not follow standard structures

Fig. 14. Mark Tobey
(1890–1976)
Skid Road Philosophers, 1942
Oil on canvas
48 x 35 in.
Private collection

Fig. 15. Mark Tobey,
circa 1930
Museum of History &
Industry, Seattle, Richard
Bennett Collection,
2006.38.406.105

Fig. 16. Roi Partridge
(1888–1984)
Early Morning, Notre Dame,
1912
Drypoint
12¹¹⁄₁₆ x 8¹⁄₁₆ in.
Honolulu Museum of Art,
gift of Eliza Lefferts and
Charles Montague Cooke,
Jr., 1932 (7071)

Fig. 17. Pavel Tchelitchew
(1898–1957)
The Thinker, 1927
Gouache, coffee, and sand
on paper
25¼ x 19½ in.
Yale University Art
Gallery, New Haven, gift
of Mr. and Mrs. Sherman
Kent
1978.115.1
This painting is repro-
duced in black and white.

Fig. 18. Mark Tobey
(1890–1976)
Coliseum, 1942
Tempera
10 x 14½ in.
Private collection

of dynamic symmetry, so the composition reflects symbolic rather than analytical elements.[8] It is very likely that Tobey either personally knew or at least knew of Tchelitchew through his circle of artist friends while living in New York in the early 1930s. Coincidentally, Tobey's "white writing" development began right after Tchelitchew's first American exhibition at New York's Julien Levy Gallery in 1934.

Seizing the opportunity to expand on this technique, the younger Morris Graves began appropriating the white-line structures of Tobey and Tchelitchew into his own work. His breakthrough painting *Bird Singing in the Moonlight* of 1938–39 is a drastic departure from his oil paintings and is indebted to Tobey's signature technique.

Tobey's homosexuality has had limited coverage in the numerous publications about his life and work. A November 1934 reference appears in the journal of Margaret Callahan, Kenneth's wife, stating, "At dinner, Kenneth and Mark discussed Mark's Bahai religion. It apparently desires the same ends as Communism, but wants to bring them about without hate or violence. And the Bahai believe there are divinities. Mark is all for it. He needs [it] to bolster him. I suspect that he has strong sexual urges towards Negroes, and this 'brotherhood of man' religion justifies it for him."[9]

Fig. 19. Mark Tobey
(1890–1976)
Mockers II, 1943
Tempera
20 x 8 in.
Private collection

Fig. 20. Morris Graves
(1910–2001)
Bird Singing in the Moonlight, 1938–39
Tempera and watercolor on mulberry paper
26¾ x 30⅛ in.
Purchase
Museum of Modern Art
14.1942
Digital image © Museum of Modern Art/Licensed by SCALA/Art Resource, NY
© The Morris Graves Foundation

His close friendships with other gay artists like Richard Bennett, Graves, and Anderson, who never hid their orientation (or married), gave him support to accept his sexuality and enjoy the benefits of intimate relationships.

In a letter to Kenneth and Margaret Callahan dated July 1937, Malcolm Roberts wrote, "Dick Bennett is here and same as ever—very anxious to see you and quite busy on a new manuscript. No news of Mark [Tobey] that's new. He seems a little more sure of himself. By that I mean he's gayer about his position sexually and last night was really quite amusing. How awful that sounds, we were just talking."[10]

Tobey must have been moved by the acceptance that his younger artist friends were enjoying, especially with important figures like the Callahans.

Around 1939, he met Swedish immigrant Pehr Hallsten, whom he fell in love with. In the mid-1950s, Pehr enjoyed a brief career as a folk painter with subject matter derived from his Scandinavian heritage. The two men lived together from 1940 until Hallsten's death in 1965.

Fig. 21. Sherrill Van Cott as pictured in his 1931 Sedro-Woolley High School yearbook Scan provided by Frank and Joline Bettendorf

In the mid-1930s, Morris Graves met a handsome young man named Sherrill Kinney Van Cott (1913–1942) from the small town of Sedro-Woolley, seventy-two miles north of Seattle.

Van Cott had briefly attended the University of Washington after graduating from high school in 1931, but was largely a self-taught artist. He first began exhibiting in the Northwest Annuals at the Seattle Art Museum in 1935 with an oil painting titled *Potato Eaters*, while Graves also showed two oils. Both artists exhibited in the annuals for the next few years, and in 1939 Van Cott began to exhibit sculpture. The few extant sculptures by Van Cott, using regional materials, appear to have been influenced by the French sculptor Henri Gaudier-Brzeska (1891–1915), who had died at age twenty-four in World War I. Graves and Van Cott developed a romantic relationship, with Graves exerting a stylistic influence on the slightly younger artist. Van Cott was also a poet, and his writings were compatible with the visual content of his paintings. He focused on insects and other animals, both real and imagined, as well as complex intertwining of the male human form in a fossil-like contained border.

By 1940, Graves began exhibiting paintings in water-based mediums, such as *Bird Singing in the Moonlight* and *Shore-Birds*, drastically changing his style under Tobey's influence. The success of these works fueled Van Cott's preference for the medium from then on. His last painting, a watercolor titled *Weeping Girl*, was exhibited at the Northwest Annual from October 7 through November 8, 1942. A month later, he was dead at age twenty-nine from cardiac failure. Twenty years earlier, Van Cott had contracted scarlet fever, which caused a severe heart problem, leaving him practically an invalid for most of his short life.

The local art scene had lost a promising talent, and Graves a lover and acolyte. He promoted Van Cott's work long after his death, and preserved many works in his own collection. In February 1945, *Fortune* magazine paid a small tribute to

Man is likened unto a lizard of many directions

Hiding in the dried sticks of a burned forest

Or a hermit crab sidling through pebbles and tide-wash.

I have built a shell around me and I cling to a rock.

I change my colors with the leaves.

I burrow into the earth and nurse my confusion.

Once I ran to the mountains but fear came between me and the sun,
	and the moon itself became a black disk.

Millions upon millions of lives I have given up to the Beast.

My skin lies rotting on the beaches.

My plumage dries in the high rocks.

Two crumpled shells in a ravaged nest is my history.

Fear I know and fear I promote.

Fear is my master—I am driven into hiding.

[Through it I abuse myself.

I conquer and subdue, protect and demonstrate.]

I am devoured by fear

I run screaming into the jaws of it and

End up in its belly.

Man in his true form, repossessed, will be a glorious sight.

I shall gather myself from all parts of the earth.

I shall sit in the sun and draw all life around me, and become all of life.

I shall open my many throats to psalms more beautiful than I now
	know.

I shall walk out from under the shadow and shed my disguise.

These shapes I have assumed through the ages [the moment] of hiding,
	I shall bury in some

Remote spot when I become Adam.

—Sherrill Van Cott

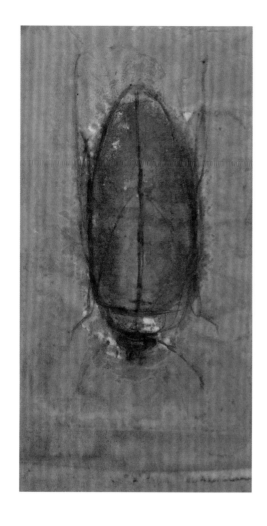

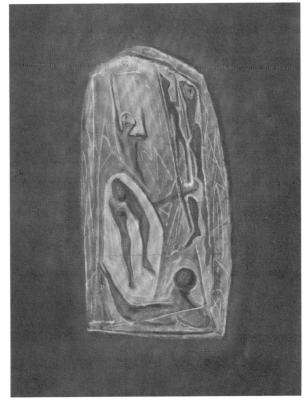

(opposite page)
Fig. 22. Sherrill Van Cott
(1913–1942)
Beetle, circa 1940
Gouache
12½ x 6½ in.
Private collection

(above left)
Fig. 23. Sherrill Van Cott
(1913–1942)
Untitled, circa 1940
Gouache
12½ x 9½ in.
Private collection

(above right)
Fig. 24. Sherrill Van Cott
(1913–1942)
Untitled, circa 1940
Gouache
9½ x 7½ in.
Collection of Lawrence
and Judi Mroczek

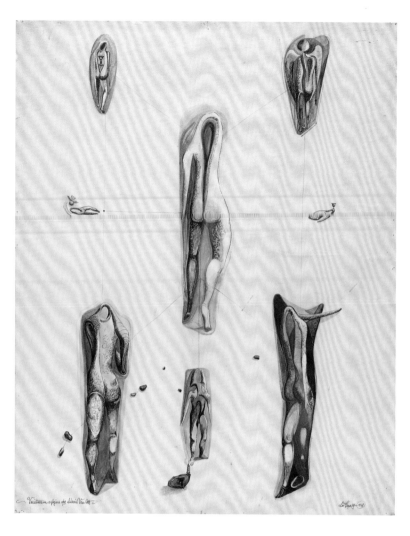

Van Cott and Graves, exposing the work to some of the younger generation of gay artists, like Leo Kenney and Ward Corley.

In a December 1959 letter to Morris Graves, Corley wrote, "I am painting lately again. . . . I am deeply influenced by you—Mark [Tobey]—and (really) Sherrill Van Cott. I have the things of his that you gave me and Richard, of course, has others and I keep putting off looking at them although I think of them often. Maybe that sounds foolish."[11]

Kenney paid tribute to Van Cott in a 1948 painting titled *Variations on a Figure by Sherrill Van Cott*, and his influence can be seen in Kenney's works like *Reclining Dreamer*.

~

Not surprisingly, male forms continued to inhabit the work of the local gay artists.

Richard Bennett had enjoyed a national and international reputation as a printmaker and illustrator since the 1920s. His illustrations contain numerous images of brawny men and lumberjacks, which were compatible with the celebration of labor and the working class in much WPA art of the Depression. A peculiar watercolor by Morris Graves titled *If Eye Be Lifted Up* shares several characteristics with a Paul Bunyan figure by Bennett.

In both paintings, a male figure is embracing a large wood beam or tree. The Graves painting shows the figure mounted by the wooden object while seated precariously on a lectern. There is a church to the right and a chalice superimposed over the figure's head. The brawny figure in Bennett's illustration is also in a suggestive embrace with a large tree taking the cruciform shape. In both works, the

Fig. 29. From left: Richard Bennett, Guy Anderson, and Edmund Tolk, circa 1945
Collection of the Museum of History & Industry, Seattle
2006.38.406.69

Fig. 30. Guy Anderson, circa 1945
Museum of History & Industry, Seattle
Richard Bennett Collection, 2006.38.406.68

singular figures are encased in a swirling pattern of water suggesting movement and an erotic subtext.

Graves, Anderson, and Richard Bennett remained friends throughout the 1940s, and Graves would often visit the couple at their cabin at Robe Ranch, where they all shared ideas and produced work in the Northwest wilderness. Tobey would also visit occasionally, but his disdain for outdoor activities led Margaret Callahan to remark, "Nature in the raw for Mark Tobey means dinner in the open at a city park such as Golden Gardens or Volunteer Park."[12]

Bennett joined his friends Thomas Handforth and Handforth's lover Edmund Tolk in an eight-month teaching position at Seeman School in El Monte, California. The experimental school was geared toward educating young men with special needs. After Bennett returned to Robe Ranch in spring 1944, Handforth became ill with scarlet fever and convalesced with care provided by Anderson and Bennett in their cabin. Like Van Cott's, Handforth's heart was damaged from the effects of scarlet fever, and he died prematurely a few years later in 1948.

For the July 1946 issue of *Art News* magazine, artist and writer Kenneth Callahan penned an article entitled "Pacific Northwest" at the request of the editor. The intention was to give some national recognition to lesser-known artists of the region rather than focusing exclusively on Tobey and Graves. Callahan made several points that attempted to explain the region's stylistic preferences: "Based on broad intellectual concepts and bound to nature as a fundamental theme, the painting movement characteristic of the Pacific Northwest is today just about fifteen years old. . . . It must be recognized at the outset, however that no standardized formulas set our painting apart in a fixed 'regional school,' for the painting styles of the Oregon-Washington area are unified rather than uniform."

Callahan unfortunately disregarded the international achievements of earlier Northwest artists, many of them women and minorities. However, he did state in his article that "contrary to popular belief on the eastern seaboard, though the region is geographically somewhat isolated, the Pacific Northwest artists have not been unaware of influences which have swept the art of Eastern United States centers since the Armory Show. Especially in the past twenty years, an artist sitting on a mountain side in Washington State is at most three weeks behind his eastern brethren in knowing 'what's going on.'"

Fig. 31. Guy Anderson
(1906–1998)
Icarus, 1949
Oil on canvas
32 x 42 in.
Collection of Robert and
Shaké Sarkis

Fig. 32. Guy Anderson
(1906–1998)
Martyrdom of St. Sebastian,
1950
Oil on composition board
31 x 11 in.
Seattle Art Museum, gift
in memory of Eunice P.
Clise from her children
48.30

Although the prominent artists in the Northwest dismissed being categorized into a homogenous style, their work did share similar characteristics, especially the art of those involved with each other romantically. Around 1950, Guy Anderson began creating a body of work using primarily male figures floating above landscapes or disks and mythological and religious figures, with the saints and mythical characters nude or scantily clad. He also introduced elements of formline design derived from Northwest Coast Native American design.

Younger gay artists like Leo Kenney grasped the conceptual and spiritual elements of their older mentors but often elevated them to an even higher level. By the time Callahan's article appeared in *Art News*, Kenney had created one of his early masterpieces and an iconic image of midcentury Northwest art, *Inception of Magic* from 1945.

This painting is a concise amalgamation of regional, historical, and international influences. The main form, a truncated torso, mimics almost exactly the contour of the Belvedere Torso, the famous ancient marble fragment that was a source for artists ranging from Michelangelo to Rodin. It epitomizes male strength and beauty, and the contrapposto pose was influential for generations of artists. Another fascinating aspect of Kenney's painting is the placement of a design that appears to be a representation of *anahata*, the heart chakra in Hindu and Buddhist traditions, reflecting Kenney's interest in variant forms of religion and spiritual teachings. The heart chakra is usually associated with balance, purity, and serenity. The painting is laden with intertwining symbols from different cultures, and with biological forms representing external human

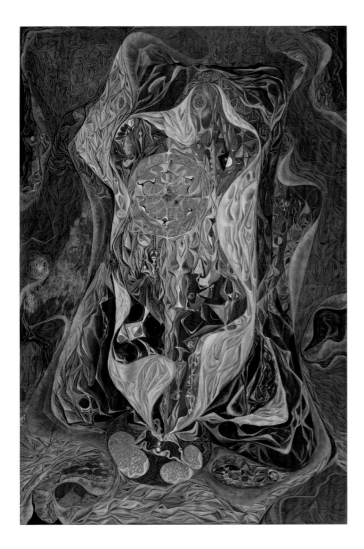

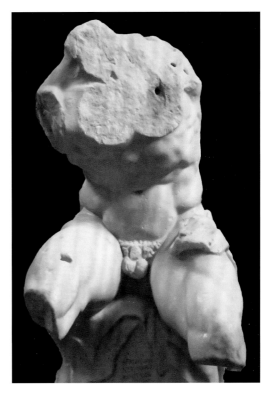

physical characteristics like sex organs as well as internal microscopic shapes like corpuscles and arteries, in addition to the symbolic urn and chalice forms.

Another of Kenney's masterworks is *Night Blooming Vessel* of 1956, painted eleven years after *Inception of Magic*. In it, Kenney has codified the symbols of his mentors: the unfolding lotus and the Egyptian sun disk superimposed over the neck of an ancient urn.

In many of Kenney's paintings, the figures are gender neutral and are often crying and layered with the iconography of chalices and urns. According to his biographer, Sheila Farr, Kenney was raised Catholic and was fascinated by symbols of the church, including chalices, vestments, and transfiguration. Farr also noted that although Kenney was gay, she was unaware of any long-term romantic relationships he had with men.[13]

Kenney, self-effacing and humble, never had the self-confidence to recognize fully his enormous talent. In a May 25, 1964, diary entry, he wrote, "Am so worried—I don't know why—about Morris Graves['s] reaction to my pictures. Everyone says they are related to his constructions and I fear he may not like them or resent them in some way."

In a June 12, 1964, entry in his diary he responded to the news of one of his paintings being purchased by Morris Graves by writing, "He is unique while I am a hybrid." But what he failed to realize is that his assimilation of influences is precisely what made his and Graves's work unique.

This is an entry from April 9, 1965: "I think my roots are in my own con-sciousness and have no outer form at all except in the pictures I make and the process of making them which seem to correspond often with the outer world and make me seem a part of it. My life and work both seem to be sensible only as reflec-tions of each other. When I am in a good period, I live in the light of this reflection and it seems enough."[14]

Another masterwork by Kenney, just recently rediscovered, is the symbolic and Surrealist portrait of his close friend Jan Thompson titled *The Priestess*. The painting appears to have been inspired by a work by the iconoclastic painter John D. Graham (1886–1961) titled *Marya (Donna Ferita, Pensive Lady)*, from 1944. Once again, Kenney's Egyptian references are evident and the mystical folding and unfolding of the forms, along with visible vessel shapes, give the feeling of the priestess being created through paranormal forces. Thompson herself was indeed a central figure of inspiration and a muse to most Northwest gay artists of that generation. The fact that she posed for the painting in a worn sweatshirt that is visible at the neckline gives an anchor to the human quality of the financially strapped artists.

When Morris Graves began his exploration of water-based mediums in 1939, he brought his vision down to earth by observing the more sinister sides of nature. His *Wounded Gull* of 1943 reflects the angst of human warfare infringing on nature. The gull is set inside a turbulent landscape with crashing waves capped by bloodred tinges encroaching on the bird. Graves produced a number of paint-ings with themes of the vulnerability of life and nature. Painted on thin Japanese papers, these works display a fragility enhanced by the delicate materials used to create them.

Graves's friend and fellow artist Clifford Wright fell under this influence as well, producing what appears to be a response to Graves's wounded-bird paint-ings in his own *Dead Woodpecker*. In a May 1948 diary entry, Wright explained,

Fig. 37. John D. Graham (1886–1961)
Marya (Donna Ferita, Pensive Lady), 1944
Oil on Masonite
48 x 48 in.
Photo courtesy of the Allan Stone Collection, New York

Fig. 38. Leo Kenney
(1925–2001)
*Study of Jan Thompson—
The Priestess*, September
1949
Ink and watercolor on
pink paper
23 x 18½ in. (sight)
Collection of Merch and
Alice Pease

Fig. 39. Leo Kenney
(1925–2001)
The Priestess, 1951–53
Oil on canvas
46¾ x 32½ in.
Collection of Dr. Alvin
Friedman-Kien and Ryo
Toyonaga

Fig. 40. Leo Kenney
(1925–2001)
Voyage for Two, 1953
Gouache on Chinese
paper
19¾ x 23½ in.
Seattle Art Museum, gift
of the artist
66.87
Photograph by Elizabeth
Mann

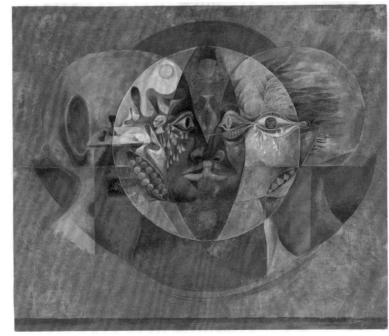

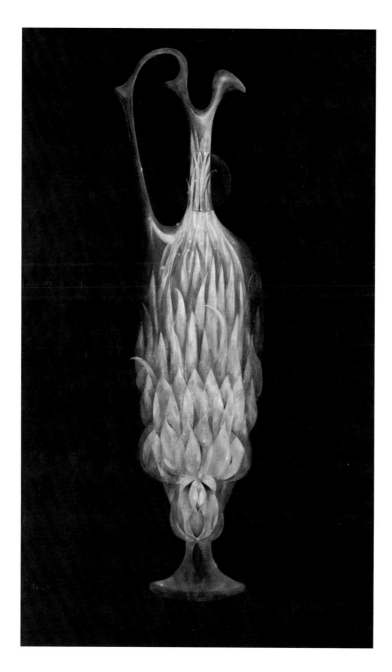

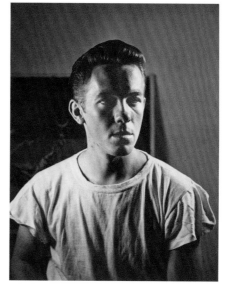

Fig. 41. Leo Kenney
(1925–2001)
Night Blooming Vessel, 1956
Oil on canvas
50 x 30 in.
Collection of Michael and
Danielle Mroczek

Fig. 42. Portrait of Leo
Kenney, Seattle, 1947
Photograph by Frank
Murphy
Collection of Merch and
Alice Pease

Fig. 43. Leo Kenney
(1925–2001)
Swimmer (unfinished), 1962
Tempera and gouache
16 x 29¾ in.
Collection of Merch and
Alice Pease

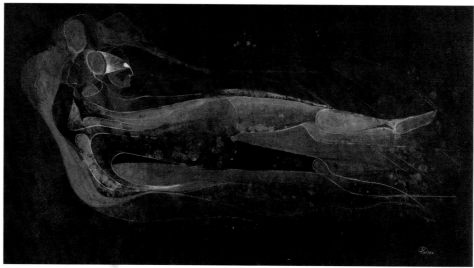

Fig. 44. Leo Kenney standing in front of a mural he created for the studio of photographer Frank Murphy, circa 1946
Photograph by Frank Murphy
Collection of Merch and Alice Pease

Fig. 45. Morris Graves (1910–2001)
Wounded Gull, 1943
Gouache on paper
26⅝ x 30¼ in.
Acquired 1945
© Morris Graves Foundation
The Phillips Collection, Washington, DC

Fig. 46. Clifford Wright (1919–1999)
Dead Woodpecker, circa 1948
Gouache on illustration board
8 x 16 in.
Private collection

"Yesterday, one of the gardeners brought me the still warm carcass of a giant pileated woodpecker which I have been making drawings of a la Morris Graves. It broke its neck by flying into a window. It is fifteen inches long from top-knot to tail-tip with black, gray, white and brilliant red markings. Two paintings, four by four-ish are cooking. A couple of laundry-paper sizes have come out well recently. The big ones are on brown wrapping paper."[15]

Wright was not the only artist inspired by Graves. His style was being co-opted by several national artists of the period. These included Darrell Austin (1907–1994) and Jan Stussy (1921–1990), whose painting *Hurt Bird*, from 1947, was denigrated by art critic Arthur Millier as being "done in the now-epidemic Picasso–Morris Graves manner. I shed tears, but not for the bird."[16]

American artist Carlyle Brown (1919–1963) used Graves's work as a template with additional inspiration from Pavel Tchelitchew, discussed earlier in this essay. Graves was a friend of Brown's, even visiting him in Italy in 1949. Although Brown was married to a woman, he also shared Graves's polyamorous inclinations and had a male lover as well. Whether the two artists had a physical or romantic affair has not yet been determined.

Fig. 47. Carlyle Brown (left) and Morris Graves, Florence, Italy, 1949
Morris Graves Papers, Coll. 326, Box 127, Folder 2-7
Special Collections & University Archives, University of Oregon Libraries, Eugene

With all his international success, Graves developed an unfortunately inflated ego and became difficult, even turning on close friends. After Kenneth Callahan's 1946 article in *Art News*, he felt slighted that the author should imply that he copied Tobey's signature style. He wrote a scathing letter to the editor defending his reputation: "For reasons which need not be reviewed in this letter, Kenneth Callahan has a twenty year history of inability to retain the friendships of the painters in the Puget Sound area. Mr. Tobey's influence has been unquestionably great. Callahan states that Mr. Mark Tobey influences 'Me.' To the contrary, the obvious being for the reason of envy of their ability to so live that they can devote their entire life to painting. . . . I have at no time lived in a 'Summer Colony' as stated by Callahan but in [a] sparsely inhabited coastal area [of] which he has long shown a psycho-pathically resentful envy as an environment for my way of life which he rather posed as native to himself alone but economically impossible for him to achieve. Also, the descriptive adjectives used by Callahan in his mention of my present studio are used to continue his determination to discredit me as a war objector and as a painter. I cannot believe that an article so colored by personal feelings that it includes numerous reworks which are not true is consistent with the policy of the Editors of *Art News*. Yours Sincerely, Morris Graves.

"PS The article has caused several sincere and capable painters unnecessary harm."[17]

This letter, which became part of a barrage of attacks against Callahan, is to a degree unjust. Although he did have an advantage in the community by being the main art critic for several publications and his wife Margaret being the other, and he did serve in a high position at the Seattle Art Museum, his record shows support for his fellow regional artists, even consistently favoring the three gay artists he was associated with.

Fig. 48. Carlyle Brown
(1919–1963)
Untitled, 1962
Gouache
10½ x 12 in.
Collection of William
Coniff

In her diaries, Margaret Callahan expressed her anger and hurt in an entry from 1946: "It has been a disturbing fall in many ways. Kenneth was asked by the editor to write an article for *Art News* that avoided promoting the usual big names. The responses to the article from Mark, Morris and Guy in the form of letters to *Art News* and verbally by phone, attacked Kenneth personally. It has left me with feelings of uncertainty about friendships and human relationships in general. I wondered if we had been at fault, and I searched into past events and attitudes. But I am certain that Mark, Morris and Guy are the unfair ones. I think they are some-how driven by their homosexuality and need to feel superior. But their anger and bouts of jealousy cause loneliness in me. As our friend Don Bear said in his letter, 'Ah me! Caught between the fairies and the Pharisees.'"[18]

A year later, Margaret Callahan was still trying to make sense of the attacks on her husband and focusing on the artists' sexual orientation as a possible explanation. In 1947 she wrote that Mark Tobey and Guy Anderson "were here at lunchtime yesterday. We were looking at Henry Moore's things in *Life* magazine and the Penguin book. Mark feels that there is something strange and wrong with Moore's feeling toward women. 'When I look at all these twisted forms, with the navel all pulled out and the tortured things he does with them, I say to myself, what *is* it between himself and women. What is wrong? He must hate them to do these dreadful things.' I said I thought he tried to ally all forms in nature, seeing the female form in relationship to stone and driftwood, etc. No. Mark thought it some-thing deeply psychological and unresolved in his own nature. I think homosexuals too often resent any preoccupation with fertility."[19]

Graves was not faring very well in his love life at this time. He had been involved with a man named Yonemitsu (Yone) Arashiro, who fell hopelessly in love with him but was taken aback at Graves's contradictory nature.

The extant letters between the two men reveal a chronology of hopeful, romantic love, followed by Yone's desperate attempt to resign himself to a hopeless loss of the idea of romantic love. In a letter dated November 13, 1952, he wrote to Graves, "You are building your life with one justifiable selfishness. My downfall is that I need someone to love and share the hopes and dreams that belong to

nowhere—no other—or ever anywhere. A selfish love for two people—for their inner self alone. If I must walk this life alone, I would do so. I cannot comply or try to discharge this inner feeling. So, I am going to resign myself to a solitary life & live another kind of life void of all emotional ties."[20]

Graves's life was in transition at this time. He had met and fallen in love with Paul Mills (1924–2004), a Seattle-born museum professional who had attended the University of Washington and was working at the university's Henry Art Gallery as assistant curator in 1952 and '53. Mills, who was fourteen years younger than Graves, was living a closeted existence, but that didn't stop Graves from falling for him. Their relationship was brief but intense. Surviving letters show Graves for once as the shunned partner. Mills addressed his conflict in an undated letter to Graves: "I'm at last beginning to learn something you have learned for yourself and have tried to tell me—the importance of calming down. I have also discovered, by watching myself and seeing what I get confused about and when I get along well, that homosexuality is something that creates too much of a strain on me and makes life difficult for me—hence I had better give that up. The next chapter of my life is going to be devoted to developing a nice, calm 'middle.' I have investigated the extremes of experiences a little too thoroughly."

Graves responded, "This is what I cannot withhold letting you know: You are in my thoughts almost constantly—but those earlier thoughts which (during the months before winter) were set in motion by you (and willingly together) are now thoughts cheated of their long & urgently needed expressions. You have killed half of my heart—half of my spirit. You have replaced a kind of growing buoyancy with a negative vacancy. You have, at last, by your behavior, put a kind of solid vacancy into my spirit—into my whole way of being & breathing & searching and that which in my life was, by you, once invited into a renewed living & expanding

Figs. 51, 52, 53.
Life magazine, September
28, 1953
With featured article
"Mystic Painters of the
Northwest," one of the
catalysts in forming the
national identity of what
would later be referred to
as the Northwest School
Cascadia Art Museum
archive

& creating experience has found finally only the drying effect of your smashing &
that is why you, whom I loved, I now feel only hatred for."

Mills, resigned to his stand, replied, "Morris, the answer seems to be 'no' and
quite a final one. And it would only make things more difficult for both of us if we
were to see each other again."[21]

Mills went on to marry a woman and had children. They remained married
until his wife's death in 1999, after which he came out as a homosexual and became
an activist in California. His son, Mike Mills, wrote and directed an award-
winning film titled *Beginners* in 2010 based on his father's complicated life.

Within a few years of the end of his relationship with Mills, Graves met a
young man named Richard Svare and had a long-term, productive relationship
with him.

～

By the middle of the twentieth century, the regional identity of a Northwest school
of art was established in the local community.

In a 1952 art review in the *Seattle Daily Times*, writer Elise Kelleher used
the term in an encompassing way: "Included in the exhibit are paintings, drawings, sculpture and ceramics, the work of 52 artists widely representative of the
Northwest School."[22]

The exhibition she refers to, sponsored by Mount Zion Baptist Church, a
highly regarded venue at that time, included a wide spectrum of artists including
George Tsutakawa, Glen Alps, and Paul Bonifas, all of whom had their own significant reputations at the time.

The term eventually began to focus almost exclusively on Tobey, Graves,
Anderson, and Callahan. This began when, in 1953, *Life* magazine featured an

article titled "Mystic Painters of the Northwest," which brought national focus to the region. Soon, the term would inhibit rather than expand the local production. The irony is that by the time this article came out, the personal friendships of the artists had dissipated.

Tobey and Graves were obviously the favored artists with the most coverage. One of the Graves paintings reproduced in the article is an outstanding 1952 oil titled *Preening Sparrow*. Graves shows a wide range of influences in this return to oil painting. The vulnerable sparrow is being eyed by the sinister predator, which is either bewildered by it or about to devour it. The painting departs from his standard Asian influences and bears a remarkable similarity to the fresco in the burial chamber of Nefertari, wife of Pharaoh Ramses II in the Valley of the Queens, circa 1250 BCE. The fresco depicts the gods Hathor and Ra-Horakhty in the persona of a falcon with a solar disk floating above its head.

The role of Egyptian art is understudied in relation to the Northwest aesthetic, but solar and lunar disks appear frequently in the work of Kenney, Anderson, Graves, and others.

Fig. 54. Morris Graves (1910–2001)
Preening Sparrow, 1952
Oil on canvas
53¼ x 26⅝ in. (sight)
Private collection
Illustrated in *Life* magazine, "Mystic Painters of the Northwest," September 28, 1953

Fig. 55. Fresco in the burial chamber of Nefertari, wife of Pharaoh Ramses II, Valley of the Queens, circa 1250 BCE
Depicting the gods Hathor and Ra-Horakhty
Image from the Yorck Project DVD *10,000 Masterpieces of Painting*, 2002

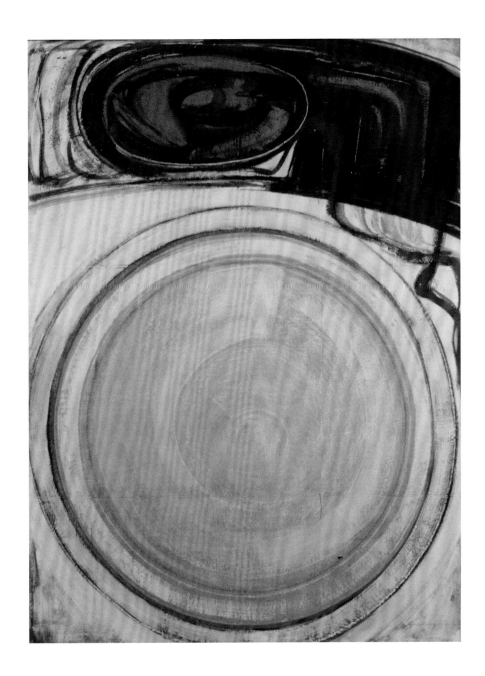

Fig. 56. Guy Anderson
(1906–1998)
The Birth of Adam, 1969–70
Oil on tar paper on
plywood
96 x 72 in.
Collection of Robert and
Shaké Sarkis

~

Unlike Graves and Tobey, who would eventually leave the Northwest, Guy
Anderson remained here and settled in the town of La Conner, where he continued to flourish as a painter and mentor to younger artists. Never one for self-
promotion, he allowed his national reputation to falter in favor of developing his
art. His romantic life after Richard Bennett is not well known, although there are
references to his life and orientation in an unpublished manuscript by his friend
and fellow artist Wes Wehr: "There was something wistful about Guy, and even
about some of the stories he told me. 'I was in Wenatchee for a while. I went to the
YMCA pool for a swim one evening. The most handsome young Italian-looking
man joined me in the swimming pool. We were the only ones there. He was like
a figure in a Signorelli painting. I couldn't take my eyes off of him. It didn't seem
to bother him at all. In fact, he seemed to enjoy my admiring him so openly.
We talked for a long while and swam together. I liked him very much, he was so
beautiful. There was something serious about him. Then he said he had to go. I
went back to that pool every evening at the same time for almost a week. He never

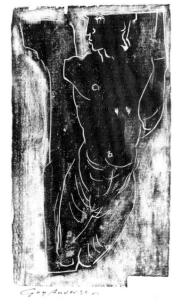

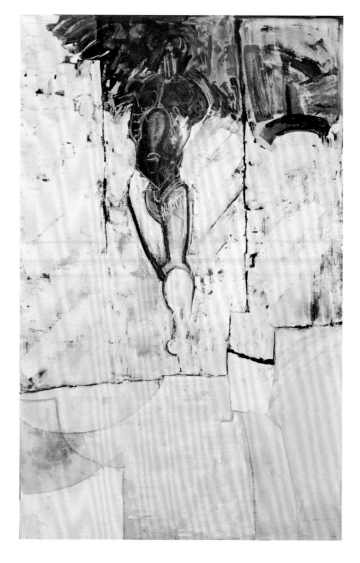

Fig. 57. Guy Anderson
(1906–1998)
Christmas card, circa 1960
Relief print
Collection of Robert and
Shaké Sarkis

Fig. 58. Guy Anderson
(1906–1998)
Icarus, 1969
Oil on canvas
81 x 51 in.
Collection of Ulrich and
Stella Fritzsche

Fig. 59. Guy Anderson
(1906–1998)
Fiery Night, 1985
Oil on paper
60 x 48 in.
Collection of Mel and
Leena Sturman

Fig. 60. Mark Tobey,
circa 1958
Courtesy of the
Matsudaira family

Fig. 61. Malcolm Roberts
(1913–1990)
Untitled, 1940–50
Gouache and tempera on
Kraft paper (fragment)
Size and current location
unknown
Scan from slide, Martin-
Zambito Archive

This satirical still life by
Malcolm Roberts com-
bines the "white writing"
developed by Mark Tobey
with the flowing washes
typical of the style of
Morris Graves. The imag-
ery includes the ubiquitous
urn form that appears in
the work of many artists
connected with Tobey,
Graves, and their acolytes.
Roberts incorporates a
flaccid penis shape within
the flowers and uses the
white writing to irrever-
ently convey hairy testicles
and scrotums.

reappeared. I've never forgotten him. Let me see now, that must have been around 1940 or so, when I was working in Spokane on the Public Art Project.'"

Wehr also discussed Graves's difficult personality: "Guy Anderson stated, 'Don't let Morris keep throwing you off. Just keep in mind that he is at least fifty percent put-on.' Was Morris sort of a Zen Master? Some people seemed to think so. 'Morris was a real brat. One day he discovered a socially acceptable way of kicking people in the shins and insulting them. They called it Zen. I always felt it was simply bad manners on Morris's part.'"[23]

By the late 1950s, Mark Tobey's career had begun to reach a pinnacle. He won first prize in the XXIX Venice Biennale in 1958 and two years later moved with his partner Pehr Hallsten to Basel, Switzerland. In 1961, Tobey became the first American artist to receive a retrospective at the Musée des Arts Décoratifs, Palais du Louvre, where three hundred of his paintings were exhibited. The following year, he was given a retrospective at the Museum of Modern Art in New York.

The younger generation of artists like Kenney would resume in building upon what their older mentors originated. Tobey's "white writing" became a hallmark that could even be subject to satire. This is seen in an undated painting fragment by Malcolm Roberts where he mimicked the style of Graves's work with the ubiquitous chalice or vessel encased in the white writing of Tobey. In this instance, however, Roberts included a flaccid penis, scrotum shapes, and testicles, using the technique irreverently as body hair on the genital forms.

Kenney, after focusing on figurative work in his early career, refined the techniques he had learned from his mentors while including inspiration from Pavel Tchelitchew. In his diary entry dated April 29, 1964, Kenney wrote, "Will Sanderson sent Tchelitchew catalogue. Those late linear works are just incredible— if he could have painted Paradise!? Maybe I will do it for him."

Fig. 62. Pavel Tchelitchew
(1898–1957)
Fruit of Paradise, 1933
Pastel and watercolor on
blue-green paper
25⅞⁄₁₆ x 19⅛ in. (sheet)
Yale University Art
Gallery, New Haven, from
the collection of Richard
Park Beard
2009.188.4

Fig. 62a. The Crown
Chakra, plate 1, C. W.
Leadbeater, *The Chakras*,
1927
Courtesy of the
Theosophical Society in
America
Image provided by Robert
Resnikoff

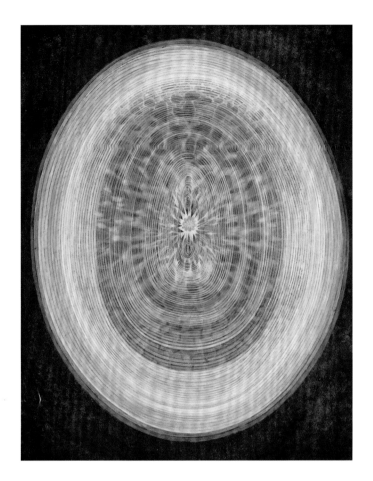

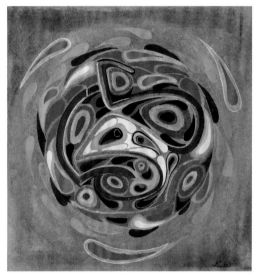

Fig. 63. Leo Kenney
(1925–2001)
Seed and Beyond, 1964
Gouache on Chinese
paper mounted on painted
composite board
19½ x 15⅛ in. (sheet)
20⅞ x 16⅝ in. (mount)
Seattle Art Museum,
Eugene Fuller Memorial
Collection
64.139
Photograph by Elizabeth
Mann

Fig. 64. Leo Kenney
(1925–2001)
Indian Circle, 1963
Tempera and gouache on
paper
8 x 7½ in.
Collection of Merch and
Alice Pease

That same year Kenney produced an extraordinary work titled *Seed and Beyond II* displaying a debt to both Tobey and Tchelitchew. He would concentrate on these mandala and chakra forms in his art for the remainder of his life. The works are brilliantly painted with great technical proficiency, but the intricacy of the details in his style allowed him to create only a small body of work.[24]

Kenney remembered Ward Corley as another continuing influence even after the artist's death. In a letter to Jan Thompson dated August 14, 1968, he stated, "So impressed by the way Ward's painting holds up. 'Timeless' is the word. It exists (and *all* his late work) outside of 'now' concerns. It's that very quality that I aspire to. I will go on striving for it—and hope to attain it. The painting is 'nourishment' to the spirit. Isn't that what we need?—Fuck A.R.T. !!!!"[25]

The Northwest aesthetic fostered a legacy of inspiration even outside of painting and into the realm of crafts. Jack Lenor Larsen, the internationally renowned fabric designer, developed under this influence as a young gay man in Seattle. His retrospective at the Musée des Arts Décoratifs, Palais du Louvre, in 1979–80 made him and Mark Tobey two of only four Americans to be so honored.

NOTES

1   It is not known if Anderson had any interaction with Paul Cadmus and Luigi Lucioni at the Tiffany Foundation, although it is likely. I was not allowed to view Anderson's archive, controlled by his executor, for this project.

Artist Yvonne Twining Humber was the recipient of a Tiffany Foundation scholarship in 1932 and '33 and befriended Cadmus and Lucioni. A heterosexual woman, Humber recalled to me that this was her first opportunity to form a bond with homosexual artists, and she was somewhat shocked when she was asked out on a date by artist Edna Reindel, which she respectfully declined.

2   Sheryl Conkelton and Laura Landau, *Northwest Mythologies: The Interactions of Mark Tobey, Morris Graves, Kenneth Callahan, and Guy Anderson* (Seattle and London: Tacoma Art Museum and University of Washington Press, 2003), 38–39.

3   The painting was in Pries's private collection until he gave it to his friend Duane Shipman around 1964. See Jeffrey Karl Ochsner, *Lionel H. Pries, Architect, Artist, Educator: From Arts and Crafts to Modern Architecture* (Seattle and London: University of Washington Press, 2007), 188–89 and 351 (chapter 8, note 51).

4   Conkelton and Landau, *Northwest Mythologies*, 41 and note 30.

5   Dr. Richard Fuller's sexual orientation has not been established, although several of my personal friends who knew him (Yvonne Twining Humber, Attorney John D. McLauchlan, and Doris Jensen Carmin) told me in confidence that he was gay. Fuller was married very late in life to a woman named Betti Morrison, who in basic terms could be described as a social climber. Fuller had a devoted live-in butler named Les who was described by a family member as being "queer as a three-dollar bill." It was not uncommon in that era for a wealthy man to have a lover live with him under the guise of a servant; however, in Fuller's case, this is just a possibility and not a fact based on any evidence. Considering Fuller's wealth, good looks, and standing in the community, it would be hard to believe he couldn't find a wife in his youth and middle age.

6   Letter from Malcolm Roberts to Margaret and Kenneth Callahan, July 1937, Martin-Zambito Archive.

7   Karin Breuer, *Mac Harshberger: Art Deco Americain*, exhibition catalog (San Francisco: Fine Arts Museum of San Francisco, 1986), 20.

8   Thank you to artist Gary Faigin for his insightful explanation of the methods used in Tchelitchew's paintings.

9   Brian Tobey Callahan, *Margaret Callahan: Mother of Northwest Art* (n.p.: Trafford Publishing, 2009), 103.

10   Letter from Malcolm Roberts to Margaret and Kenneth Callahan, July 1937, Martin-Zambito Archive.

11   From Morris Graves Papers, Early December (1959), Ward Corley letter to Morris Graves, Special Collections & University Archives, University of Oregon Libraries, Eugene.

The romantic relationship between Morris Graves and Sherrill Van Cott was verified to me by two separate sources, architect Robert M. Shields and artist Jan Thompson.

Van Cott's poetry was kindly provided to me by Lawrence and Judi Mroczek.

Van Cott's medical information from Washington State Department of Health, Division of Vital Statistics, Certificate of Death.

12   Callahan, *Margaret Callahan*, 174 (summer 1942).

13   Interview with Sheila Farr, April 6, 2019.

14   Leo Kenney diary entry, April 9, 1965.

15   Copy of a diary excerpt from Wright's woodpecker painting dated May 3, 1948, and affixed to the back of the painting's frame. It also states, "This painting was originally owned by Howard Griffin (poet, close friend of CW, secretary to WH Auden) who sold the painting to *Poetry* magazine editor Nicholas Joost in 1955." Joost died in 1980 and I acquired this and one other Clifford Wright painting in the early 1990s. The painting is currently in a private collection in Seattle.

16   Arthur Millier, "State Water Color Show Has Quality," *Los Angeles Times*, September 21, 1947, part III, 4. The painting remains in the permanent collection of the Los Angeles County Museum of Art.

17   Letter to the editor of *Art News*, dated 1946, Morris Graves Papers, Special Collections &
      University Archives, University of Oregon Libraries, Eugene. It doesn't appear that the letter was
      published in the magazine but copies of it must have been sent to the Callahans and probably
      others in the community.

18   Callahan, *Margaret Callahan*, 333.

19   Callahan, 258.

20   Letter from Yone Arashiro to Morris Graves, November 13, 1952, Morris Graves Papers, Special
      Collections & University Archives, University of Oregon Libraries, Eugene.

21   Correspondence between Paul Mills and Morris Graves, undated, Morris Graves Papers, Special
      Collections & University Archives, University of Oregon Libraries, Eugene.

22   Elise Kelleher, "Annual Church Exhibition Has Art for Everyone," *Seattle Daily Times*, April 30,
      1952, 33.

23   Wesley Wehr, *Three Stories*, 2003, 10, 24; unpublished manuscript provided by Wehr to David Martin.

24   Leo Kenney diary, April 29, 1964, Leo Kenney archive, courtesy of Merch and Alice Pease.

25   Letter from Leo Kenney to Jan Thompson, August 14, 1968, Leo Kenney archive, courtesy of Merch
      and Alice Pease.

CONVICTED OF SODOMY

1160 Chas Wesley, waiter, King Co., 1893, sodomy, 43 yo, 7 yrs.

1401 John Morris, sailor, Pierce Co., 1895, sodomy, 33 yo, 10 yrs.

1403 James Murphy, printer, Pierce Co., 1895, 25 yo, 10 yrs.

1404 Charles Righter, none, Pierce Co., 1895, 19 yo, 10 yrs.

1460 William Barry, laborer, Spokane Co., 1895, attempted sodomy, 19 yo, 6 yrs.

1461 Richard Edwards, teamster, Spokane Co., 1895, attempted sodomy, 25 yo, 6 yrs.

1511 Jos. Manholland, barber, Walla Walla Co., 1896, sodomy, 33 yo, 10 yrs.

1672 Thomas Nicholas, laborer, Kitsap Co., 1897, assault with intent to commit infamous crime against nature, 30 yo, 12 yrs.

1702 Patrick Finley, sailor, Jefferson Co., 1897, sodomy, 38 yo, 10 yrs.

1930 Frank Romans (½ Indian), shoemaker, Yakima Co., 1898, attempt to commit sodomy, 28 yo, 5 yrs.

2060 John Brown, boilermaker, King Co., 1899, attempted sodomy, 47 yo, 4 yrs.

2061 Chas. Sanders, stonemason, King Co., 1899, attempt sodomy, 34 yo, 3 yrs.

2213 Dan Moran, laborer, Walla Walla Co., sodomy, 1900, 18 yo, 10 yrs.

2282 George Gray, bookkeeper, King Co., sodomy, 1900, 39 yo, 14 yrs.

2303 John Blackman, sawmill man, Pierce Co., 1900, 30 yo, 2 yrs.

2341 A. B. Hunt, farmer, King Co., 1901, assault to commit sodomy, 43 yo, 7 yrs.

2496 Frank Lewis (Negro), cook, King Co., 1901, sodomy, 24 yo, 10 yrs.

2498 Frank McIntosh, miner, King Co., 1901, sodomy, 45 yo, 10 yrs.

2522 Jacob Anderson, tailor, Spokane Co., 1901, sodomy, 37 yo, 2 yrs.

2546 Herbert Edwards, tailor, Whatcom Co., 1901, sodomy, 31 yo, 12 yrs.

2641 J. O. Hanch, King Co., clerk, sodomy, 1901, 26 yo

2684 Frank McGuire, laborer, King Co., attempt to commit sodomy, 1902, 24 yo, 1 yr.

3072 George S. Johnson (Negro), electric engineer, King Co., sodomy, 1903, 31 yo, 12 yrs.

3141 Sannan Kahn (E. Indian), waiter, King Co., assault to commit sodomy, 1903, 23 yo

3153 Edward D. Long, cook, Jefferson Co., assault to commit sodomy, 1903, 31 yo, 5 yrs.

3172 William Joseph McLanglin, tile setter, King Co., attempted sodomy, 1903, 36 yo, 8 yrs.

3265 Frank Van Loton, painter, Spokane Co., assault to commit sodomy, 1904, 41 yo, 2 yrs.

3291 Herbert C. Rollason, sailmaker, King Co., attempted sodomy, 1904, 27 yo, 9 yrs.

3296 George Carey, laborer, Chelan Co., assault to sodomy, 1904, 35 yo

3303 George Scott Smith, carpenter, Snohomish Co., assault against Nature, 1904, 56 yo, 3 yrs.

3334 Patrick Kirby, sailor, Jefferson Co., assault to commit sodomy, 1904, 25 yo, 2 yrs.

3369 William Jones, laborer, King Co., sodomy, 1904, 22 yo, 1 yr.

3414 W. L. McKernon, laborer, King Co., assault to commit sodomy, 1904, 20 yo, 1 yr.

3646 Frank Cario, laborer, Adams Co., sodomy, 1905, 30 yo, 10 yrs.

6154 Charles Gaffney, laborer, Benton Co., sodomy, 1911, 38 yo

6187 Christopher Wassis, laborer, Spokane Co., sodomy, 1911, 32 yo

6188 James Lollerhide, laborer, Asotin Co., against nature, 1911, 45 yo, 1–10 yrs.

6206 George McElroy, shoemaker, Grant Co., sodomy, 1911, 26 yo

6298 J. F. Hankins, painter, King Co., sodomy, 1911, 36 yo

6344 Harold Douglas, laborer, King Co., sodomy, 1913, 63 yo

6406 William H. Ha . . . [illegible], miner, Snohomish Co., 1913, 28 yo

6409 Joe A. MaGill, cook, Spokane Co., 1913, 46 yo

6452 Jago Sing (India), laborer, Thurston Co., sodomy, 1912, 23 yo

6453 Don Sing (India), laborer, Thurston Co., sodomy, 1912, 42 yo

6454 Bram Sing (India), laborer, Thurston Co., sodomy, 1912, 32 yo, 6–10 yrs.

6491 Clayborn H. Rafferty, laborer, Whatcom Co., attempt to commit sodomy, 1912, 30 yo, 1–5 yrs.

6493 John Ryan, miner, Cowlitz Co., sodomy, 1912, 25 yo, 2–10 yrs.

6607 David Gunreth, porter, Whitman Co., sodomy, 1912, 37 yo

6670 George Newham, clerk, Spokane Co, sodomy, 1913, 51 yo

6765 Joe A. Magill, laborer, Spokane Co., sodomy, 1913, 41 yo, 1–10 yrs.

6775 Thomas Tasus, laborer, King Co., sodomy, 1913, 30 yo, 1–10 yrs.

6783 James Cameron, laborer, Columbia Co., sodomy, 1913, 30 yo

6839 Adam J. May, laborer, King Co., sodomy, 1913, 44 yo

6904 John Doe (C. L. Grant), logger, Skagit Co., sodomy, 1913, 31 yo, 1–10 yrs.

6911 Tony Jovich, laborer, Pierce Co., sodomy, 1913, 42 yo, 1–10 yrs.

The Lavender Lens:
Gay Photography in Washington State

David L. Chapman

Before 1893 in Washington State there wasn't even a word for homosexuality—at least in the lawbooks. In the distant past of our region, those who committed *illum crimen horribile quod non nominandum est* (that horrible crime that is not named) might have been shunned, ignored, or attacked, but not prosecuted legally. If men pursued their erotic desires with other adults, behind closed doors or in darkened alleys, the law pretty much left them alone—as long as violence was not involved.

In 1893 all that changed when an anti-sodomy law was passed by the legislature and the official pogrom against gay people was off to a rousing start. Soon there were more than enough words—some old, some new—to describe this offense: sodomy, buggery, perversion, the detestable crime against nature, and many others.[1] There is not only a rich variety of names but also a great diversity of physical and personality types among gay men—from sissies to he-men and everything in between.

Homosexuality is just one of the many variations in human behavior, but it is one that has been at home in the Northwest for a very long time indeed. Despite its formerly remote location and primitive amenities, Washington State has hosted a remarkable group of people whose stories have been recorded in both quietly subtle and loudly dramatic ways.

For much of the nineteenth century, virtually the entire Pacific Northwest from Victoria in the north to Portland in the south was very sparsely populated. Unlike the urban centers of civilization far to the east, this was a place where people who wanted a new start might move.

If these settlers wanted to record photographic images of the land or its inhabitants, that was not always easy. Prior to the 1900s, photographic images often involved pricey, cumbersome equipment and the services of skilled professionals. Even greater problems ensued if one wanted to take pictures of the state's gay population; perhaps the biggest obstacle to this was that there was never any real understanding of who they were. Before the middle of the twentieth century, the concept of a gay social subcategory was seldom recognized. Most people considered homosexuality to be an act, not a lifestyle.[2]

Necessity, however, often bred breeding of a different sort. This was because in places like the nineteenth-century Northwest, where there was a huge gender disparity (men outnumbered women more than fifteen to one in 1890), sexual interaction was often fluid, and people sometimes indulged in different varieties as opportunity or necessity dictated.[3] If, for instance, a lonely, liquored-up logger in a

Fig. 1. Jon Arnt (1906–1982)
John Curtis with totem
pole, circa 1955
Toned gelatin silver print
10 x 8 in.
Private collection

remote camp desired a bit of sexual relief, his options were often quite limited and he had to take what he could get from whoever would give it to him.

If Victorian Northwesterners thought about it at all, most would probably have considered homosexuality to be an alternate and generally infamous activity but not something with its own unique mores and culture. Ironically, gays were sometimes flamboyantly visible, but few people "saw" them—at least not as a distinct and separate group. Fairies, pansies, and other visibly effeminate men were certainly out there, but in the nineteenth century they were seldom lumped together in a definable subspecies. Those men who exhibited traditionally masculine traits but who participated in homosexuality remained for the most part hidden. So even if a gay person stood before the camera in full, extravagant drag, he might have been considered a remarkable (and possibly despicable) rara avis, but he probably would not be recognized as a member of a distinct social and sexual group. In short, the technology for gay photography was there in the earliest days of Washington State but not the vision.[4]

If early photographs of gay men are rare, those portraying lesbians are even rarer. A few images have survived, but these represent only a tiny fraction of the number taken by and of gay men. It is easy to understand how female social subservience, financial dependence, and technological inexperience could contribute to this situation. Women who cross-dressed as men were surprisingly common in the frontier West, and when their gender was discovered, it often created a sensation. A case in point was Seattle native Nell Pickerell (1882–1922), who dressed as a man, called herself Harry Allen, and was as rough and pugnacious as any male street tough. It was said that two lovesick women committed suicide after discovering that the dashing Harry was actually Nell. In later times, lesbian women became

Fig. 2. Electric Studio, Seattle
Two affectionate men identified only as H. T. and R. D., circa 1910
Real photo postcard
3⅜ x 5⅜ in.
Chapman Collection

Fig. 3. Two shirtless lumberjacks, Olympic Peninsula, circa 1935
2¾ x 4½ in.
Chapman Collection

Fig. 4. Three shirtless men, Eastern Washington, circa 1930
2⅞ x 3⅞ in.
Chapman Collection

Fig. 5. Varsity football
player Steve Slivinsky
attired for his part in
the *Ballet Moose* at the
University of Washington
Press photo dated
March 13, 1937
10 x 8 in.
Chapman Collection

Fig. 6. Drag king known
only as Nick Arthur who
emceed frequently at the
Garden of Allah nightclub
7 x 5 in.
University of Washington
Libraries, Special
Collections
PH Coll 673.29

a little more visible and some sat for portraits. One of these was Nick Arthur, a
noted drag king who often appeared at local venues in the late 1940s and early
1950s. It is said that Nick was very proud of her widow's peak hairline.[5] By and
large, however, most nineteenth- and early-twentieth-century lesbians remained
deeply concealed in the social fabric of Washington State.

Sometimes society's blindness to the homosexuals among them proved to be a
boon to those who chose to live together quietly as "bachelor friends" or who sur-
reptitiously enjoyed viewing risqué photos of men in abbreviated attire. Although
many gay men had long been interested in photos of nude athletes (and others),
is a photograph of a naked man, regardless of the subject's sexuality, automati-
cally a homosexual photograph? Identifying a "gay" photograph has always been
a notoriously slippery prospect. Is it an image of a gay person, is it taken by a gay
photographer, or is it simply a picture that might appeal to a gay audience? One
critic has defined homosexual photography as "those images which consciously or
unconsciously portray or evoke homoerotic associations shared by the creator and
viewer."[6] The modifiers "consciously or unconsciously" are the key to a broader
sense of gay imagery. A "gay photograph" should therefore be a picture that
appeals to a gay audience (or at least a broad portion of it).

Within these general parameters, homosexual photography can be divided
into a few distinct subcategories. The first is news or documentary in nature, and
it includes journalistic reporting. The second is vernacular photography that
includes amateur pictures, snapshots, and inexpertly produced novelty photos of
usually anonymous subjects. A third group consists of physique photos. These are
images of muscular young men wearing next to nothing; their ostensible purpose is
to display the subject's musculature, but they also include an unmistakable element

of homoeroticism. Another segment of gay photography is the drag photo. The purpose of these is to display men in their often elaborate female costumes and makeup; many of the subjects are performers in bars or other entertainment venues. Perhaps the most respected subgenre of gay photography is the art photo. As the name implies, the purpose of this genre is to display the nude male body in an aesthetically pleasing way.[7]

There was one remaining type of photographic representation that permitted the region's homosexuals to be immortalized in silver, albumin, or mercury. But there was a darker reason for making and preserving these images.

It is a melancholy fact that in the earliest days of Washington's existence as a separate political entity, the only verifiable form of photography that featured a man who committed a homosexual act was the mug shot. It was only after someone who had committed an offense was arrested, booked at the police station, and photographed that his image was preserved. These artless and unimaginative pictures are the only way that today we can look into the faces of men who committed sodomy and were somehow caught at it.[8]

Naturally, there exist a few snapshots or studio photos of men or women showing a socially acceptable level of affection, but not much beyond that, especially in the remoter areas of the Pacific Northwest. These playful images might have portrayed same-sex affection, but they might just as easily be ambiguous pictures of friendship that are misinterpreted by modern viewers. However, it is hard to quibble with the evidence of someone who was arrested for "the infamous crime against nature."

Despite their institutional format, mug shots can reveal the fine gradations of feelings that these men had as they were being photographed. We can look into their eyes and read expressions of fear, defiance, regret, uncertainty, ignorance,

Fig. 7. Francis Hill worked on a ranch near Spokane, where he posed for this snapshot circa 1950.
3 x 2½ in.
University of Washington Libraries, Special Collections
uw40253 phcoll1028 11d

Fig. 8. Francis Hill moved to Seattle, where he often became "Frances." Here she poses demurely on a television set for this snapshot, 1956.
5 x 3½ in.
University of Washington Libraries, Special Collections
uw40254, phcoll1028.1 _146

Fig. 9. Harta Studio
Exotic dancer Robin
Raye in a triple exposure
showing him as a man,
a woman, and an exotic
dancer; Raye performed at
Seattle's Garden of Allah
nightclub, circa 1955
10 x 8 in.
University of Washington
Libraries, Special
Collections
uw40258 phcoll673.239
_1963

Fig. 10. Jackie Starr was a
top female impersonator
at the Garden of Allah,
and she is shown here in a
charming informal snap-
shot from circa 1948 with
her "husband," Bill Scott.
The two were "married"
in a ceremony in which
Nick Arthur (see fig. 6) was
"best man."
3⅝ x 2¾ in.
University of Washington
Libraries, Special
Collections
uw40255 phcoll673.259d

worry, or a thousand other emotions that were welling up in their minds as they sat for these pictures.

The men in this rogue's gallery were from all parts of the state—rural and urban, east and west of the Cascades. The youngest in these pictures was only eighteen years old and the oldest was sixty-three; they date from 1893 to 1913. A man who was convicted of sodomy could expect a very harsh sentence of up to twenty years in prison at hard labor, even where no coercion or violence was involved. How many of the subjects of these mug shots showed in their pained facial expressions that their lives were about to change forever? A long stretch at Walla Walla or some other state institution was the result of a few moments of drunken tussling or stolen pleasure.

The circumstances of their cases varied; some involved force, some were consensual, and almost all involved alcohol. With only a few exceptions, these men were from the working class, since rich men had the money to hire eloquent lawyers or leave the region quickly.[9] They included African Americans, East Indians, "half-breeds," immigrants who could barely speak English, and blue-collar whites. The majority worked in all-male environments where they were isolated from society; they were miners, loggers, or sailors, or they were cut off from other, more conventional relationships by poverty. The most common profession given was "laborer," and the majority of the prisoners were young men between the ages of eighteen and thirty-five. When their pent-up desires got the better of them, these lusty young workers cast good judgment aside and acted on urges that ended up destroying their futures. Now they are memorialized in these once-shameful images, but modern viewers can easily see the tragedy, disruption, and melancholy in their faces. They had been apprehended for committing an offense that today is not a crime—not counting those poor souls who were so frustrated that they forced

themselves on another. One thing is certain: these men's "crimes" represent only a tiny fraction of the gay sex that was taking place at the time.[10] The men shown here are merely the ones who were caught and who could not defend themselves properly.

Some photographs were just as unstudied as mug shots, but they showed a side of gay life that was less intense and more intimate. These were the vernacular photos of queer subjects taken by amateurs. Although they might have a few aesthetic rough edges, they can display contemporary gay life in a way that is hidden to mainstream photographers. Frequently these images were taken outdoors and were homemade; at other times they might have been taken in small storefront studios that specialized in quickly made or tourist photographs. These often-jokey images might use sly, camp humor as a souvenir of a time, a place, or an event. Sometimes vernacular images were taken to record a man's musculature, sometimes to remember a fond friendship or an association that was important though perhaps fleeting. They might not have been originally produced by or directed at a gay audience, but they nevertheless appeal to homosexuals because of their subject matter. These include attractive, often shirtless men who were captured on film in backyards, at work, or even in photographic studios.

What secret message is conveyed by a cabinet photo from the 1890s of a trio of male Graces who pose in nightshirts? Other images are less opaque. Some photos simply celebrated the delights of friendship, as in the image of a couple of buddies dressed like cowboys, perhaps concealing their real feelings for one another by making suggestive moves with their drawn revolvers. The one uniting feature of these photos is that because of the subject matter, they aimed at a very narrow audience—often either the subject or one or two others. They were not created for wide consumption. Some have an obvious gay or camp subtext; others might convey unintended homoerotic meanings to later and more alert viewers.

Fig. 11. Elite Photo Studios
Three young men in nightshirts
Tacoma, circa 1893
Cabinet photo
6½ x 4¼ in.
Chapman Collection

Fig. 12. Radium Portrait Studio
City dudes identified only as Al and Percy
Seattle, circa 1915
Real photo postcard
Approx. 5⅜ x 3⅜ in.
Chapman Collection

Fig. 13. Raul Hoyt is winner of the "Miss Hubba Hubba of 1946" contest, a mock beauty pageant held at the University of Washington. Acme Press photo dated January 26, 1946
9 x 7 in.
Chapman Collection

Closely connected to vernacular photos are those that were taken for journalistic purposes. These newspaper shots might display men participating in sports (while showing their physiques in a state of undress) or doing something that is typically girlie (like wearing women's clothes). A straight man might have donned a frilly woman's frock just for laughs, but gay men might get a bigger chuckle out of it because a massive football player or some other paragon of heterosexuality has compromised (even in jest) his own manliness.

When photos display men who crossdressed in a more determined or expert way, the genre subtly changes to the drag picture. Northwesterners have been cross-dressing for quite a while, but in the middle decades of the last century, when many men posed for photos in full regalia, a sort of golden era began. Seattle's first drag bar, the Garden of Allah, opened in 1946, and this proved to be not only a gathering place for gay people but also a way for men (and some women) to show their talents at transvestism.[11] Fortunately, many of these photos have been preserved, and they provide both a window into the lives of postwar gay men in the region and a look at the liberating effects of dressing the way one wants.

While some local gays were getting in touch with their feminine sides, others were more interested in the aesthetic and erotic delights of traditional masculinity and muscularity. Thus, one of the most popular forms of gay photography is the physique photograph. Due to a physical-culture movement that swept the region, the country, and the world in the late nineteenth century, more and more people were concerned about maintaining their health and their appearance. It did not take long for books and magazines to show would-be athletes what a strong man looked like. Perhaps not surprisingly, many homosexuals quickly realized that the images of scantily clad, handsome, and muscular men in these sports-centered publications were very exciting.

Although photos of nude men had appeared almost as soon as photography was invented, physique photography blossomed from the 1940s to the mid-1960s.[12] The ostensible purpose of physique photography was to display muscular development and to encourage others to build their muscles as part of cultivating a strong, healthy, and attractive appearance. Images of strong young men flexing their biceps, spreading their latissimi dorsi, or crunching their abs were the norm, but certain photographers discovered that they could make a good deal of money selling to gays if they recorded the musculature of virile subjects with just a soupçon of eroticism. A knowing look at the camera, a provocative pose, or a tantalizing bulge in the model's trunks could mean the difference between a photo that emphasized the musculature and one that hinted at something a bit more exciting.

The most successful physique photographers began taking pictures and sending them to legitimate bodybuilding magazines like *Strength & Health* and *Your*

Physique, and in return for use of the photos for free, the publishers gave the photographers space for ads in the backs of the periodicals. These ads promised more photos and often hinted that the good stuff that could not be published in the magazines was available for sale directly from the source. Selling overtly suggestive or sexually charged images was strictly forbidden, so the men in the pictures had to cover up their privates, and they generally did this in physique photos using a "posing pouch," a cloth sack that was strung around the waist and that concealed the genitalia (though just barely). Some cameramen took photos of totally nude models, but this was asking for trouble, since the legal and postal authorities took a dim view of such things. The excuse that the images were artistic and not sexually explicit generally got little traction with the authorities. To them smut was smut.

Most of the photographers were in the major cities of the East and West Coasts, but one of the finest and most prolific physique photo studios was run by Jon Arnt in Seattle. The photographer was born in Beloit, Kansas, in 1906, but in the early 1940s he moved to Seattle, where he found work taking photos at Boeing Aircraft. Sometime around 1945 Arnt began his own photo studio, and for two decades he recorded the usual array of marriage, anniversary, and other formal portraits. He also became the official photographer for Seattle University, where he took pictures of sports teams, prom couples, faculty members, and various campus scenes. What the priests at the Jesuit university did not know (at least so one assumes) was that the Kansas native was also recording the glories of local manhood.

Arnt would visit nearby gymnasiums and invite a few of the better-looking men to come to his studio on East Pike Street and pose for his camera. Many times the photographer would convince the men to disrobe completely and would take nude pictures of them. This was not so odd in the early days, since it was assumed that before the images were published the photographer would black out the private parts by inking in a posing strap. If Arnt had tried to market the pictures

Fig. 14. Jon Arnt
(1906–1982)
The parade float of the Totem Club in Seattle's Seafair celebration featured (left to right) Dave Solhaug, Davie Trammell, and Dick Hofeditz, press photo, August 1954
10 x 8 in.
Chapman Collection

Fig. 15. Jon Arnt
(1906–1982)
Seattle resident Richard Hofeditz was a prominent local bodybuilder.
circa 1954
Toned gelatin silver print
10 x 8 in.
Chapman Collection

of the models when they were au naturel, he could have been arrested and sent to prison. Still, some of these nudes did survive unretouched, and now they are extremely rare. Arnt was famous for his bronze-toned photos, and there is a great warmth and richness in these images. Most of the men whom he photographed were presumably heterosexual, but they were captured with an eye toward the sensuality that was conveyed by their bodies. It was Arnt's appreciation for beauty that lends a special luminous quality to his masterful images.

Arnt was apparently well connected in the burgeoning Seattle homosexual community, and he recorded other gay subjects. He took a few photos of the female impersonators at the Garden of Allah, as well as at least one moody portrait of ballet impresario and Seattle native Robert Joffrey. Arnt was truly not just a regional master but an equal to others all over the world. He would occasionally send photos to a few early crypto-gay publications that maintained the illusion that they promoted exercise and a healthy life. They fooled very few.

Arnt continued his photography business until the mid-1960s, but he seems to have gradually decreased his involvement in physique studies. This is almost certainly related to the fact that the laws against obscenity were beginning to break down around 1966–67, and it soon became possible to exhibit not just nude photos but pictures of actual sex acts.[13] At this point the great majority of physique photographers called it quits. They had never wanted to produce pornography; art was their goal (with a little erotic spice stirred in). The Seattle photographer had to find another way to make a living, so surprisingly he found employment as the city's night coroner. It must have been a grisly business, but it left Arnt free to pursue his picture taking during the day. Around 1972 he retired to a little residence on Camano Island, and it was there he died on January 23, 1982.[14]

There is little question that Jon Arnt was the region's best physique photographer. It is thanks to him that a few of Seattle's handsomest and best-proportioned men have been beautifully and skillfully preserved for all time. But Arnt was

Fig. 18. Jon Arnt
(1906–1982)
Black Panther tattoo
circa 1955
Toned gelatin silver print
7½ x 9½ in.
Chapman Collection

not the only physique artist operating in Washington State at this time. Another Washington man, Carl Natelli (1913–2008), was only slightly less prolific, and his work was published in both gay and bodybuilding magazines. Some of his best work was done with the bodybuilder Edmund Pinnell around 1958.

Photographer Natelli worked in conjunction with another artist, William M. MacLane (1926–2000), who acted as a distributor for the work of a number of artists and photographers from the region and beyond. MacLane had been a combat artist during World War II, and he continued to make art his profession when he returned to Washington after the war. He worked in pencil-and-ink drawings that portrayed sailors, soldiers, and surfers in addition to Northwest subjects like rugged lumberjacks and beachgoers. Most of MacLane's works reflect the vocabulary of the midcentury physique genre: muscular models, sexually charged scenes, but no overt sex displayed. His artwork is clearly designed to appeal to a gay audience since his scenes always show a heavy sensuality and (when there are two or more figures) there is a subtle but obvious sexual tension to the scenes. MacLane was prosperous enough in 1953 to build a starkly modern house overlooking Portage Bay that was featured in the *Seattle Times* in 1955. The artist worked in a variety of mediums including pen and ink, watercolor, and oils. In 1982, MacLane sold all his remaining works and moved to Bothell, where he lived another twenty years, quickly fading from public view.[15]

The final Washington State photographer who produced thousands of male nudes is Grenville Michael Scott. He was born in Tacoma in 1922, but much like Imogene Cunningham, another Northwest artist who was thoroughly grounded in the values and atmosphere of the region, Scott did most of his best work in

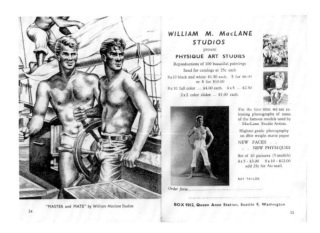

Fig. 19. Two photo
advertisements for William
M. MacLane Studios,
Seattle; the artist's portrait
taken at his residence on
Delmar Drive is in the
upper left corner of both
pieces, and his various
artwork is arrayed around
him, circa 1958.
3¼ x 8⅜ in. each
Chapman Collection

Fig. 20. Double-page
advertising spread for
MacLane Studios, Seattle.
In addition to the artwork,
there is also a physique
photograph of model Ray
Taylor from *Adonis: The
Art Magazine of the Male
Physique*, no. 5, May 1959.
5¾ x 8¼ in.
Chapman Collection

Fig. 21. Double-page
advertising spread for
MacLane Studios, Seattle;
paintings by MacLane
(*The Studio* and *Moracas*),
from *Adonis: The Art
Magazine of the Male
Physique*, no. 10, September
1960
5¾ x 8¼ in.
Chapman Collection

California. His parents separated and divorced shortly after he was born, and he
and his mother lived in Tacoma for the next twenty years.

After attending Stadium High School, Scott went to the University of
Washington and pledged at the Sigma Chi fraternity in 1941, but after Pearl Harbor
he left school in 1942 to join the army. Apparently, his duties in the service did not
prevent him from returning to the UW, and he is shown in uniform in the 1944
Tyee as a member of the Purple Shield Society. He finally graduated in 1947, and
sometime around 1950 moved to San Francisco, where he found work in advertising for the National Distillers Corporation. It was in the Bay Area where he
began to discover and expand his photographic talents, as well as his sexuality.
San Francisco was mobbed with servicemen who were returning from the Pacific
theater, and a surprising number of them ended up in Scott's bed, as well as being
recorded on black-and-white film and, occasionally, in color transparencies.

Grenville Scott eventually moved to Los Angeles, where he bought a gra-
cious home in the Toluca Lake neighborhood of the San Fernando Valley. There
he installed a pool and had tall cinder-block walls built around his little domain,
where he often held wild parties for his friends and paramours. From the late 1950s
to the early 1980s, Mike Scott (as he usually called himself) began taking photos
with an astonishing frenzy. He took thousands of black-and-white images and even
more color slides and transparencies. This was a risky business at the time because
these photos were almost exclusively of male nudes—and not coyly posed or
attired in posing pouches. Since he did not intend to sell his images, he could make
them as bold and sexy as he wished. Mike Scott continued taking photos well into
the 1980s, but by then he had slowed down and his preferred format changed to

Polaroid instant photos. Then in 2013, while the ninety-two-year-old Washington native was crossing the road near his home, he was struck by an SUV and died after a few weeks in the hospital. Fortunately, his photographs survived more or less intact.[16]

Like much gay art and photography, the images in this exhibition have survived time, neglect, and social disapproval to form a precious link to the past. From the hapless sodomites of a century ago to muscular sports stars, from virile young physique models to outrageous drag queens, from repression to liberation—these long-forgotten glimpses of gay life in Washington State can finally be seen and appreciated again. The love that dared not speak its name can finally be shouted loud and clear.

Fig. 22. Grenville Michael Scott (1922–2014) Two male figures Scan from original negative made in San Francisco, circa 1955 Chapman Collection

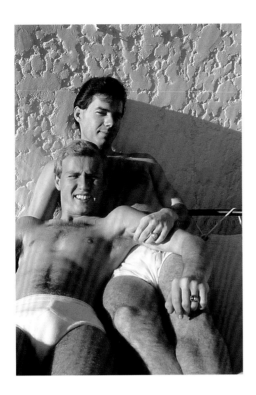

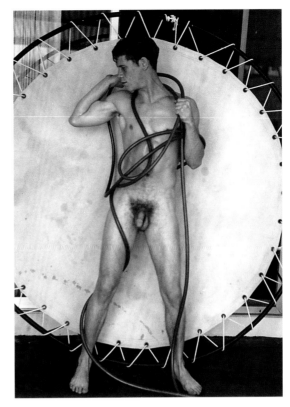

Fig. 23. Grenville Michael
Scott (1922–2014)
Two male figures
Color slide photographed
in the San Fernando
Valley, circa 1965
Chapman Collection

Fig. 24. Grenville Michael
Scott (1922–2014)
Male figure with garden
hose
Black-and-white
photograph from original
negative made in the
San Fernando Valley,
circa 1965
Chapman Collection

Fig. 25, Grenville Michael
Scott (1922–2014)
Male figure with
phonograph record
Black-and-white
photograph from original
negative made in San
Francisco, circa 1955
Chapman Collection

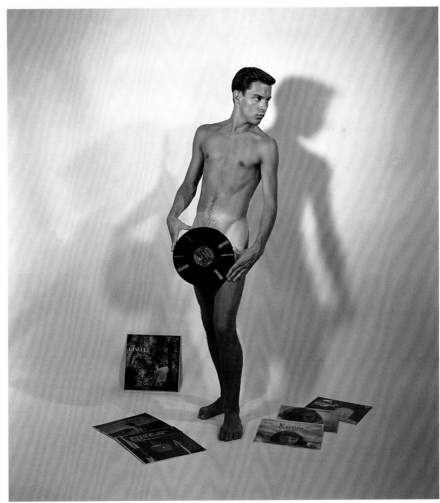

1   For a fuller report on Washington's sodomy laws, see Gary L. Atkins, *Gay Seattle: Stories of Exile and Belonging* (Seattle: University of Washington Press, 2003), 13–33.

2   This concept is explored most fully in Michel Foucault's *The History of Sexuality*, vol. 1: *The Will to Knowledge*, part II: "The Repressive Hypothesis." According to John D'Emilio in *Sexual Politics, Sexual Communities: The Making of a Homosexual Minority in the United States, 1940–1970* (Chicago: University of Chicago Press, 1983), 32–35, a true gay subculture did not emerge fully until after World War II.

3   The 15-to-1 statistic is found in Peter Boag, *Same-Sex Affairs: Constructing and Controlling Homosexuality in the Pacific Northwest* (Berkeley: University of California, 2003), 18. Also see Jana Bommersbach, "Homos on the Range: How Gay Was the West?" in *True West*, November 1, 2005, https://truewestmagazine.com/old-west-homosexuality-homos-on-the-range/.

4   Historian George Chauncey, in *Gay New York: Gender, Urban Culture, and the Making of the Gay Male World, 1890–1940* (New York: Basic Books, 1994), 2–3, calls the supposed blindness of the majority toward gay people the "Myth of Invisibility." He says sophisticated New Yorkers saw homosexuals perfectly well and many went slumming in "pansy bars" to laugh at the queers. This may have been true in New York, but not necessarily in Washington State.

5   The biography of Nell Pickerell/Harry Allen is found in Knute Berger's article at https://crosscut.com/2014/06/nell-pickerell-transgender-youth-knute-berger, and Nick Arthur's biography is in Don Paulson and Roger Simpson, *An Evening at the Garden of Allah: A Gay Cabaret in Seattle* (New York: Columbia University Press, 1996), 57–68.

6   Donald Mader, "Photography," in Wayne R. Dynes, ed., *The Encyclopedia of Homosexuality* (Abington: Routledge, 1990), vol. 2, 993.

7   There have been many books on the subject of gay photography, but most deal almost exclusively with art photos. One exception is Pierre Borhan, *Hommes pour hommes: Homoérotisme et homosexualité masculine dans l'histoire de la photographie depuis 1840* (Paris: Éditions des 2 terres, 2007). Published in English as *Men for Men: A History of Gay Photography* (London: Jonathan Cape, 2008).

8   In legal terms, sodomy is any sexual act that is considered "unnatural" or immoral. This means that technically the law can also be used to prosecute heterosexuals, but in practice its victims have been almost exclusively homosexuals. See https://www.law.cornell.edu/wex/sodomy.

9   Another reason for the heavy preponderance of working-class men is that, according to Alfred Kinsey, during the first decades of the twentieth century men at the lowest end of educational and class levels were more likely than others to engage in homosexual activity. Kinsey reported that "common day laborers engaged in more homosexual activity than any other group of men." See Chauncey, *Gay New York*, 118–19, and Boag, *Same-Sex Affairs*, 22.

10 Since sodomy was a felony that required a jury trial and a preponderance of evidence, most men who were detained by the police for homosexual activity were charged with "disorderly conduct," a misdemeanor that merely required a hearing before a judge. See Chauncey, *Gay New York*, 185.

11 See Paulson and Simpson, *An Evening at the Garden of Allah*.

12 For more complete analysis of physique photography, see David K. Johnson, *Buying Gay: How Physique Entrepreneurs Sparked a Movement* (New York: Columbia University Press, 2019). Also see Thomas Waugh, *Hard to Imagine: Gay Male Eroticism in Photography and Film from Their Beginnings to Stonewall* (New York: Columbia University Press, 1996).

13 See Johnson, *Buying Gay*, 215–20.

14 Details of Jon Arnt's life were pieced together from various newspaper accounts (including Arnt's obituary in the *Seattle Times*), the *Seattle City Directory*, Ancestry.com, and interviews with former models.

15 Biographical details on William M. MacLane came mainly from an article in *Physique Pictorial*, vol. 6, no. 2, summer 1956, 14–15. Other facts came from various newspaper articles, including the *Seattle Times*, September 4, 1955. Carl Natelli's obituary provided details of his life (*Seattle Times*, November 22, 2008).

16 Grenville Michael Scott's biography was gleaned from various newspaper articles, Ancestry.com, real estate records, Seattle and San Francisco city directories, and the *Tyee*, the University of Washington yearbook.

Fig. 26. Grenville Michael
Scott (1922–2014)
Three male figures
Black-and-white
photograph from original
negative made in San
Francisco, circa 1955
Chapman Collection

Biographies

Richard Bennett
(1899–1971)

Richard Francis Bennett was a nationally known printmaker, painter, and illustrator, born in Ireland but raised and educated in Washington State. He divided his time between New York City and the Pacific Northwest and was considered one of the leading children's book author-illustrators of his time. He also produced an important body of work in the field of relief printmaking (woodblock prints and wood engravings) for which he received national recognition.

Born in County Cork, Ireland, the first of four children, Bennett moved to the Pacific Northwest with his parents in 1903 at the age of four. His family owned and operated a farm in Bellevue, near Lake Sammamish, and it was there that Richard developed his lifelong love of nature. The talented young man also excelled in music, playing both piano and violin. After graduating from Redmond High School, he moved to Seattle, where he lived with two of his aunts and attended the UW with their support.

At the university, he studied English and drama in addition to fine arts. He produced illustrations for the student publication, the *Sun Dodger*, a satirical magazine that lampooned current issues of the day. Like those of his fellow UW contemporaries Thomas Handforth and Mac Harshberger, his early works were inspired by the gay English illustrator Aubrey Beardsley (1872–1898).

By 1922, Bennett had befriended Glenn Hughes (1894–1964) of the UW's Drama Department. He became involved in Hughes's various theatrical productions, acting in leading roles and occasionally designing the stage sets and costumes. Hughes and his company were key figures in Seattle's early live theater culture.

Bennett's acting career started in 1922 when he was featured in three of Hughes's productions; *A Bright Morning* by Serafín and Joaquín Alvarez Quintero; *Mother of Pierrot* by Hughes; and Shakespeare's *As You Like It*, in which he played the character Touchstone.

The following year he continued his association with Hughes, creating stage sets and costumes as well as acting in Edmond Rostand's *The Romancers*, Shakespeare's *A Midsummer Night's Dream*, and Charles Perrault's *Bluebeard*.

Around 1924, Bennett accepted a teaching position as director of dramatic arts at a private school in South Bend, Indiana, spending the summer months back in Seattle. By now, he had focused on printmaking and specifically woodcut. His prints were featured in national publications like the *Forum* and the *Dial*.

In 1928 he moved to New York City to attend Columbia University, where he

Richard Bennett (right) in drag in a comical theater production at the Moran School, Bainbridge Island, WA, circa 1924
Collection of the Museum of History & Industry, Seattle
2006.38.406.115

Richard Bennett
(1899–1971)
Untitled, 1943–48
Tempera
10 x 7½ in.
Collection of the Museum
of History & Industry,
Seattle
2006.38.1

Richard Bennett
(1899–1971)
Clearing Land, 1943–48
Tempera
10 x 7½ in.
Collection of the Museum
of History & Industry,
Seattle
2006.38.2

received a master's degree. He needed a stable income, so he accepted a position at the Rye Country Day School in Rye, New York. He remained there for five years and also taught for one year at the Ethical Culture Fieldston School in New York City.

With growing success in the visual arts, he switched his focus to a graphic-arts career and ended his theatrical aspirations.

In 1928 the *Book League Monthly* included the article "Wessex, the Hardy Country, Four Wood Blocks by Richard Bennett" in its December issue. This article paid tribute to the recently deceased Thomas Hardy (1840–1928), the great English novelist and poet. A woodcut titled *Thomas Hardy's Birthplace* became one of six Bennett woodcuts purchased by the noted collector Blanche Adler and eventually gifted to the Baltimore Museum of Art.

In 1929, Bennett spent the summer with relatives in County Cork, drawing inspiration from his native culture. Back in Seattle, a group of artists from the UW started the Northwest Printmakers Society, and Bennett won the purchase prize in their first exhibition later that year. He exhibited with the organization until 1934.

His artistic career was now in full force. The book *Dial* used one of his woodcuts as the cover for their summer 1930 edition, and the American Institute of Graphic Arts selected Bennett's woodcut *The Shelter* as one of the Fifty Prints of the Year to travel across the US. This was significant because the selection was made by one of the country's leading artists, John Sloan (1871–1951), and included some of the major printmakers of the period.

Bennett's career was following the same trajectory as that of his close friend Thomas Handforth. Both men attended the UW as English majors, and like Bennett's parents, Handforth's mother, Ruby Shera, was an Irish immigrant.

Handforth also developed his reputation through printmaking (primarily etching and lithography) and book illustration.

Bennett's first national book-illustration commission was for *The York Road* by Lizette Woodward Reese, published by Farrar & Rinehart in 1931.

The following year his woodcut *Paul Bunyan* was used as the frontispiece for James Stevens's *The Saginaw Paul Bunyan*, which contained illustrations by Bennett and was published by Alfred A. Knopf. Bennett would later produce the definitive Paul Bunyan illustrations for *Legends of Paul Bunyan*, edited by Harold W. Felton in 1948.

In 1935, Doubleday published *Skookum and Sandy*, the first of seven original children's books that Bennett wrote and illustrated himself. The story revolved around a young boy and his pet goat in the Native American settlement at La Push, on the Washington coast. The book won the prestigious Literary Guild Award.

His *Shawneen and the Gander*, 1937, won the Junior Literary Guild Award and became so popular that he read the book (using his best Irish brogue) on a live St. Patrick's Day radio broadcast on NBC. He had the honor of riding on the float that day in the Fifth Avenue parade accompanying First Lady Eleanor Roosevelt, a member of the Literary Guild herself.

With a flourishing career in New York, he was able to travel throughout the world in search of inspiration for his art and illustrations. He often returned to the Northwest for extended periods to be with his family and reconnect with his artist friends. He often brought East Coast friends to Washington State as travel companions, including painter Theodoros Stamos (1922–1987) and Leslie Marchand (1900–1999), the Lord Byron scholar whose parents lived in Seattle.

Richard Bennett
(1899–1971)
Untitled, 1943–48
Tempera
7½ x 9⅞ in.
Collection of the Museum of History & Industry, Seattle
2006.38.3

Richard Bennett
(1899–1971)
Sunday, 1943–48
Tempera
10¼ x 7¼ in.
Collection of the Museum
of History & Industry,
Seattle
2006.38.45

Richard Bennett
(1899–1971)
Untitled, circa 1935
Woodblock print
11½ x 8½ in.
Collection of the Museum
of History & Industry,
Seattle
2006.38. 309

Richard Bennett
(1899–1971)
Untitled, 1943–48
Tempera
10¼ x 14 in.
Collection of the Museum
of History & Industry,
Seattle
2006.38.77

Bennett had now established himself as a leading illustrator of children's books, and in 1943 he was honored with a solo exhibition of his prints at the University of Washington's Henry Art Gallery.

Around that time, one of Bennett's Seattle friends, artist Guy Anderson, had purchased a rustic cabin at Robe Ranch, near Granite Falls, that featured magnificent views of the Stillaguamish Valley and Mount Pilchuck. Anderson had just ended consecutive relationships with painters Morris Graves and Malcolm Roberts when he and Bennett became a couple. Bennett was in the process of completing a nine-month teaching experience at the experimental Seeman School in El Monte, California, where his friend Handforth and Handforth's lover Edmund Tolk were teaching.

From 1943 until 1948, Bennett lived intermittently with Anderson in his cabin and spent the winter months working in New York at his studio on East Fiftieth Street, where he was illustrating between two and four books per year. During his time with Anderson at Robe Ranch, he was extremely prolific as a painter, often producing homoerotic imagery of the region's lumberjacks. His book *Mick and Mack and Mary Jane*, from 1948, is set near Mount Pilchuck and is loosely based on his life with Anderson.

In 1944 the Seattle Art Museum honored Bennett with a solo exhibition of his prints, securing his reputation as one of the region's most accomplished artists.

By 1949 his romantic relationship with Anderson was coming to an end and he once again traveled to Ireland. The work produced there formed the basis for yet another solo exhibition at SAM, where in 1951 they featured his Irish drawings.

Bennett spent the ensuing decade producing numerous illustrations for many prominent authors. Although he never pursued representation by galleries in New York City, his fine art paintings were shown in prominent Seattle venues including the Otto Seligman Gallery, which also represented Mark Tobey and many of the region's other prominent artists.

By 1961, Richard Bennett's health began to fail and he returned to Seattle to have surgery. He remained there for most of the year in the care of his mother and two sisters, Kathleen and Helen. When he was well enough to return to New York, his close circle of gay friends cared for him and he resumed work in his studio apartment.

Unfortunately, this was short-lived. In 1963, Bennett suffered a debilitating stroke in his apartment. As soon as it was safe for him to travel, he returned to the Northwest, where he was placed in a nursing home in Redmond. He was confined to a wheelchair, and although he gradually regained some of his manual abilities, his artistic career had come to an end.

In 1970 the Lake Washington School District decided to name their newest elementary school after him. The Richard Bennett Elementary School is now a

part of the City of Bellevue's school system. The school is situated on the land that had originally been farmed by the Bennett family and to this day contains reproductions of his work in the school's public spaces.

Bennett died in his beloved Pacific Northwest on September 16, 1971, in Redmond.

Book illustrations

Richard Bennett created woodblock print illustrations for over two hundred publications throughout his career.

Initially, he collaborated with Glenn Hughes on his *New Plays for Mummers, A Book of Burlesques* (1926) and produced two chapbooks: *England and Ireland: Twelve Woodcuts*, 1927, and *Puget Sound: Twelve Woodcuts*, 1932.

Bennett's books that he wrote and illustrated:

Skookum and Sandy, 1935 (set in La Push)

Shawneen and the Gander, 1937

Hannah Marie, 1939

Mister Ole, 1940 (set in Redmond)

Mick and Mack and Mary Jane, 1948 (set near Mount Pilchuck)

Little Dermot and the Thirsty Stones, 1953

Not a Teeny Weeny Wink, 1959

Richard Bennett
(1899–1971)
Untitled, 1943–48
Tempera
7½ x 9⅞ in.
Collection of the
Museum of History &
Industry, Seattle
2006.38.3

Legends of Paul Bunyan, compiled and edited by Harold W. Felton, illustrated by Richard Bennett (New York: Alfred A. Knopf, 1947) Collection of the Museum of History & Industry, Seattle 2006.38.403.158

Mick and Mack and Mary Jane, written and illustrated by Richard Bennett (Garden City, NY: Doubleday, 1948) Collection of the Museum of History & Industry, Seattle 2006.38.403.164

Bennett completed illustrations for over two hundred publications including two Northwest favorites by the noted Seattle author Betty MacDonald: *The Egg and I* (1945) and *Mrs. Piggle-Wiggle* (1947).

SOURCES

David F. Martin, *The Art of Richard Bennett* (Seattle: University of Washington Press, 2010)

"Student Returns Here as Professor to Practice Old Art of Woodcutting," *Seattle Daily Times*, Aug. 14, 1927, 8

"Book Illustrator Praises Northwest," *Seattle Daily Times*, Aug. 18, 1957, 100

Margaret B. Callahan, "From Stump-Ranch Boy to Artist-Author," *Seattle Daily Times*, Nov. 2, 1947, 83

Richard Bennett
(1899–1971)
Loggers, 1943–48
Tempera
10 x 10¾ in.
Collection of the Museum
of History & Industry,
Seattle
2006.38.4

Richard Bennett
(1899–1971)
Untitled, circa 1950
Ink and tempera
10 x 15 in.
Collection of the Museum
of History & Industry,
Seattle
2006.38.23

Richard Bennett
(1899–1971)
Splitting Shakes, 1943–48
Tempera
10 x 7½ in.
Collection of the Museum
of History & Industry,
Seattle
2006.38.47

Richard Bennett
(1899–1971)
Untitled, 1943–48
Tempera
10 x 13 in.
Collection of the Museum
of History & Industry,
Seattle
2006.38.40

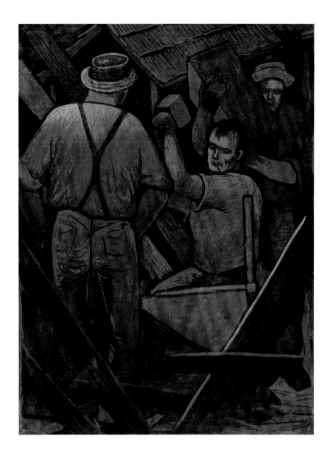

(top left)
Richard Bennett, circa 1960
Collection of the Museum of History & Industry, Seattle
2006.38.406.140

(top right)
Richard Bennett, circa 1919
Collection of the Museum of History & Industry, Seattle
2006.38.406.160

(bottom left)
Richard Bennett, 1919
Collection of the Museum of History & Industry, Seattle
2006.38.406.168

(bottom right)
Richard Bennett at Robe Ranch, circa 1945
Collection of the Museum of History & Industry, Seattle
2006.38.406.165

Richard Bennett
(1899–1971)
Dancers in the Kitchen, circa
1930s
Ink
11¼ x 9 in.
Collection of the Museum
of History & Industry,
Seattle
2006.38.113

Richard Bennett
(1899–1971)
Rodeo (also titled *Roundup*),
circa 1935
Woodblock print
9 x 7 in.
Private collection
Inscribed to his lover,
Guy Anderson

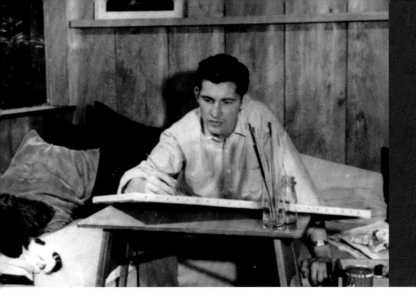

Ward Corley
1920–1962

"This is tempting fate but when I am *at* painting, I sink entirely into it with heart and soul and all the talk about it ceases to make me nervous or reduced to despair. What is inescapable and legitimate and so very gratifying is that besides doing what is *only* meaningful one makes one's living." —Ward Corley

William Ward Corley was one of five children born to Ollie and Alice Corley in Brighton, Iowa. Little is known about his early life spent in Iowa, Arkansas, and Oklahoma.

Primarily a self-taught artist, he had a very short period of production due to his untimely death at age forty-two.

As a young man he was employed as a salesman and was starting to experiment with acting as a career until he enlisted in the army the day after the attack on Pearl Harbor in 1941. He transferred to the Marine Corps and saw active duty.

After the war, Corley came to Seattle in 1945 for an unknown reason, and slowly became part of Seattle's gay artistic circles. He was briefly involved with architect Robert Shields and later had a long-term relationship with Monte Edgar Brown (1914–1999), who had a distinguished career as a captain in the Marine Corps during World War II. It is not known if the two men met in the marines or if Brown was the reason Corley moved to Seattle. Monte Brown came from a prominent and successful family that owned and operated the *Daily Journal of Commerce*, where Ward found employment until 1959.

Corley's beginnings as a painter are unknown; there are no records of him studying in any art institution or even with private instructors. In period articles, he is listed as self-taught. His stylistic variations ranged initially from a type of hard-edged magic realism and moved to Native American–inspired imagery, using a reduced palette of grays and browns and finally broadening to the fully chromatic "bouquet" motifs inspired by Les Nabis painters such as Pierre Bonnard and Jean-Édouard Vuillard.

Corley first exhibited in the Northwest Annual at SAM in 1949, when he appears to have reached initial maturity as an artist. He also exhibited at the Henry Art Gallery at the University of Washington in 1951 and 1959. He wasn't included in SAM's Northwest Annual again until 1958 through 1961, with all the painting titles listed simply as *Bouquet*.

Portrait of Monte Brown,
circa 1948
Courtesy of the Estate of
Robert Shields

Ward Corley (1920–1962)
Room with White Table, 1953
Oil on Masonite
42⅛ x 50⅛ in.
Seattle Art Museum, gift
of the Virginia and Bagley
Wright Collection

Richard Gilkey (left) and
Ward Corley, 1946–60
University of Oregon
Libraries, Eugene
Morris Graves Collection
1727210_Coll326_b140_
f15_39_001a

Corley's work was the subject of a group exhibition at SAM in 1953–54 titled *Four Pacific Northwest Painters*, which featured him, William Ivey, Jack Stangl, and Corley's close friend Richard Gilkey. In 1957 he moved to La Conner, where he shared a studio with Gilkey and worked among other artists who felt an affinity with the landscape and atmosphere of the Skagit Valley.

In 1958, Corley began losing weight and having symptoms of an illness that was debilitating but undiagnosed. On the advice of his doctor, he returned to Arkansas to be under the care of his parents to assist in his recovery.

From there, he wrote to his friend Richard Svarre, "I can hardly wait to get back to that nervous, morbid, bleak Northwest. Arkansas is so perversely relaxed that you can feel it coming through the woodwork even. I'd rather have the miseries there than the happies here, far removed from battle."

To assist Ward with his mounting medical expenses, the Seattle art community rallied to his side while he was trying to recuperate in Arkansas. Local collectors and advocates such as Virginia Wright, Betty Bowen, Robert Shields, and Jan Thompson held a fundraiser for him at the home of Virginia and Bagley Wright, with a benefit cocktail party and sale of art donated by many of Corley's friends, including Mark Tobey, Morris Graves, and Guy Anderson.

Corley was both moved and embarrassed by this much-needed support. However, it would have been difficult to find a more beloved person than Ward Corley at that time.

In a letter to Betty Bowen dated April 4, 1959, he stated: "It strikes me that customarily the finish to an artist's mortal career—if caused by ill health—should be collapse at the easel in poverty and a pool of Alizarin Crimson, although if my easel got wind of such an idea it would simply collapse first for spite. At the risk of sounding deliberately flippant, which is not my intention, all I will add in the way of frivolous thoughts is I suddenly feel like a gilded leech—mounted in chiseled splendor— gift wrapped—from Cartier's.

"In other words, if one is able to react to so much kindness—support—concern I shall dwell on this many times for years with wonder, and permit myself now and then a madness of happiness, because I believe it is necessary—also such feelings find their way into painting."

Unfortunately, his health continued to deteriorate, and he returned briefly to Seattle to have exploratory surgery that revealed he had terminal liver disease. He went immediately to Stanford University Hospital and then Berkeley for treatment from a liver specialist named Dr. Snell.

In a letter to Morris Graves dated April 21 of that year, Corley wrote, "My week-end in San Francisco was made extremely pleasant because of Monte (prior to becoming set up here in Palo Alto). He had me in the finest suite—as those things go—in the St. Francis, even asking them to give me quarters that were not modern, but with antique furniture or at least French in feeling. . . . The result was a kind of high-powered almost savage elegance that was so pleasant under the circumstances and after Arkansas."

To boost his spirits, his closest friends arranged for an exhibition of his paintings in the Seattle Art Museum's activities room in April 1959. The museum's founder, Dr. Richard Fuller, sent a telegram to Corley through mutual friend Scott Seifert that stated, "Dear Ward, without question your art show was one of the greatest of its type in the Northwest history."

Returning to Arkansas had proved both beneficial and stressful, as his parents were unaware of his homosexuality. In a letter dated June 9, 1959, he wrote to Jan Thompson, "I think my mother thinks that you and I are sweeties cause I have 3 of your cards laid out casually on my bedside table along with bottles of pills, book, etc. and they all begin dearest dearest Ward and end with much much love. Ain't it crazy what transparent little frauds delicate men catch themselves doing. Some of them even wear wedding rings like they've been divorced."

Unlike Corley, his boyfriend Monte Brown had a very supportive family in Seattle who were aware of their relationship. Ward returned to Seattle to live with Monte in a home built directly behind Monte's parents' that included a studio where he could paint. They continued to support Ward through his illness and even cared for him in their own home when he was particularly weak.

Corley lived his final years in the company of close friends, reading literature, listening to classical music, and finding solace in his love of nature.

Ward Corley, 1945
Gelatin silver print
10¾ x 13¾ in.
Private collection

Ward Corley (1920–1962)
Untitled, circa 1948
Oil on board
17⅜ x 23⅜ in.
Collection of Philip L. Brown

Ward Corley (1920–1962)
Interior, 1949
Oil on canvas
24½ x 29½ in.
Collection of Nathan
Hinds

Ward Corley (1920–1962)
Bella Coola, 1949
Tempera on panel
48 x 36 in.
Collection of David and
Janet Starr

Ward Corley died on March 16, 1962. The Seattle Art Museum held a retrospective exhibition of forty-five of his paintings from October 17 to November 25 of that year, likely representing the majority of his output.

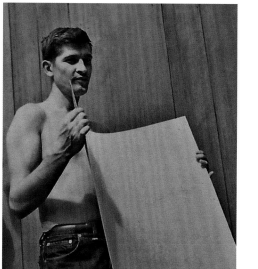

Ward Corley (1920–1962)
Crew Cut, circa 1950
(caricature of Robert Shields)
Graphite
Courtesy of the Estate of Robert Shields

Ward Corley (1920–1962)
Robert with His Silly Old Saddle Shoes, circa 1950
Graphite
Courtesy of the Estate of Robert Shields

Ward Corley, circa 1948
Courtesy of the Estate of Robert Shields

SOURCES

Louis R. Guzzo, "Artists Go to Aid of Ailing Ward Corley," *Seattle Daily Times*, Apr. 6, 1959, 41

"William Ward Corley, 42, Artist, Dies," *Seattle Daily Times*, Mar. 17, 1962, 21

Numerous e-mail exchanges and conversations with John Curran, cousin of Monte Brown

"Kenneth Callahan: Group Show Combines Four Varied Styles," *Seattle Daily Times*, Dec. 27, 1953, 47

Ward Corley and Sherrill Van Cott, Valley Museum of Northwest Art, La Conner, WA, 1991; brochure essays by Richard Svare and Barbara Stryker James

Jan Thompson Papers, University of Washington Libraries, Special Collections, access no. 5512-001, boxes 1, 3, 4, and 5

Betty Bowen Papers, University of Washington Libraries, Special Collections, access. no. 2441, boxes 9 and 10

Friendship and conversations with Robert Shields

Typescript of memorial by Reverend Peter Raible at University Unitarian Church, Mar. 22, 1962

Morris Graves Papers, coll. 326, Special Collections & University Archives, University of Oregon Libraries, Eugene

Ward Corley (1920–1962)
Large Bouquet, 1956
Oil on board
37¼ x 26¾ in.
Whatcom Museum,
Bellingham, WA, gift of
the Virginia Wright Fund
1976.48.4

Ward Corley (1920–1962)
Large Bouquet, circa 1960
Oil on board
32 x 25 in.
Collection of Makaiya
Bullitt-Rigsbee

Ward Corley, circa 1948
Courtesy of the Estate of
Robert Shields

Thomas Handforth
1897–1948

Thomas Schofield Handforth was born in Tacoma to Thomas Jefferson Handforth and Irish immigrant Ruby Shera. His father was co-owner of the Lindstrom-Handforth Lumber Company, which provided a substantial income for the family. Thomas, or "Scho" as he was called, displayed an advanced aptitude in drawing and painting at an early age. He graduated from Tacoma's Stadium High School in 1915 and a year later entered the University of Washington, where he studied English literature. By 1916 he had already established a reputation as a promising young artist with the Seattle Fine Arts Society, encouraged by prominent local artist John Davidson Butler. While in his teens, Handforth had studied with Butler at his studio and at the Cornish School in their first art program, which had developed out of Butler's home classes.

After leaving the UW to focus on an art career, he moved to New York to attend the National Academy of Design (NAD) in 1917, but his studies were interrupted when he enlisted in the Anatomical Artists Unit of the Army Medical Corps during World War I. He returned to New York in 1919 and resumed studies at the NAD, as well as at the Arts Students League with the sculptor-printmaker Mahonri Young, who refined Handforth's interest in intaglio printmaking.

Handforth left for Paris in 1920 and began his studies there the following year at École Nationale Supérieure des Beaux-Arts, the Académie Colarossi, and the Académie Delécluse.

John Butler had moved to Paris after serving in World War I and started to develop an artistic reputation there. For additional income, he and his wife, Agnes, opened an American-oriented café in Montmartre called Butler's Pantry.

In a letter to his mother from Place de Riz Ploare par Douarnenez Finistère, Brittany, dated 1921, Handforth wrote, "Now I have been here two weeks. John Butler had come a week earlier and made it possible for me to be taken into this very pleasant arrangement, on a beach where there are only six houses and no such things as a hotel or pension. Then a week ago, Prince Ilamaz Dadeskeliani, secretary of the Georgian legation in Paris, joined me, and is sharing my room. He is one of the most congenial people I have known, highly cultured yet a broad minded liberal in spite of his feudal family life in the mountains of Georgia, and his education, after the manner of his class, in Petrograd. An interesting souvenir he has just given me: a tiny silver watch charm in the form of a boar was presented to him by the Empress at the last Imperial Christmas party in St. Petersburg (1916)."

Tice Studios, Tacoma, WA
Thomas Handforth in his
World War I uniform, 1918
Collection of the Tacoma
Public Library

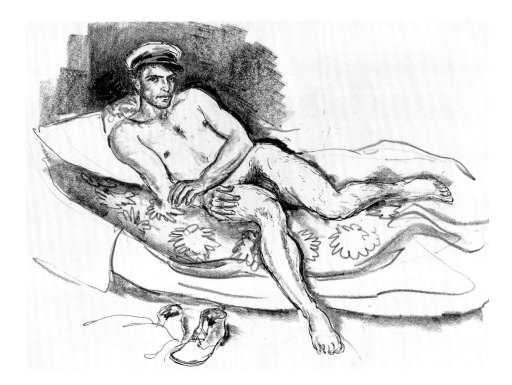

Handforth remained close to John and Agnes Butler, often washing dishes for them at their café.

As soon as he returned to Paris from Brittany, Tom rented a studio in the Parc Montsouris district, where his Tacoma artist friends Mac Harshberger and Hollande Robinson and sculptor Allan Clark also had studios. Another of Tom's friends, artist Howard Cook, also lived nearby, and Tom assisted Cook in printing some of his first etchings. The Montsouris district was also home to significant French artists, including George Braque, whose studio was next to Handforth's.

The French printmaker Jean Emile Laboureur (1877–1947) was very well known at the time, and his decorative, cubist style undoubtedly played a significant role in influencing Handforth's new modernist direction.

Always in search of models, Handforth recruited military men from the nearby garrison of French-Moroccan troops to pose for his compositions. His preference for selecting men from a wide ethnic range was in direct contrast to most of his contemporaries, who retained the standardized Caucasian ideals of strength and beauty.

In 1922, Handforth had the honor of having his etchings and oil paintings accepted into the city's prestigious Spring Salon. He remained in Paris, producing additional prints, until 1925, when he traveled to Tunisia.

The following year he returned to the Northwest, where he designed theater sets for a Chicago production by Ellen van Volkenburg, one of the pioneers of the Little Theatre Movement, who was then teaching at the Cornish School.

After producing numerous etchings and drawings with international subject matter, he turned his attention to his home region. He spent three months living with the Quileute Tribe on the Olympic Peninsula, where he interacted with the Native American inhabitants and was adopted into their tribe. The experience resulted in eleven plates that are arguably among his finest works.

After his Northwest sojourn, his wanderlust brought him back to North Africa in 1927. After first arriving in Casablanca, he traveled to Marrakech, where, in a letter to his mother dated February 12, 1928, he wrote, "If you look back in last

September's *Aria* and in other numbers, you will see articles of travel on the Niger by Leland Hall, also articles in *Harper's* magazine for last year and perhaps you have seen his new book *Timbuctoo* (Harpers & Co.). He has a delightful house here much larger than mine; we entertain each other and smoke kiff together and tell each other of the wonderful visions we are seeing, tho in truth I get nothing but the most ghastly sickly feelings in my stomach from the smoking."

He returned to Paris and London in 1928 in an attempt to market his work and produce additional plates. That year the Fogg Museum at Harvard purchased a number of his etchings, followed by the New York Public Library and the Bibliothèque nationale de France.

The following year he illustrated the book *Toutou in Bondage* by the American writer Elizabeth Jane Coatsworth, and returned to the Northwest just as the stock market was about to crash.

In 1930, Handforth traveled to Mexico for inspiration and a change of climate. He had illustrated another book, *Tranquilina's Paradise* by Susan Smith, that was released that year.

He may have been aware of the artistic atmosphere in Taxco, where just two years earlier, the gay artist and silversmith William Spratling (1900–1967) had purchased a home. Before arriving in Taxco, Handforth stopped in Colima and was arrested for "sketching only the worst types of Mexican people for the purpose of creating an unfavorable opinion of the country in the United States." Repercussions from the Mexican Revolution that had ended ten years earlier still affected the way the country wanted to be perceived by the outside world. After his release, he continued to Taxco, where he remained for a year.

Back in Seattle, the Northwest Printmakers Society (NWPS) held their first exhibition in 1929. Handforth won a purchase prize in their second annual exhibition the following year for his etching *Opistat*. The year ended with Handforth winning a prestigious Guggenheim Fellowship that allowed him to travel to China in 1931.

En route to China, Tom stopped in New York to spend time with friends, including writer-photographer Carl Van Vechten. In a letter to his mother dated January 12, 1931, written in Brooklyn, he said, "What a life! . . . With the exception of Carl Van Vechten, who looking like a white-haired Mikado, seated in a stiff kimono among the treasures of his study, was all enthusiasm about my proposed picture book, and who, too greatly honored by my seeking his good wishes, approved of <u>anything</u> that I might do, upon which he kissed my hand, and it seemed to me, that that was enough of the subject for the moment, tho I had intended to ask him if he might not write me an introduction. . . . As happens in this perverse world, New York is beginning to appeal to me now as it never has before, so maybe I won't mind coming back after seeing Singapore. I have been seeing Harlem on some gay parties with some of the inner circle. Van Vechten saw sketches that I made, and wished that he had seen them sooner, as he would have had me do the deluxe edition of his *Nigger Heaven* which is now in preparation and being illustrated by an Englishman who has never been in the states. Anyway, he now thinks that he wants me to do some other books of his. Whether this is a passing fancy or a fixed idea, it is at least a pleasing compliment. The Herr Dr. Magnus Hirschfeld left Jan. 3 for Chicago, California and point[s] thru the Orient

Carl Van Vechten
(1880–1964)
Thomas Handforth
with unidentified man,
circa 1935
Gelatin silver print
9¾ x 7⅝ in.
Collection of the Tacoma
Public Library

Carl Van Vechten
(1880–1964)
Thomas Handforth,
circa 1935
Gelatin silver print
9⅞ x 7¾ in.
Collection of the Tacoma
Public Library

"Symptoms of going
native: I can no longer
exist without a fan—it is a
more important accessory
than hat, necktie, gloves,
cane or sox, and much
more useful; one keeps an
assortment for different
occasions; palm for sport
wear, small black with
silver lettering for dress,
very large plain Indian red
for rickshaw riding, hand
painted gold fish on white
for ordinary morning
wear, and a specially
choice shrimp design done
in the fewest possible
strokes by the famous
and venerable Mr. Chee,
for cocktail parties—and
I almost forgot, a very
simple woven straw fan
for use while at work."
Excerpt from a letter from
Handforth to his mother
dated July 20, 1932

to Berlin. He has given me a hearty invitation to come to stay with him there—but a few points on the globe may have to be left until the next life."

By March of that year Tom had arrived in Japan, staying at the Imperial Hotel designed by Frank Lloyd Wright. In a letter to his mother dated March 19, 1931, he described meeting with his friend Dr. Magnus Hirschfeld, the legendary physician and sexologist of the Weimar Republic, who was one of the pioneering advocates for gay and transgender rights throughout the world: "Dr. Hirschfeld arrived from L.A. and Honolulu. We were both equally glad to see each other—he proposed that we continue our travels together thru the Orient—which may be possible to a certain extent. We have already had pleasant times together visiting the 'Coney Island' of Tokyo, Japanese movies, and merely strolling in the parks or on the 'Broadway' of the city. . . . I have tried to refrain from buying things but have acquired a few prints for one example: the first volume of Hokusai's *Views of Fuji* of which the two books from Joseph Lougheed are the 2nd and 3rd volumes.

"Today I saw Mt. Fuji for the first time; it was covered low with snow and it is so perfect in form that it seems more a spirit mountain than a real one."

While in Japan, he rekindled his friendship with sculptor Isamu Noguchi, an old friend from his Paris days. The two men sought out artistic inspiration and attended productions of Noh theater. From Kyoto he wrote his mother on April 2, "Again I have been very fortunate in that Isamu Noguchi came here just two days before me and we have been going about all the time together. His father, Yeon [sic; correct name Yone] Noguchi is well known throughout Japan as an author and poet (he has also written many books of art criticism in English). Kyoto is the centre of pottery and porcelain manufacture and Isamu is here to learn the process to apply to his sculpture[;] we have been visiting many potterers and artist craftsmen—it is a grand way to see Japanese life as one is always served tea and cakes and expected to squat for at least two hours over a charcoal brazier before starting in on the formality of saying goodbye. . . . And another dinner with Lilian Miller who does color wood block prints and is 'managed' by Mrs. Whitmore; she is spending the year here with a Miss Hayes, former secretary to L. Adams Beck who recently died."

Like Handforth, Lilian May Miller (1895–1943) was a renowned American printmaker. She was born in Japan and produced beautiful color woodcuts inspired by ukiyo-e prints of the previous century. She too was gay, and when she wasn't wearing a kimono to promote her work, she preferred men's attire, had short cropped hair, and referred to herself as "Jack," a nickname bestowed on her by her father.

Back in Seattle, Handforth's family and friends continued to promote his work. He was given a very successful show in 1933 at the Harry Hartman bookstore. Hartman was an early promoter of prints and photography through his Seattle bookstore, a tale made poignant by the fact that he was completely blind.

When Handforth returned to Peking that year he taught himself the art of lithography, purchasing a press and stones, guided by Albert W. Barker's 1930 publication *Lithography for Artists*.

His lithographs produced an entirely different effect than his etchings, and the public responded favorably to his new choice of medium. In 1934 the Library of Congress purchased his lithograph *Donkey Boy* for their permanent collection, and he won another purchase prize from the NWPS for his lithograph titled *Motherhood*. His hometown honored him in 1935 with a solo exhibition of his prints and drawings at the Seattle Art Museum.

For the remainder of the decade he continued to travel throughout the world receiving numerous awards, exhibitions, and, in the US, purchases.

Mei Li, written and illustrated by Thomas Handforth, 1938 Doubleday Books for Young Readers; reissue edition (April 1, 1955) Collection of the Tacoma Public Library

Thomas Handforth and his life partner, Edmund Tolk, circa 1945 Private collection

During that time, over a period of two years, he wrote and illustrated his most famous publication, *Mei Li*, based on the life of the youngest adopted daughter of Helen Burton, his influential friend from Peking. The book won him the prestigious Caldecott Medal for Illustration in 1939, the same year he produced another successful publication, *Faraway Meadow*.

By 1940, Handforth had returned to the US and bought property in Avila, California, with his lover, Edmund Eisen Tolk (1910–1985), a brilliant and highly regarded German scholar. The couple led an interesting and successful life, befriending talented people such as the lesbian mystic poet Ella Young, who was introduced to them by their Seattle artist friend Richard Bennett. Like Handforth's mother and Bennett's parents, Young was a native of Ireland. She had a following in Seattle and gave a lecture in 1926 at Cornish for young children, on the existence of fairies and elves derived from Irish folklore. For reasons never fully

Thomas Handforth
(1897–1948)
Black Eros, 1928
Drypoint and etching
7¹⁵⁄₁₆ x 8¹³⁄₁₆ in.
Philadelphia Museum of
Art, gift of Mrs. Merle
Shera, 1987-64-18
© Estate of Thomas
Handforth
State proof before the
aquatint background

Photographic copy of
a circa 1930 drawing by
Thomas Handforth
Collection of the Tacoma
Public Library

Thomas Handforth
(1897–1948)
*Island Horses (Vancouver
Island)*, 1926–29
Etching
8 x 10¼ in.
Private collection

explained, but perhaps because of her suspect association with the Theosophical Society and mysticism, she was detained in Victoria, BC, in 1931 and not allowed back in the US for five months. The authorities might have been aware of an incident upon her arrival in the US in 1925, when, according to writer Kevin Starr, she "had been briefly detained at Ellis Island as a probable mental case when the authorities learned that she believed in the existence of fairies, elves, and pixies."

The couple's idyllic existence was ended in 1942 when Tolk, who was born in Vienna, enlisted in the American military in service to his adopted homeland. He was allowed to serve even though he was not an American citizen. However, after his discharge he was unable to remain in Avila because of its coastal location and his alien status, even though he had served this country during the war. (Tom also reenlisted in the military for six months that same year.)

In 1943 the couple began teaching at the experimental Seaman School in El Monte, California. The students were young men with various forms of mental health issues and learning disabilities. The two men remained at the school for three years, with Richard Bennett joining them for one of the terms.

Aircrew training recruiting poster, circa 1943, designed by Thomas Handforth
19⅞ x 15 in.
Collection of the Tacoma Public Library

While teaching art at the school, Handforth contracted scarlet fever in 1944. Once he was able to travel, he went to convalesce at Richard Bennett and Guy Anderson's cabin at Robe Ranch for a month. Bennett wrote, "Most of the time was spent in sketching trips, and working on a picture book for children. Tom I always found a delightful companion, willing to share in all the duties of that primitive life."

In 1945 the Seattle Art Museum gave him his second solo exhibition focusing on his drawings and watercolors.

In 1946 the two men sold the Avila house and Tolk accepted a professorship at Manhattan College as a German scholar in 1947. Tom moved to a secluded property at Menlo Park in Northern California, where his health began to deteriorate, likely from the scarlet fever's debilitating effects on his heart.

He died of a heart attack in Los Angeles at age fifty-one in 1948.

Edmund Tolk went on to receive his PhD at Columbia University in 1954 and remained a highly regarded professor at Manhattan College until retiring in 1980.

SOURCES

Tacoma Public Library, Thomas Handforth Papers

Various authors, the *Horn Book* magazine, Oct. 19, 1950

Several interviews with Richard Bennett's sister Helen Johnston in 2008 and 2009

Numerous conversations, e-mails, and meetings with Peggy Hartzell, Handforth's niece and author of the 2014 book *Thomas Handforth: Artist*

Thomas Handforth
(1897–1948)
Untitled, circa 1938
Conté crayon
22 x 15 in.
Collection of the Tacoma
Public Library

Thomas Handforth
(1897–1948)
Untitled, circa 1940
Pastel
24 x 18¼ in.
Collection of the Tacoma
Public Library

Thomas Handforth
(1897–1948)
Untitled, Paris, 1938
Conté crayon and ink
24 x 18¼ in.
Collection of the Tacoma
Public Library

Thomas Handforth
(1897–1948)
Untitled, circa 1940
Conté crayon and ink
11¼ x 15½ in.
Collection of the Tacoma
Public Library

Thomas Handforth
(1897–1948)
Untitled, circa 1940
Ink
15 x 12 in.
Collection of the Tacoma
Public Library

Thomas Handforth
(1897–1948)
Untitled, circa 1940
Ink
15 x 12 in.
Collection of the Tacoma
Public Library

Thomas Handforth
(1897–1948)
Untitled, circa 1938
Pastel
13 x 19⅝ in.
Collection of the Tacoma
Public Library

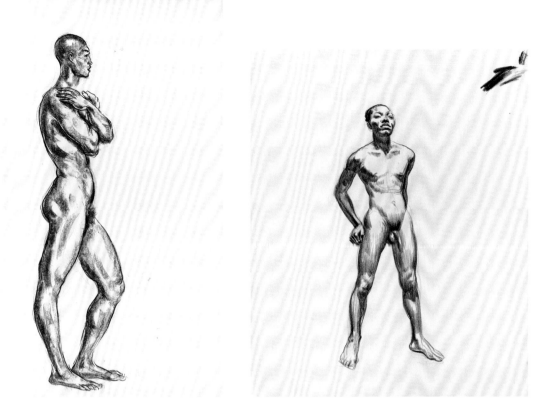

Thomas Handforth
(1897–1948)
Untitled, circa 1935
Graphite and Conté
crayon
24 x 18¾ in.
Collection of the Tacoma
Public Library

Thomas Handforth
(1897–1948)
Untitled, circa 1935
Conté crayon
16¾ x 13¾ in.
Collection of the Tacoma
Public Library

Thomas Handforth
(1897–1948)
Untitled, circa 1938
Conté crayon
10¼ x 22⅞ in.
Collection of The Tacoma
Public Library

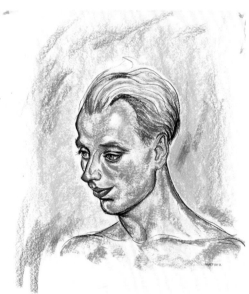

(top left)
Thomas Handforth
(1897–1948)
Untitled, 1945
Conté crayon
24 x 19 in.
Collection of the Tacoma
Public Library

(top right)
Porter Woodruff
(1894–1959)
*Portrait of Thomas
Handforth*, circa 1921
Pastel
20 x 13 in.
Collection of the Tacoma
Public Library
Woodruff was a leading
American illustrator
known for his work with
Vogue magazine in Paris in
the 1920s.

(bottom left)
Thomas Handforth
(1897–1948)
Untitled, circa 1935
Conté crayon
24 x 19 in.
Collection of the Tacoma
Public Library

(bottom right)
Thomas Handforth
(1897–1948)
Portrait sketch of Edmund
Tolk, circa 1942
Pastel
24 x 18 in.
Collection of the Tacoma
Public Library

Thomas Handforth
(1897–1948)
Untitled, circa 1940
Conté crayon and ink
24 x 17¾ in.
Collection of the Tacoma
Public Library

Thomas Handforth
(1897–1948)
Untitled, circa 1940
Watercolor
24 x 18 in.
Collection of the Tacoma
Public Library

Mac Harshberger
1901–1975

Holland Robinson
1890–1959

Frank McCoy "Mac" Harshberger was one of four children born in Tacoma to Frank M. Harshberger, a prominent local attorney, and Arloa Richardson Harshberger. He was raised in an artistically inclined family.

Mac attended Tacoma High School (later renamed Stadium High School) in Tacoma and produced illustrations for the school's yearbook, the *Tahoma*. His senior yearbook photograph was accompanied with the statement, "A Brilliant Artist with Brush or Pen, He will make his way in the world of men."

After graduating in 1919, he attended the University of Washington and studied primarily under Ambrose Patterson. He became involved with the school's drama clubs and designed stage sets for productions by Glenn Hughes. He also provided illustrations for student publications. Around this time, he met musician Harry Gye Robinson who was born in Urbana, Ohio, to Oscar Sidney Robinson. Harry moved to the Northwest at an early age, settling initially in Yakima, where he was employed as an organist. He eventually made his way to Tacoma, where he developed a successful career in regional vaudeville circuits as early as 1907, when he received recognition as the piano accompanist for dancer Nina Payne (1890–1971), a Tacoma native.

How Robinson and Harshberger met is not known, but the two became lovers and had a productive joint career that spanned several decades. By 1921, Robinson was already active in New York, where some of his musical compositions were published. He was likely there working with Payne, who first appeared on the New York stage in 1910 in *La Somnambule* at the American Music Hall and would later travel to Cuba to perform.

By this time, Harry began using the pseudonym Hollande Robinson, with a variation of sometimes omitting the "e" at the end of the given name. When Nina Payne completed her run with the Keith and Orpheum circuits, she and Hollande left for Paris in 1921. Nina was soon dancing with American expatriate Harry Pilcer (1885–1961), before signing with the Folies Bergère the following year.

Following Mac's studies at the UW, he left for Paris in 1922 to join Hollande, and they began living together. Hollande was now flourishing in Paris with Payne, writing music for her, designing some of her stage sets and costumes, and writing and illustrating her sheet music. He even designed a futuristic sketch of her used to create a Nina Payne doll.

Atelier Binder for Studio Manassé
Nina Payne in costume from the Rudolf Nelson revue *Confetti*, Nelson Theater, Berlin, 1925
Collection of Visual Studies Workshop, Rochester, NY

Frank McCoy (Mac)
Harshberger, Jr. (1901–1975)
Holland Robinson, circa
1926
Oil on canvas
36⅜ x 30½ x 1½ in.
Wolfsonian–Florida
International University,
Miami Beach
Gift of the William
Whitney Collection,
2009.13.5
Photograph by Lynton
Gardiner

Holland Robinson
(1890–1959) and Mac
Harshberger (1901–1975)
Studio label for the
Harshberger and
Robinson Studio
Inscribed in French "To
the Singing Cat"
Private collection

from the studio of
holland robinson
and
mac harshberger

**steinway building
new york city**

au
chat
qui
chante

Harry had now started using the acronym "Hagyro" for his artistic signature, taking the first two letters of his first, middle, and last names. Nina Payne, although forgotten today, was a major entertainer in Paris during the 1920s. She was known for her modernist or "Futurist" dances and elaborate costumes. One of the featured performers at the Folies Bergère, she befriended the legendary lesbian American expatriate Loïe Fuller, the "Electric Salome" of the Belle Epoque, as well as Josephine Baker, whose revue she eventually joined. Payne traveled in artistic circles that exposed Mac and Hollande to some of the great talents of the era. She dated composer Vladimir Dukelsky (1903–1969), who was involved with Serge Diaghilev's Ballet Russes and the extraordinary dancers, artists, and composers associated with the legendary entrepreneur. Dukelsky later changed his name to Vernon Duke and went on to compose some of the great standard songs of the twentieth century, including "April in Paris" and "Autumn in New York."

Mac (and possibly Hollande) studied at the Académie Ranson under Maurice Denis (1870–1943) and Francois Quelvee (1884–1967). As a result of his firsthand exposure to the Ballet Russes, Mac became highly influenced by the work of the company's designer, Leon Bakst, as well as by the illustrations of Aubrey Beardsley. Mac and Hollande rented a studio in the Parc Montsouris district of Paris, where their Tacoma friends Allan Clark and Thomas Handforth also had studios, with Handforth's next to George Braque's. After a year in Paris, Mac returned to the Northwest, but went back to Paris in 1923 with Hollande, who had been briefly in

New York. In Paris, Mac received commercial commissions as well as working with Hollande and Payne.

Mac and Hollande moved to New York in 1925 and secured a studio in the Steinway Building, on Fifty-Seventh Street near Carnegie Hall, to resume their careers in music and graphic arts. That year, Hollande wrote and illustrated a satiric but disturbing book titled *Nursery Rhymes for the Petits Francais* that he had begun in Paris. The text was created by using articles about violent crimes and murders found in the newspaper *Le Journal* and stylized after popular children's stories like "Jack and Jill," accompanied by his gruesome, decorative illustrations.

Also in 1925, they self-published a book titled *Carcassonne and Company*, a whimsical chronicle of their travels throughout France by train, which featured Mac's beautifully designed illustrations. The following year they began an association with the Albert and Charles Boni Publishing Company and collaborated with Mac's sister Kay on several titles.

Mac and Kay Harshberger and Holland Robinson, c. 1926
Gelatin silver print
3¾ x 2¼ in.
Wolfsonian–Florida International University, Miami Beach, Florida, gift of the William Whitney Collection, XC2009.07.11.50.3
Photograph by Lynton Gardiner

Katharine "Kay" Harshberger (1893–1974) was known in Northwest art circles as a writer, collector, and benefactor, and promoted many artists in Seattle and Tacoma—but especially her brother Mac. Although the siblings came from a reasonably successful family, Kay's resources greatly expanded when she married Count Jean de Landry, a wealthy heir who subsidized many travel expenses for Kay, Mac, and Hollande.

Robinson's light-classical songs and other compositions were very popular with a wide range of concert performers. He even occasionally performed himself on radio and in theater. He appeared in a 1928 revue at New York's Selwyn Theatre, sharing the stage with Cornelia Otis Skinner, the Denishawn Dancers, and Radiana Pazmor.

The following year, with the stock market crash and the ensuing economic depression, Harshberger's and Robinson's careers took a downturn.

Mac had developed a relatively successful career in commercial advertising and eventually accepted a position at the Pratt Institute in Brooklyn, where he taught decorative and commercial illustration from 1937 to 1960. While teaching, he also became employed by the firm Jenter Design out of New Jersey. This association led to him designing a mural and decorative panels for two pavilions at the 1939 New York World's Fair.

These projects, including a large mural for the South Carolina Building, were described in the *Seattle Daily Times* on May 28, 1939: "Instead of the statistic-ornamented dioramas depicting state after state in the usual fair exhibit style, very high interior wall panels are used as backgrounds for streamlined single figures (you know, the kind you cut out in rows from folded papers). Each bears a scene typical of a region or industry. . . . Another of Mac's outstanding designs is the exhibit of Wonder Bread which extends the childhood theme of balloons into the whole fantastic and colorful world of Alice in Wonderland."

By now, Harshberger and Robinson were living apart but not too far from each other, and they maintained a close friendship. Robinson started to decline physically and emotionally, but had one last honor when some of his music was

Mac Harshberger
(1901–1975)
Horace Terrell, circa 1928
Watercolor and ink on
illustration board
12⅛ x 10 in.
Honolulu Museum of Art,
gift of Rose Dequine and
Daisy Brigg, 1988
20523

Orland Campbell
(1890–1970)
Portrait of Holland Robinson,
1933
Oil on canvas
18¹³⁄₁₆ x 15⅛ in.
Courtesy of the
Pennsylvania Academy
of the Fine Arts,
Philadelphia, gift of Mrs.
Elizabeth de C. Wilson
1981.10

performed at a "Victory Concert" at the Metropolitan Museum on January 10, 1943. Mina Hager performed selections from his "Zoological Soliloquies" on a program that also featured the music of Wagner, Poulenc, and Bach. Unfortunately, the high-profile concert never led to any additional jobs.

In a desperate letter to a Mr. Dies of the G. Schirmer company dated July 4, 1943, Mac wrote, "I am writing in the interest of a friend of mine, Holland Robinson, who, I believe, met you at the time you were doing jury duty together. Naturally during this very cursory acquaintance-ship you could not know him personally nor have any interest in him. But I have known him for twenty years and know him to be a person of great talent both in serious and lighter music as well as a person of brilliant mind and an extraordinarily refined and sensitive person. Years ago, he had an amazingly interesting life but in the last twelve years the succession of misfortune after misfortune has finally beaten him down—and he is now flat. Naturally this has affected his personality. You might say—if this is true—it must be his own fault. Perhaps—but certainly in no tangible way. He has sold his Steinway grand piano, his typewriter and all his fine books. He was dispossessed from his apartment and in the meantime has come to stay with me in my apartment but is unhappy here in his indigent condition. He goes out each day to employment offices but is quite discouraged not to get even a typing job or a night clerk in a small hotel—which naturally he is not fitted for in the least. Now, the reason that I am writing you is that Holland told me of meeting you and I just can not sit by and watch the destruction of a really brilliant personality without doing something to try to salvage that valuable personality and that talent. All he needs is some insignificant job which would give him just enough to support himself and give him back some self respect. He is too humiliated and broken to let anyone know his present condition. So he will go only to the usual business employment agencies and it is only natural they have nothing for him. The only thing I want to ask of you is if you should happen to know by any chance any one he might go to or any place he might find a job—with only enough salary to give him that economical security which is necessary to every man—where his exceptional musical ability and knowledge and intelligence may be used to advantage."

Mac assisted Hollande as much as possible, but there are no records of Robinson's life after this letter was written.

Around this time, Mac had developed another relationship with close friend Horace H. Terrell (1906–1980), who had graduated from Pratt in 1927. Terrell had maintained a very good career in New York as an interior decorator and was a positive support after the stress from Hollande's declining condition. The two moved into Terrell's home at Westport, Connecticut, around 1950 and remained there until Mac's death in 1975.

The Harshberger-Robinson legacy was solidified when Mac's cousin William Whitney inherited Mac and Kay's artistic estates. He arranged for a 1986 exhibition titled *Mac Harshberger Art Deco Americain* at the Fine Arts Museum of San Francisco, Achenbach Foundation for Graphic Arts. He also left a bequest of some of Mac's art to that institution's permanent collection.

In 1989, Whitney, with the assistance of Mitchell Wolfson Jr., sponsored a musical revue titled *Goodbye Tacoma* that presented the music of Hollande Robinson and the art of Mac Harshberger. The story revolved around the four Tacomans—Kay and Mac Harshberger, Hollande Robinson, and Nina Payne—during their success in Paris during the 1920s. The production benefited San Francisco's Art Deco Society and was held at several venues in San Francisco.

A representative collection of works by Harshberger and Robinson is now part of the permanent collection of the Wolfsonian–Florida International University, Miami Beach, Florida.

SOURCES

Interviews with Mac Harshberger's cousin John Butler

Important biographical information provided by Larry Wiggins, accountant, the Wolfsonian-FIU, Miami Beach, Florida

Letter from Mac Harshberger to Mr. Dies dated July 4, 1943, Martin-Zambito Archive, Seattle

Karin Breuer: Mac Harshberger Art Deco Americain, exhibition catalog, the Fine Arts Museum of San Francisco, 1986

"Seattle Girl the Queen of the Folies Bergere," *Seattle Daily Times*, Sept. 24, 1922, 84

William W. Whitney, *The Elegant Art of Mac Harshberger*, brochure from Art Deco Weekend, Miami Design Preservation League, 1989

"Artist Doesn't Starve in Garret, Harshberger," *Seattle Daily Times*, Sept. 1, 1939, 21

Virginia Boren, "Walk a Little Faster," *Seattle Daily Times*, May 28, 1939, 44

http://www.jazzageclub.com/personalities/nina-payne/

John Richardson, *A Life of Picasso*, vol. 3: *The Triumphant Years, 1917–1932* (New York: Alfred A. Knopf, 2010)

(opposite page)
Mac Harshberger
(1901–1975)
Holland Robinson and Mac Harshberger (Exponents of Depressionistic Art), circa 1932
Woodcut with hand coloring
14.6 x 10.1 cm (image)
Fine Arts Museums of San Francisco, gift of William W. Whitney
1986.1.65

Mac Harshberger
(1901–1975)
Holland Robinson and Mac Harshberger Send the Season's Greetings, circa 1934
Woodcut with hand coloring
13.6 x 10.2 cm (image)
Fine Arts Museums of San Francisco, gift of William W. Whitney
1986.1.63

Mac Harshberger
(1901–1975)
Jingle Bells (wheeze) Jingle Bells (wheeze) Jingle all the way (wheeze wheeze) Holland Robinson and Mac Harshberger, circa 1933
Woodcut in brown with hand coloring
13.5 x 9 cm (image)
Fine Arts Museums of San Francisco, gift of William W. Whitney,
1986.1.64

HOLLAND ROBINSON AND MAC HARSHBERGER
(EXPONENTS OF DEPRESSIONISTIC ART)

holland robinson and ◄◄◄
mac harshberger ◄◄◄◄◄
send the season's greetings ◄◄

JINGLE BELLS (WHEEZE) JINGLE BELLS (WHEEZE)
JINGLE ALL THE WAY — (WHEEZE—WHEEZE)

HOLLAND ROBINSON & MAC HARSHBERGER

Mac Harshberger
(1901–1975)
Untitled, circa 1928
Ink on illustration board
17 x 13⅝ in.
Private collection

Mac Harshberger
(1901–1975)
Untitled, circa 1928
Ink on illustration board
12¼ x 10¼ in.
Private collection

Mac Harshberger
(1901–1975)
*Tigellin—Un Jeune Romain
(Gladiator)*, circa 1924
Ink on illustration board
12½ x 8⅝ in.
Private collection

Mac Harshberger
(1901–1975)
Illustration from the book
Whispering Whirligig,
written by his sister, Kay
Harshberger, 1933
Pacific Book Association
Johnson-Cox Company,
Tacoma, WA
Private collection

Mac Harshberger
(1901–1975)
George Sand, 1927
Original illustration for
Loose Lyrics of Lovely Ladies,
1928
Ink on illustration board
19½ x 15 in.
Private collection

Mac Harshberger
(1901–1975)
Helen of Troy, 1927
Original illustration for
Loose Lyrics of Lovely Ladies,
1928
Ink on illustration board
19½ x 15 in.
Private collection

Mac Harshberger
(1901–1975)
Cleopatra, 1927
Original illustration for
Loose Lyrics of Lovely Ladies,
1928
Ink on illustration board
19½ x 15 in.
Private collection

Mac Harshberger
(1901–1975)
Mona Lisa, 1927
Original illustration for
Loose Lyrics of Lovely Ladies,
1928
Ink on illustration board
17⅝ x 14½ in.
Private collection

(top left)
Mac Harshberger
(1901–1975)
Sheet music for Hollande
Robinson composition
"Nipponese," poem by
Katharine Harshberger,
1922–24
Collection of Peter Mack

(top right)
Mac Harshberger
(1901–1975)
Sheet music for Hollande
Robinson composition
*Sérénade aux cinq chats
noires*, 1924
Collection of Peter Mack

(center left)
Hagyro (acronym
for Harry [Hollande]
Robinson) (1890–1959)
Sheet music for Robinson
composition "Chimera,"
1924
Collection of Peter Mack

(center right)
Hollande Robinson
(1890–1959)
Sheet music for Robinson
composition *Six Rhymes
from Walter de la Mare's
"Peacock Pie,"* 1924
With coat of arms
depicting a sly reference
to his name: Holland,
robin, sun
Collection of Peter Mack

(bottom)
Mac Harshberger, c. 1926
Gelatin silver print
2⅜ x 2½ in.
Wolfsonian–Florida
International University,
Miami Beach, gift
of the William
Whitney Collection,
XC2009.07.11.50.1
Photograph by Lynton
Gardiner

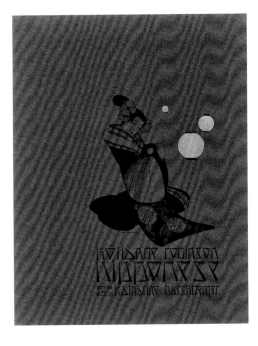

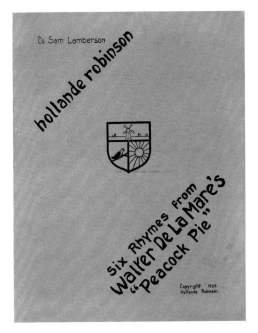

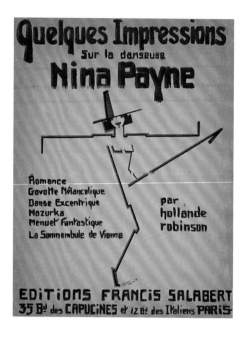

Hagyro (acronym
for Harry [Hollande]
Robinson) (1890–1959)
Sheet music for
compositions by Robinson
*Quelques impressions sur la
danseuse Nina Payne*, 1922
Private collection

Hollande Robinson
(1890–1959)
Frontispiece illustration
from his publication
*Nursery Rhymes for the
Petits Francais*, 1925,
self-published
Private collection

Mac Harshberger
(1901–1975)
Untitled (tennis set),
circa 1928
Watercolor
22 x 29⅛ in. (sight)
Thomas Reynolds Gallery,
San Francisco

Mac Harshberger
(1901–1975)
Untitled, circa 1924
Watercolor and graphite
on illustration board
20 x 15 in.
Private collection

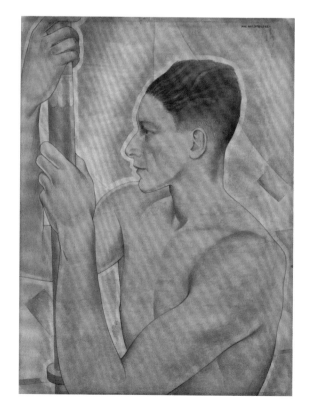

Mac Harshberger
(1901–1975)
Untitled (Horace Terrell in
bathtub), circa 1928
Watercolor
12¼ x 8 in.
Private collection

Hollande Robinson
(1890–1959)
"Sing a Song of Six
Francs," illustration
by Robinson from his
publication *Nursery Rhymes
for the Petits Francais*, 1925,
self-published
Private collection

Mac Harshberger
(1901–1975)
Couture fashion design,
circa 1922
Watercolor
19 x 13¼ in. (sheet size)
Thomas Reynolds Gallery,
San Francisco

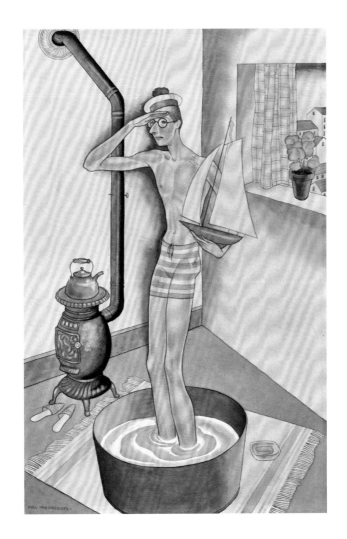

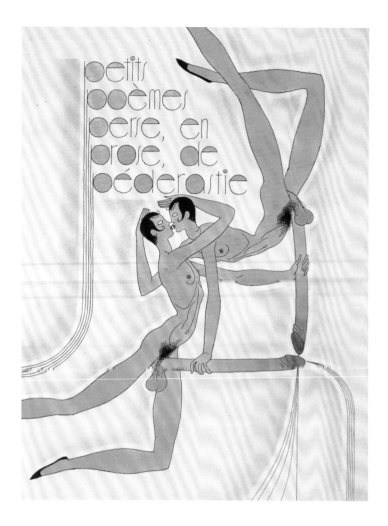

Mac Harshberger
(1901–1975)
Interior page from *Petits poèmes perse, en prose, de péderastie*, date unknown
13⅜ x 10¼ in.
Wolfsonian–Florida International University, Miami Beach
Mitchell Wolfson, Jr. Collection, TD1989.42.7
Photograph by Lynton Gardiner

The exaggerated size of the genitalia of the two figures was likely inspired by Harshberger's admiration for the English author and illustrator Aubrey Beardsley (1872–1898), who was a major influence on his art.

Mac Harshberger
(1901–1975)
Interior page from *Petits poèmes perse, en prose, de péderastie*, date unknown
13⅜ x 10¼ in.
Wolfsonian–Florida International University, Miami Beach
Mitchell Wolfson, Jr. Collection, TD1989.42.7
Photograph by Lynton Gardiner

Mac Harshberger
(1901–1975)
Interior page from *Petits
poèmes perse, en prose, de
péderastie*, date unknown
13⅜ x 10¼ in.
Wolfsonian–Florida
International University,
Miami Beach
Mitchell Wolfson, Jr.
Collection, TD1989.42.7
Photograph by Lynton
Gardiner

Mac Harshberger
(1901–1975)
Interior page from *Petits
poèmes perse, en prose, de
péderastie*, date unknown
13⅜ x 10¼ in.
Wolfsonian–Florida
International University,
Miami Beach
Mitchell Wolfson, Jr.
Collection, TD1989.42.7
Photograph by Lynton
Gardiner

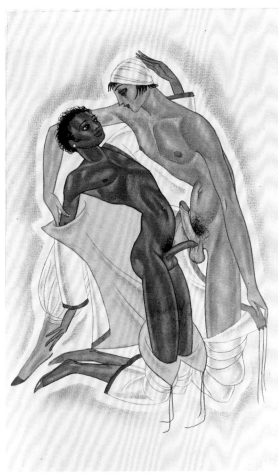

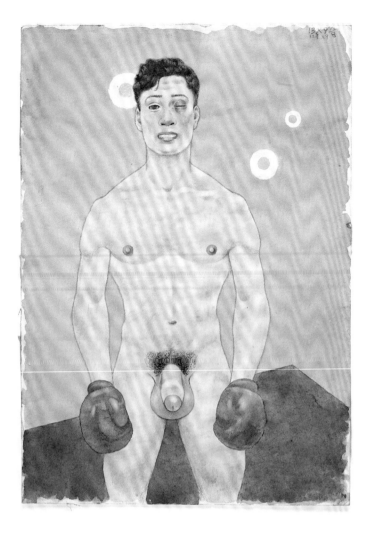

Mac Harshberger
(1901–1975)
Le Boxeur, 1920–39
Watercolor and graphite
on paper
14 x 10 in.
Wolfsonian–Florida
International University,
Miami Beach
Mitchell Wolfson, Jr.
Collection, TD1991.111.1
Photograph by Lynton
Gardiner

Mac Harshberger
(1901–1975)
*Young Nude Male with
Bracelets and Lily*, 1920–39
Watercolor, colored pencil,
and graphite on paper
14 x 10 in.
Wolfsonian–Florida
International University,
Miami Beach
Mitchell Wolfson, Jr.
Collection, TD1991.111.6
Photograph by Lynton
Gardiner

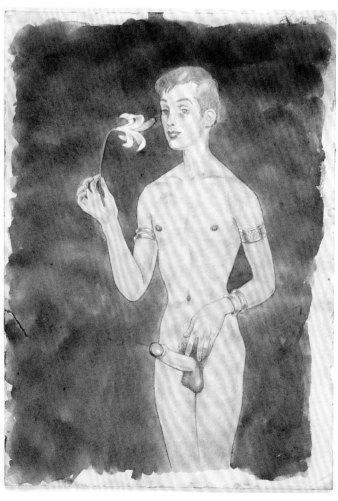

Mac Harshberger
(1901–1975)
*Le matin suivant la nuit
dernière*, 1920–39
Watercolor, colored pencil,
and graphite on paper
15 x 10⅛ in.
Wolfsonian–Florida
International University,
Miami Beach
Mitchell Wolfson, Jr.
Collection, TD1991.111.12
Photograph by Lynton
Gardiner

Mac Harshberger
(1901–1975)
*Two Young Males on a Bed
Engaged in Mutual Fellatio*,
1920–39
Watercolor and graphite
on paper
9⅛ x 12 in.
Wolfsonian–Florida
International University,
Miami Beach
Mitchell Wolfson, Jr.
Collection, TD1991.111.7
Photograph by Lynton
Gardiner

Jule Kullberg
1905–1976

Jule Helen Kullberg was born an only child in Saint Paul, Minnesota, and moved as a baby with her parents to Seattle the year of her birth. Her mother, Pauline Broadum Kullberg, was a German immigrant, and her father, John Emil Kullberg, was a Swedish immigrant who worked as a salesman and real estate investor. Mr. Kullberg was interested in parapsychology and, as a member of the Seattle Psychic Research Society, lectured on his own psychic experiences as well as the practice of automatic writing.

Jule studied at the University of Washington, graduating with a BA in dramatic art in 1927. During her time as a student, she designed stage sets and props for various UW productions. She later entered the University of Oregon on a Carnegie Scholarship, and consequently studied with Dong Kingman at Mills College in Oakland, California, and with George Grosz in New York.

While attending the University of Washington, Kullberg met a fellow student, Orlena Harsch (1904–1995), who was pursuing a career as a teacher. Harsch came from both an artistic and academic family. Her father, Howard Harsch, was an extremely talented photographer who had studios in Seattle and Yakima. Her brother, Alfred E. Harsch, became a prominent Seattle attorney and professor at the University of Washington, serving in their School of Law for thirty-five years.

Orlena and Jule, circa 1945
Photograph courtesy of
Gretchen Harsch

After graduating from the UW, Kullberg taught public speaking, science, and world history at Prosser High School in Washington before accepting a teaching position in the Bothell school district in 1928. Orlena also joined the Bothell faculty by 1932. It was around this time that the two women started living together as a couple. When Jule accepted a position to teach drama and English at Seattle's Broadway High School in 1935, Orlena moved in with Jule in her parents' home until they rented an apartment on Capitol Hill that same year. Jule had always liked to sketch and paint in watercolor, though her education had been primarily in the dramatic arts. One of her friends, artist Edmond James Fitzgerald, admired her paintings and encouraged her to return to the university to advance her art education. With a new focus on the visual arts, she became a very active member of Women Painters of Washington (WPW), one of the region's most prominent arts organizations.

Jule Kullberg (1905–1976)
Painted chest of drawers,
circa 1936
36½ (H) x 45½ (W) x
24½ in. (D)
Collection of Gretchen
Harsch

Orlena secured a teaching job at Highline High School, in nearby Burien, where she also became involved in the school's theater productions. Around this time, the couple purchased a cabin on Whidbey Island for weekend getaways and as a summer residence. In the late 1930s, they began following their lifelong passion for travel by visiting Jule's aunt Emma Olson, who lived outside Gothenburg, Sweden.

As the new decade began, they had purchased a home on Seattle's Queen Anne Hill and then sold the cabin and built a larger country home at Coupeville, also on Whidbey Island. The women did much of the construction work themselves, and Jule decorated the interior and exterior of the home as well as customizing the furniture with designs based on Pennsylvania Dutch and Swedish iconography, celebrating her own paternal heritage. The Coupeville area attracted a number of lesbian couples who also found the beauty of the island a safe refuge from the city.

Orlena began working at Seattle's Queen Anne High School in 1943, initially teaching French and then becoming the school's head counselor. She was active in the Administrative Women in Education organization, assisting international students after the war.

Jule became a prominent member of the Northwest Watercolor Society and began showing her work in their annual exhibitions at the Seattle Art Museum in 1943. She would be involved with that organization for the next thirty years, exhibiting twenty-one watercolors during the period of her membership.

Jule's teaching position changed in 1946 when Broadway High School students were redirected to other districts as the school merged with the neighboring Edison Technical School. The following year the couple spent a month during the summer on a driving trip to allow Jule to sketch up and down the West Coast. Since Jule never learned to drive, Orlena indulged her partner's artistic pursuits by driving her wherever she thought she would find inspiration. Their love of the ocean caused them to purchase yet another home, this time at Arch Cape on the Oregon Coast, where Jule could paint and entertain friends and family.

Jule Kullberg (1905–1976)
Seattle from Queen Anne Hill, 1954
Watercolor
18 x 23⅜ in.
Collection of the Lea family

The new Broadway-Edison became a school for adults as well as accommodating World War II veterans to assist in their training and reintegration into the job market through the GI Bill. Jule continued her position at the technical school and became head of their flourishing art department by 1953, hiring prominent local artist friends such as Jacob Elshin, Fay Chong, and Yvonne Twining Humber to teach night classes. This school became the starting point for numerous future successful Northwest artists, including Doris Totten Chase, who had taken painting classes there at the beginning of her career.

In 1948 the Northwest Watercolor Society held its first national exhibition at the Riverside Museum in New York. Five of Jule's watercolors were among the 101 paintings exhibited by forty-three artist members of the organization. This was a significant honor for the contributing artists and a validation of their talents and advocacy of the difficult medium.

Jule and Orlena were both savvy in financial matters, and besides their teaching jobs, they had extra income from investments in apartment buildings in Seattle. This allowed them to build a new studio home in 1948 on Seattle's posh Queen Anne Hill with a spectacular view of the city and Puget Sound.

They would often open their home to artists and arts organizations, especially WPW, which held its annual Christmas parties there for several years. Jule honed her art skills and learned printmaking as well. In 1950 she taught screen printing for members of WPW and became their president in 1954. Her artistic ambitions were generally aimed at teaching and promoting younger artists, although she exhibited her own work in group presentations locally as well as in New York, Hawaii, and California.

Jule and Orlena never hid the fact that they were a couple. Their families and artist friends accepted their relationship as a matter of fact and gave them their support and love.

In 1963 both women took sabbaticals from their educational careers and indulged in a nine-month trip around the world. Their financial acumen had

allowed them to travel extensively, with regular trips to Hawaii, Palm Springs, and other locations that welcomed gay visitors.

Jule retired from teaching in 1965 to concentrate on travel and painting. Orlena soon followed suit. From February 4 through April 20, 1971, actor Richard Chamberlain rented Jule and Orlena's home through discreet connections in local gay circles. The actor, who was closeted at the time, could live freely with his then boyfriend in a nonthreatening atmosphere. While Chamberlain occupied the upstairs quarters of their home, the women went to Honolulu, Alaska, and the Oregon Coast to give him some privacy.

Jule and Orlena continued to support their former students, younger artists, and professional women as time and finances allowed.

When Kullberg died in 1976, there was no mention of Harsch in her obituary, even though the women had been a couple for over forty years. Orlena, in tribute to her life partner, set up the Jule Kullberg Memorial Award with both the Northwest Watercolor Society and WPW. Before Orlena's death in 1995, most of Kullberg's paintings were dispersed to friends and students without record.

SOURCES

Interview with Orlena Harsch's niece, Gretchen Harsch, Dec. 6, 2018, and archival materials in Gretchen Harsch's possession

"Jule Kullberg First Lady of Art at Edison School," by Roland Ryder-Smith, *Seattle Daily Times*, June 2, 1956, 73

"April Showers Exciting Hours," by Dorothy Brant Brazier, *Seattle Times*, May 10, 1971, 21

Jule Kullberg (1905–1976)
Untitled Eastern
Washington landscape,
1952
Watercolor
15½ x 22½ in.
Private collection

Jule Kullberg (1905–1976)
Untitled (China) circa 1960
Watercolor
9 x 11¾ in.
Collection of Gretchen
Harsch

Jule Kullberg (1905–1976)
Dock at Pusan, circa 1960
Watercolor
9 x 11¾ in.
Collection of Gretchen
Harsch

Jule Kullberg (1905–1976)
Untitled, circa 1948
Watercolor
11 x 15 in.
Collection of Ron Endlich

From left: unidentified
friend, Orlena Harsch,
Jule Kullberg, and Richard
Chamberlain, 1971
Photograph courtesy of
Gretchen Harsch

Orlena Harsch and Jule
Kullberg at their Queen
Anne home, circa 1952
Photograph courtesy of
Gretchen Harsch

Interior of the Harsch-
Kullberg home, circa 1955
Photograph courtesy of
Gretchen Harsch

Jule working on the
Whidbey Island cabin,
circa 1956
Photograph courtesy of
Gretchen Harsch

Jule Kullberg (1905–1976)
Untitled, circa 1950
Oil on Masonite
24 x 18 in.
Collection of Lindsey and
Carolyn Echelbarger

Jule Kullberg (1905–1976)
Surf Watchers, circa 1955
Watercolor
21½ x 29 in.
Private collection

Orlena and Jule, circa 1936
Photograph courtesy of
Gretchen Harsch

Christmas card: *The Three Ring Circus*, 1950s–'60s
Offset print with watercolor
Collection of Gretchen Harsch

Christmas card: *Three Mere Maids*, 1950s–'60s
Collection of Gretchen Harsch

Christmas card: Jule and Orlena on a magic carpet and their pet poodle, Lisa, 1950s–'60s
Collection of Gretchen Harsch

Howard Harsch Studio
Jule Kullberg, circa 1930
Photograph courtesy of
Gretchen Harsch

James & Merrihew Studio
Jule Kullberg, circa 1928
Photograph courtesy of
Gretchen Harsch

Howard Harsch Studio
Silhouette portrait of
Orlena, circa 1930
Photograph courtesy of
Gretchen Harsch

Howard Harsch Studio
Silhouette portrait of Jule
Kullberg, circa 1930
Photograph courtesy of
Gretchen Harsch

Howard Harsch (1878–
1963) was a talented
Northwest studio
photographer. He
created beautiful, artistic
photographs of his
daughter Orlena and her
life partner, Jule Kullberg.

Del McBride
1920–1998

Delbert John McBride was born in Olympia, the eldest of three sons of Albert McBride and Pauline McAllister McBride. His family was of mixed European ancestry but also included significant Native American heritage from the Quinault, Cowlitz, Puyallup, and Nisqually tribes.

As a teenager, McBride displayed a mature talent for drawing and design, and he made art his major when he entered the College of Puget Sound (now University of Puget Sound) in 1938. He remained there until 1940, when he enrolled at the University of Washington while simultaneously joining the National Youth Administration under President Roosevelt's New Deal. It was during this time that he met Dr. Erna Gunther (1896–1982), director of the University of Washington's Anthropology Department and, from 1930 to 1962, director of what is now known as the Burke Museum. Dr. Gunther was an internationally recognized authority on Pacific Northwest Native American tribes. Through Gunther, Del McBride learned about his ethnic and artistic heritage, which would soon have a major effect on the direction of his artistic output.

After his studies at the UW were completed, he moved to Los Angeles in 1941 to study at the Art Center School (now Art Center College of Design), working primarily under Joseph Henninger (1906–1999), a successful painter, illustrator, and cartoonist. The school had a strong curriculum that would assist McBride in his desire to become a commercial artist. He then moved to San Francisco in late 1942. During his time in California he explored his homosexuality and began creating gay-oriented subject matter, but only showed these works to close friends. By 1944 he had moved back to the Northwest and enrolled again at the UW, where he studied with Walter Isaacs (1886–1964) before contracting tuberculosis that required him to recuperate for nearly a year.

He then resumed his art studies at Seattle's Cornish School (now Cornish College of the Arts), where he worked with James E. Peck (1907–2002), whose sophisticated watercolor technique became an influence in McBride's preference for water-based mediums. For the next four years he worked as a commercial artist with the Tacoma Engraving Company. In 1950, McBride and his brother Albert "Bud" and cousin Oliver Tiedemann started the Klee Wyk Studio, which is discussed in the main essay (page 46).

In 1954 he reentered the University of Washington, graduating the following year magna cum laude with a teaching certificate. By this time his art had fallen into two distinct categories: surrealistic and biomorphic abstractions that reflected his interest in his native heritage, and homoerotic male figure compositions. He

became aware of the gay New York artist Paul Cadmus (1904–1999) and copied some of his drawings and etchings for study purposes. He also made versions of other popular paintings of the period that contained nude or partially clad male figures, such as *The Bathers* of circa 1928 by the bisexual artist John Steuart Curry (1897–1946), whose work affected and validated his own emphasis on male forms.

McBride spent the next several years in various teaching positions, including ones at Peninsula High School in Gig Harbor and the University of British Columbia.

His artistic output became mainly focused on designs and production for Klee Wyk Studio, but he continued his secret production of homoerotic images.

Due to the repressive social attitudes toward homosexuality in the 1950s, McBride sought out discreet national publications and organizations aimed at gay men and their suppressed libidos. He collected erotic photographs from various studios, including Bob Mizer's Athletic Model Guild (AMG), whose nearly naked models were promoted under the guise of aesthetic source material or as role models for the attainment of a physical ideal. According to Del's brother Bud, McBride made an erotic film accompanied with graphic illustrations that were submitted to AMG, but neither the film nor any record of publications containing his illustrations has been located. Del also belonged to the Frontier Athletic Club based out of San Diego and Tijuana, Mexico, and received their awkward, handmade, mimeographed newsletter that promoted the sale of erotic photographs of sexy men. He would later subscribe to the post-Stonewall International Phallic Society newsletter, based out of Las Vegas, another venue for male erotica.

Around 1959, he met the esteemed scholar and archaeologist Clark W. Brott (1934–1993), who became his close friend, confidant, model, professional peer, and sexual partner. Brott was curator and director for the Washington State Historical Society (WSHS) in Tacoma from 1960 to 1962, but also became involved in the Klee Wyk Studio as a photographer. Although married with children, he was primarily attracted to men, which was a source of personal conflict for many years. Judging by their lifelong correspondence in McBride's archive at WSHS, he was also McBride's most significant love. Although McBride would confide in Brott when interested in other men, whether for relationships or sexual conquests, his emotional attachment seemed most centered on his relationship with Brott, even after their physical relationship had ended.

Although McBride exhibited in numerous regional exhibitions, his career as a painter was about to shift from artist and designer to curator and historian. One of his last significant national exhibitions was the 16th Annual Indian Artists Exhibition at the Philbrook Art Center in Tulsa, Oklahoma, in spring of 1961. McBride exhibited two paintings in the exhibition that included such luminaries as Pablita Vellarde (1918–2006) and Fritz Scholder (1937–2005). After his entry into the museum field, he restricted his artistic output to male figure drawings, which he did for his own pleasure and rarely showed to anyone. Hiring beautiful male models was a way to be in contact with nude men within the context of fine art as middle age set in and his sexual life began to diminish.

Delbert J. McBride,
circa 1945
Martin-Zambito Archive

At this time, the Klee Wyk Studio was entering its final year. McBride decided to get out of the financially stressful retail business and entered the museum world of curation, writing, and administration.

He accepted the position of curator of art at Spokane's Cheney Cowles Memorial Museum (now the Northwest Museum of Arts and Culture), where he remained until 1966, when he became the curator for the Washington State Capitol Museum in Olympia. He remained in that position until 1982, conducting international research on Native American arts and culture and assisting in numerous projects as a leading expert in the field.

McBride and members of the Klee Wyk Studio were the subjects of several retrospectives at the Washington State Historical Museum in Tacoma, the repository for most of the studio's work. Their reputations were established and preserved largely through the efforts of Northwest art historian Maria Pascualy.

SOURCES

Maria Pascualy, "Delbert J. McBride, Native American Artist, Designer, Curator, Historian," *Columbia* magazine, winter 2017–18, 13–19

Maria Pascualy, "Klee Wyk: Artists on the Nisqually Flats," *Columbia* magazine, winter 1998–99, 12–15

Washington State Historical Society, Delbert J. McBride Papers

Martin-Zambito Archive, Seattle

Numerous conversations over many years with Bud McBride and Richard Schneider

Page R. Hosmer, "Young Tacoma Artist's Work Will Be Shown," *Tacoma News Tribune*, Oct. 1949, clipping not dated or paginated

Information concerning John Steuart Curry's bisexual orientation came from my close friendship with Curry's assistant, artist William Ashby McCloy (1913–2001); McCloy also shared a studio with Grant Wood in Iowa.

Delbert J. McBride
(1920–1998)
Untitled, circa 1942
Oil on paper
15 x 16¼ in.
Private collection

Delbert J. McBride
(1920–1998)
Untitled, circa 1945
Pastel and chalk
45 x 27½ in.
Private collection

Untitled, circa 1945
Oil on canvas
23½ x 19⅝ in.
Private collection

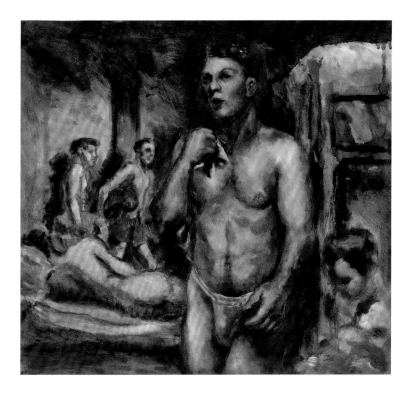

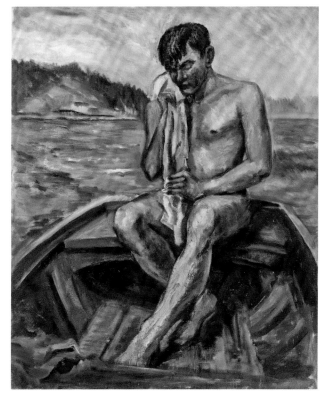

Delbert J. McBride
(1920–1998)
Untitled, circa 1945
Watercolor, gouache, and
collage
16 x 19⅞ in.
Private collection

Delbert J. McBride
(1920–1998)
Untitled, 1951
Watercolor and gouache
8½ x 11 in.
Private collection

Delbert J. McBride
(1920–1998)
Untitled (drag queen),
circa 1948
Gouache
11⅝ x 11½ in.
Private collection

Delbert J. McBride
(1920–1998)
Untitled, circa 1948
Oil on paper
22 x 13 in.
Private collection

Delbert J. McBride
(1920–1998)
The Black Cat Bar, circa
1948
Graphite drawing
11 x 8½ in.
Private collection
The Black Cat was an
important early gay bar in
San Francisco.

Delbert J. McBride
(1920–1998)
Drag Queen, circa 1950
Oil on paper
16¾ x 11¾ in.
Private collection

Delbert J. McBride
(1920–1998)
Untitled, circa 1945
Watercolor and gouache
17 x 21½ in.
Private collection

Delbert J. McBride
(1920–1998)
Untitled (locker room),
circa 1950
Oil on paper
27 x 19½ in.
Private collection

Delbert J. McBride
(1920–1998)
Untitled (sauna), circa 1950
Charcoal
18 x 24 in.
Private collection

Delbert J. McBride
(1920–1998)
Untitled, circa 1950
Oil on paper
24¼ x 17 in.
Private collection

Delbert J. McBride
(1920–1998)
Untitled, circa 1948
Ink
11 x 8½ in.
Private collection

Delbert J. McBride
(1920–1998)
Untitled, circa 1945
Graphite
11¼ x 8½ in.
Private collection

Delbert J. McBride
(1920–1998)
Untitled, circa 1950
Conté crayon
17 x 14 in.
Private collection

Delbert J. McBride
(1920–1998)
Untitled, circa 1942
Watercolor and ink
11¼ x 8½ in.
Private collection

Excerpts of Correspondence between Del McBride and Clark Brott

Del McBride had a loving professional and personal relationship with archaeologist Clark Brott for nearly forty years. Clark W. Brott (1934–1993) was raised in Southern California and educated at the University of Alaska and the University of Bonn, Germany. After marriage and fatherhood, he enlisted in the US Air Force.

Starting in the 1950s, he became an artist's model to augment his income and to explore his sexuality. Brott was a favored model for McBride as well as for sculptor Donal Hord and his photographer/lover Homer Dana, both of whom were originally from the Northwest.

In 1960, Brott became curator/director of the Washington State History Museum in Olympia, Washington. He furthered his education at the University of Washington in Seattle and completed a summer session in archaeology at the University of New Mexico, as well as one at the Summer Institute in Anthropology for Museum Curators at the University of Arizona in Tucson. In 1962, Brott accepted a position as curator with the San Diego Museum of Man, where he remained for seven years. He went on to have a distinguished career in the field of California archaeology until his death from complications of AIDS in 1993.

The majority of McBride's figure drawings and paintings of Brott have not been located.

The following are excerpts from letters exchanged between McBride and Brott, housed in the Delbert J. McBride Papers at the Washington State Historical Society, Tacoma, Washington.

THURSDAY, JANUARY 17, 1961, CB TO DM

Knowing that I do that you are a frugal sort of fellow (that's the McAllister in you), I was a bit shocked to learn my "surprise" for you will cost a neat $24. I thought I was going to obtain it for little or no cost. You don't have to take it if you don't want it, but I am sure you will like it, and you should derive not only some benefit from it (artistic) but also (I hope) some considerable pleasure. With those thoughts in mind, you might want to throw an extra $24 in your wampum belt, and if you don't have the extra, perhaps we can make up the difference by living a spartan and or unalcoholic existence for a few days. You could also save a coin or two by not taking photographs (since that film costs nearly $3.00 a roll, doesn't it?) (I am still willing to strip, of course, if the cost of things doesn't upset your plans, and I have a few interesting ideas for close anatomical studies which may be of help to you). . . . My schedule every day this week has been: rise and shower at 7:00 a.m., work at the museum from 8 a.m. to 5:45 p.m., work out at the gym for one to two hours, model for three hours for a variety of artist-types, and collapse into bed around midnight. I am looking forward to a casual trip for us.

APRIL 13, 1962, CB TO DM

Come along when you can. I look forward to some philosophic discourses over a mug of mulled wine, and as I say, I'll be happy to furnish a little naked flesh and blood if it will result in some good sculpture. There won't be any rhinestones or eye-shadow, but the hair is still there.
As ever,
Clark
P.S. When you come, be sure to bring your polaroid camera.

SEPTEMBER 3, 1962, CB TO DM

You would have gotten quite a kick out of my lecture on the NWC (Northwest coast) and Eskimo. I did a pantomime of the Cannibal dance as recorded by [Franz] Boas (although I didn't strip to the appropriate costume—I'm not that much of an exhibitionist and the ladies would faint.)

If you really concentrate, you can put out some very fine drawings. All you have to have is the right model and a little mulled wine, and you can turn out a most interesting array of work.

NOVEMBER 29, 1962, CB TO DM

Last night I spent three hours standing naked and as still as I could while thirteen students of the La Jolla Art Center life class strained through drawings of the male figure. As you well know, it is the first time I have posed for more than two people (and all of them were sober). At first I was a little apprehensive about striding out into a room filled with men and women, and my heart was really beating as I mounted the gold-velveteen-covered platform in the center of the room, which was so large and strongly lighted that I was very conscious of my near nudity and conspicuous elevation (referring to the platform). As soon as I dropped the towel that was around my waist and exposed what little that had been covered, I began the first of five-minute poses and completely forgot that I was naked at all. . . . One thing I must say, and that is that I am very appreciative of the time that we have

spent with me modelling and you sketching, because, it paid off last night. . . . I remember the first night (with dear old drunken Oliver [Tiedemann] I posed for you two, and I was very self-conscious and reluctant to strip all the way (which wasn't helped at all by O. exclaiming so loudly about "those terrific veins."

DECEMBER 7, 1962, CB TO DM

Myrna is trained not to open mail that is addressed to me personally, so you would not have to balk at an unrestrained text (although you generally are very restrained anyway). If you have something which you feel is especially personal, the museum delivery is safer, because our mail is *never* touched.

UNDATED, CB TO DM

Thanks very appreciatively for the very handsome tie. I have worn the tie many times since Christmas. It is one of my favorites. Your amusing comment about wanting to be here so you could tie it on me, made me think, "I'll bet. He'd probably wrap one end around my neck and the other end over a rafter." But the sense of distance made me secure, so I tied it around my own neck, with only occasional glances about for caution's sake. With the John Birchers hanging their 19-year-old sons as martyrs to the communists, one must be cautious in San Diego.

Delbert J. McBride
(1920–1998)
Untitled study sheet of male nudes, circa 1950
Conté crayon and ink
36 x 21½ in.
Private collection

Delbert J. McBride
(1920–1998)
Untitled study sheet of male nudes, circa 1945
Ink
10¼ x 8½ in.
Private collection

UNDATED BUT SURMISED TO BE SPRING OF 1963, CB TO DM

The modelling is still going well. I put in another session last night at Scripps. . . .
Last night a not-so-good-looking but nevertheless charming beatnik type of girl
seemed to get very excited about me, and as she left she thanked me for allowing
her to draw "your beautiful display of muscles." . . . In addition to steady increases
in my workouts (not time but poundage), I have been taking quantities of protein
supplements (brewer's yeast, wheat germ, amino acids, etc.). These not only give me
a ravishing appetite, but they seem to have a peculiar effect on my sexual desires,
and I have a difficult time keeping my penis from being as hard as a ramrod.
Several times last night my thoughts wandered to erotic subjects (especially when
I would notice this girl's eyes roaming over my body), and I could feel an erec-
tion developing under the scrap of cloth that was "covering" my nakedness. I am
especially frustrated now because my wife is medically indisposed, and there is no
proper satisfaction for my sensual urges, which are rather ravenous. . . . These people are paying $2.50 an hour, while you have worked my naked body for hundreds
of hours for free. When you come down again, I should be a somewhat improved
(because of the increased workouts) male model—stripped and free, for you. If you
bring your camera this time, I would be glad to provide the necessary body, once
again, completely stripped, if you like. . . . I went out to Donal Hord's house, not
only because I was curious to meet him, but because he wanted to look me over to
see if I was satisfactory for his type of sculpture before he hired me as a model. . . .
We went out to his huge studio, which is a separate building, and [he] asked me
to remove my clothes so he could examine me. I did and I must say I felt pretty
strange standing naked in the middle of the floor (of a large room with one whole
wall of glass) while he scrutinized every muscle in my body. His comment was that I
would do fine and that "the definition of your muscles is very good." He didn't say
so, but every indication was that his models pose entirely nude. If that's the case I
shouldn't have any trouble, as long as he won't mind some occasional movement
between my legs whenever my mind wanders to sex.

Delbert J. McBride
(1920–1998)
Untitled, circa 1950
Ink
11 x 8½ in.
Private collection

Delbert J. McBride
(1920–1998)
Untitled, circa 1948
Ink and graphite
10¼ x 8½ in.
Private collection

MARCH 22, 1963, CB TO DM

I am still participating in my moonlight vocation, although I still have yet to model for Donal Hord. If things keep sliding along, I doubt if I ever will—who knows. . . . Do you remember the slides we took of me posing when you came down for the Western Conference last October? I had given up trying to get those developed (no time) and thought I had thrown the roll away. The other day we sent a bunch of pictures into town to be developed, and yes, you guessed it: one of the rolls was that one. Judith [Judith Strupp, a co-worker] was going through the returned slides, when she exclaimed, "Well, what's this? It looks like you as an Indian." After nearly breaking my neck scrambling across the table to get the photos from her, I was relieved to find that they were pretty innocent.

APRIL 19, 1963, CB TO DM

I had been spending every weekend out in the desert surveying sites and doing a considerable amount of surface archaeology. I spent one weekend out with Donal Hord and Homer Dana. They have a four-wheel-drive Jeep wagon, and we visited 5 different sites, 3 of which are "Early Man" sites. . . . Following that weekend, I hired a muscular young lad from the gym to help me empty all of the artifact drawers and cabinets from the archaeology lab. . . . My helper (who literally bristles with brawn) did his share, and we got it moved, but you should have heard the girls' remarks about him. They would have been more cautious if they knew how unscrupulous a young stud he really is. By his own admission, he'll do anything for money or sexual pleasure. He has been at me to introduce him to the modelling market, so I finally arranged for him to take my place at the Art Center one night when I had to work here at the museum.

JUNE 3, 1963, CB TO DM

I am still modelling for Donal Hord but I stopped posing at the Art Center and Scripps. It was just too much time and effort, and I was really getting worn to a frazzle from the extra work. Donal seems to be very happy with me, and he has constructed a nice clay figure (an exercise he calls it) from the pose I have done for him. His exercises he does very meticulously, as you can well imagine, since he has worked the same pose over since I started. From the exercise, he has taken ideas for a rosewood carving (4 feet tall) of a Mexican boy with (symbolically) all the burdens of life on his back. [Homer] Dana took some more photos of me, and I will provide you with some of them, if you like. Two or three are really rather good (even if I say so), and the photography is better than before. They cost $1.00 per 8 x 10 or 50¢ for 5 x 7s. Three are in trunks, one in the nude, and two with a posing strap.

I read the book you gave me, *Song of the Red Ruby*, as I mentioned in my last letter. I enjoyed it, but it only increased my boyish, animal frustrations.

UNDATED, SURMISED TO BE LATE SEPTEMBER OR EARLY OCTOBER 1963, CB TO DM

My dear friend. . . . Nothing we have done in the last few days affects what I am telling you, for I had decided quite some time ago that the relationship between us would have to be altered. I didn't mention it in regard to this last weekend prior to our embarking on it, because you know, I enjoy our erotic pastimes as much as you do. Generally, I am a relatively weak-willed individual, and I will succumb to my erotic desires when the opportunity is presented, even when I am well aware of the damage it does to my mental well-being. In other words, I enjoy the activities we indulge in, but my Puritan upbringing always returns to haunt me, and I have been told for so many years by so many people that the satisfaction of such desires is improper, that indulging in them with you is making me increasingly neurotic. I am afraid that if I don't gather all my willpower for this one effort to break away, I am likely to become completely mentally irresponsible, and there are too many things I would like to accomplish in life to risk this inevitability. This is not an entirely selfish thought either, because I think that the thin line we have crossed between what could be good art and what is rapidly becoming a façade for eroticism is gradually destroying your potential to be a good artist—a potential I would sincerely like to see developed. As much as I hate to say this, I am afraid that from now on, you will have to include me in your group of "former" models. I hope to discontinue all modelling as soon as it is economically feasible. Not because it is sexually improper, but because it takes too much time away from the things I really want to accomplish. I must stop modelling for you for the simple reason that we all too often stray to more intimate things and the best way to avoid this altogether is to halt the principal entrée. This does not mean at all that our friendship should cease, for I hope you will always be my friend; and perhaps (I sincerely hope) this will introduce a period of an even warmer, more useful, and certainly more realistic friendship. But from this point forward, I am asking—both for you and for me—that it be a purely platonic friendship.

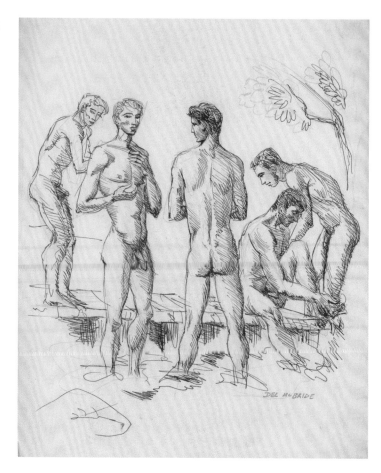

Delbert J. McBride
(1920–1998)
Untitled, circa 1948
Ink and graphite
10¼ x 8½ in.
Private collection

MARCH 31, 1966, CB TO DM

Thank you for the nice selection of drawings. There were three rather good ones in the group, and they look quite nice matted. I was hoping you might include one of the several drawings you did for the Sebastian theme, because I remember that at least two of them were really quite good. If it is not convenient to bring one of those with you, perhaps we can (with a little effort on the part of both of us) do two or three more along the same lines. In a classroom I recently modelled in, I saw several drawings (preliminary sketches for paintings, I think) by Raphael, Dürer, and Michelangelo which depicted three different and quite interesting versions of males, stripped and strung up for execution or torture. Another thing, do you still have that group of AMG drawings ("Summer Cruise") you bought for me? A friend of mine has a definite interest in seeing them, so I would like to borrow them, if I may. Would you please bring them with you?

AUGUST I, 1967, DM TO CB

Dear Clark: How are you and things in your immediate circle these days? I haven't been doing much writing and really haven't expected to hear from people but felt impelled to write tonight as I sit in my basement escaping from the television and listening to a rendition of Purcell's *Indian Queen* (quite appropriate perhaps).

NOVEMBER 12, 1967, DM TO CB

I finally got the little book *Song of the Loon* which is purple prose if I ever saw it but makes one wonder if there was a subculture going here in the Pacific Northwest in the 19th century.

SEPTEMBER 4, 1972, DM TO CB

I must still have some kind of mental block when it comes to putting paint on canvas—maybe I'm still waiting for some kind of mystical illumination—another Tamanous power vision such as did lead to a very productive decade at Klee Wyk. . . . Of course a studio, and models, and the right atmosphere would help, but until the urge to paint gets too strong to resist, it seems I may go on dreaming and making the occasional sketch. There are even a couple of art dealers in Seattle ready to give me a show if and when I'm ready. A little over a week ago at Neah Bay I

Delbert J. McBride
(1920–1998)
Clark Brott, circa 1960
Graphite and wash
9 x 6⅝ in.
Private collection

saw some Indian dancing which inspired me, by the Nootka carver Joe David and his brother. A whirling wolf dance and Wild man (Bukwiss) masked dance. The Wolf Dance has some similarities to the mayo deer dance in that the dancer, with very simple mask and painted robe, somehow gives the illusion of becoming the wolf. It was a really gripping experience.

FEBRUARY 27, 1973, DM TO CB

Thursday had to escape Olympia some way—a black sculptor friend in Portland invited me to the opening of his show—in a pool hall back of a huge tavern down on the Portland waterfront. It was really fantastic, with free-flowing beer and wine, and a Dutch lunch, a mixed-bag of people, from skid row bums (not really many of those), lots of gay people, including the artist and his sculptor friend (white) he lives with, and the owner of Denny's restaurants, also Vincent Price was to drop in. I was invited to another, bigger and more elegant party, but declined regretfully to get on a Greyhound bus and go back to work the next day.

MARCH 12, 1974, DM TO CB

Which brings me to another point—I have a new boyfriend—met him in Marin Valley California over the Christmas holidays at the home of gay friends, but he lives in Seattle. Nick likes older guys—he is quite receptive to learning about art, etc. Has a car, marvelous cook (he worked in Alaska as a hotel kitchen manager last year), is tall, dark, 23, attractive, and poor. On unemployment right now as a matter of fact. Well I never did want a rich boyfriend anyway. Don't know how it will last but it's in the fun stages right now. Wish me luck. . . .

I think my friend Patrick may have migrated south to San Diego—I had such a good time with him in Hollywood just before Christmas. . . . He usually phones me collect when time is hanging heavy on his hands—he was dating people like Rock Hudson, but the turnover rate is rather high down there.

JUNE 6, 1974, DM TO CB

I have a date with Nick for tomorrow and maybe the rest of the weekend if things work out. He's back from Anchorage, came to my birthday party May 16. . . . The Arts Commission awards banquet was that night and I kept inviting people, never dreaming they would all show up, but they did and we couldn't fit them all in at my table. At least I had the two handsomest young men sitting with me—Nick, tall dark and Hungarian, and Ray Stamford, wrestling star and son of one of my favorite arts commissioners.

A Most Important Feeling,

A Youthful Surf Boy Crouching,
Gliding-----Board and Boy Before The Wave:
Strength, And Graceful, Curling Speed
Will Tell You-----
He Belongs.

The Golden Carp-----A Crystal Pool.
With Pine Reflections Adding to the Song-----
Amber Leaves falling, Do Not
Stir This Lyric:
They Belong.

Grey-Blue Mountains Scatter
The Desert Sunset's Golden Arrows,
While sinewy Indian Warrior Spirits
Wrap Shadows Among the Dunes Where
They Belong.

An Autumn Cascades A sycamore Carpet-----
Weaving the Pattern of a Sunlit Glade,
A Boy in Love Recalls the Gentle Grip:
A hand Assuring
He Belongs

Rest In My Cradle of warmth.
Our Bodies Form The Mold and cast of Love,
While The Tender Strength of My Embrace
Whispers Gently-----
You Belong.

October 1964
c w brott

Frontier Athletic Club
Newsletter #8, 1960,
Tijuana, Mexico
Washington State
Historical Society, Delbert
McBride Papers
1998.8 Box 5, Folder 7
The Frontier Athletic
Club was an organization
based in Tijuana that
catered to gay men in
the early 1960s. It offered
inexpensive memberships
that provided a variety of
social and erotic opportunities in a discreet setting.

Delbert J. McBride
(1920–1998)
Copy of John Steuart
Curry painting *The Bathers*
(1928), circa 1942
Oil on paper
23 x 30¾ in.
Private collection

Delbert J. McBride
(1920–1998)
Untitled, circa 1950
Graphite, ink, and colored
pencil
11 x 7 in.
Private collection

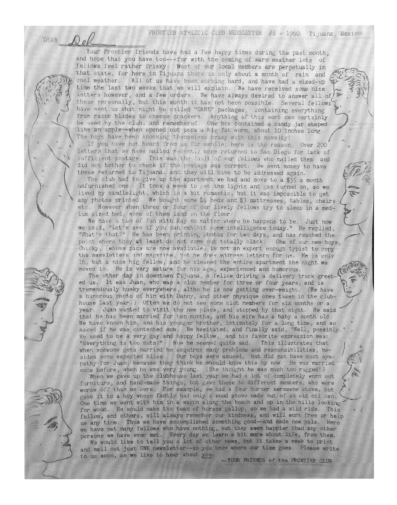

Orre Nobles
1894–1967

Orrie Nelson Nobles was born in Sumter, Minnesota, one of seven children of William Nobles and Marig Nobles, a Danish immigrant. William was a railroad telegrapher and dispatcher.

Nobles alternatively used four different spellings of his first name: Orrie, as he was named by his parents, Orie, Orré, and finally Orre. He attended Tacoma High school (later called Stadium High School) with the goal of attending the Pratt Institute in Brooklyn, New York. His classmate Dorothy Milne (Rising) had been accepted at Pratt, which increased his desire to attend as soon as he was able. Rising went on to become a noted Northwest modernist painter and cofounded the Northwest Watercolor Society in 1940.

After his high school graduation in 1913, he began working as a laborer and machinist assistant at the Chicago, Milwaukee, and St. Paul Railroad shops, first in Maple Valley and then in Puyallup, as his family lived in each town. During this time he studied violin and piano; learned how to develop photographs; sketched and painted; and used his salary to attend local theater productions and concerts. He also purchased his first Indian basket for twenty-five cents, ushering in a life-long love of collecting beautiful objects.

By 1914 he was attending Washington State Normal School at Bellingham (now Western Washington University) along with his brother William. His goal was to be an art teacher.

At Normal, his cultural interests began to take shape under the guidance of a mature and experienced faculty. The curriculum included craft-oriented classes in wood carving, metalsmithing, and, of course, painting. One of his teachers, Annette Edens, had a profound influence on his artistic direction. A graduate of Columbia Teachers College in New York, she became a mentor to him in his pursuit of becoming an art instructor.

He had a wide range of experiences in Bellingham that included attending a lecture by Helen Keller and her teacher, Anne Sullivan. It was an event that made a deep impression on him.

His diary entry for April 18, 1914, stated, "I expect many important things to come into my life in the next ten years. When I am thirty, I hope to have completed the work offered in the curriculum of Pratt Institute, N.Y. with a great deal more in other schools I desire that not one moment of my time be spent toward an end which will not do justice to my other self. I feel that I am here for a purpose, be it ever so small I wish to continue to express my ideals in terms of material beauty to even a much greater extent than have I up to the present time. I desire to use to its full extent the 'Great Within' and to divert every ounce or grain of energy to some soothing and satisfying good."

He thrived in the stimulation provided at Bellingham and received his teaching certificate. After returning home to Puyallup, he secured a job as a teacher in the town of Tahuya, near Hood Canal in a beautiful section of Washington not far from the Olympic National Forest. He began his teaching career there in September 1914. The small, one-room schoolhouse reflected the sparse population at that time. Just two years earlier, Tahuya had been home to only five families "and a number of assorted bachelors."

Teaching young people suited Orre very well; he was inquisitive, had an ebullient personality, and was concerned that the children receive a solid education, even if he could be a harsh taskmaster at times.

Nobles would commute to Tahuya in a canoe from his home at Union, across Hood Canal. At twenty years of age, he was soon dealing with his emotional and physical attraction to men. He befriended a gay couple named Tommy and William living near him on a houseboat, and they would figure prominently in his life in the next few years.

The couple were mentioned in his diary entry dated December 13, 1914, where he stated, "Sunday and a beautiful sunrise to greet us though plenty of cold to boot. I left early . . . and paid 'The Boys' a visit in their new abode. Somehow I seem to have a great liking for them but why shouldn't I? I think I should be quite satisfied to live as they do and enjoy life as I see fit."

Orre was aware of the utopian colony at nearby Home, Washington, one of several that had begun in the state at the turn of the century. These enclaves stressed the development of independent thought and the rejection of forced social norms. Some of these communities also encouraged incorporating art into everyday life, which reflected the values of the Arts and Crafts Movement. Orre subscribed to several publications by Elbert Hubbard's Roycroft Community in East Aurora, New York, and he used them to guide him in his quest for beauty and personal expression, which he could then impart to his students.

Around this time, Orre met an older man who would become his mentor and have a profound impact on the course of his life. Frank Pixley (1865–1959) came to the Northwest after the 1906 San Francisco earthquake and fire. He settled near Union, an area that enticed his entrepreneurial drive. A true iconoclast, Pixley was trying to establish a community of like-minded people driven by an artistic and creative spirit. He and his family became some of the largest landowners in the region and established the area known as Yacht Haven as his residence.

Coming from a prosperous family, Pixley brought Chinese antiques, a grand piano, and other symbols of affluence and refinement. Orre was in awe of the older man, who seemed to be living the life he himself desired: successful, well traveled, and independent, surrounded by art and music. Orre soon became a fixture in the Pixley home for dinners, parties, and community events, and they loved him as much as he did them.

In 1915, Orre and his family traveled to San Francisco to attend the Panama-Pacific International Exposition. He was still savoring the stimulation he had experienced through numerous visits to Seattle's Alaska-Yukon-Pacific Exposition six years earlier. Between the cultural exposure provided by the exposition and with raconteur Pixley's relayed adventures, Orre's wanderlust was beginning to motivate him to move ahead with his goals.

The following summer, Orre left for Hawaii, expressing what would be a lifelong need for travel and exploration. While on board the S.S. *Makura*, he kept detailed journals of the trip. One life-changing event was that he experienced what appears to be his first love. A young Australian man, Owen Griffiths, was working on board the ship, and he soon caught Orre's attention.

Orre Nobles with his mother at the Panama-Pacific International Exposition in San Francisco, 1915
Collection of the Mason County Historical Society, Shelton, WA

The two young men spent a short time together in Hawaii and a romantic relationship began to form. Orre explored the islands on his bicycle with a new "motor wheel" attachment that gave extra power outside of manual pedaling. He created experiences that he could eventually share with Owen, who had to return to his job on the ship.

The melancholy of leaving Hawaii after spending over six weeks in the tropical paradise was mitigated when he realized that Owen was on board the same ship, and they were able to continue seeing each other. When he returned home, Orre was a changed man. He had found a potential love interest and had experienced a new and exciting culture.

He returned to his teaching position at Tahuya but now realized the potential lying outside the confinement of his small-town life. Owen surprised him by coming to Union so that they could spend a prolonged period together to see if their relationship could survive. At first the situation seemed idyllic, with Orre having a companion who would have wonderful dinners ready for him when he returned from work and provided a steady supply of physical affection. The joy was soon marred by his mentor Pixley, who did not like Owen or the obvious relationship they were having. He was rude and unwelcoming to Owen and displayed this disapproval, causing Orre to be uncomfortable in social situations. Whether Pixley was disdainful of homosexuality or was jealous of the lost adulation from his younger friend, his actions caused a rift between them.

After a while, Orre became tired of Owen and the mundane life he might represent. His desire to travel and expand his potential soon ended the relationship. After Owen left the Northwest, Orre became more involved with his couple friends William and Tommy and had regular sexual experiences with them. The arrangement allowed him to receive the physical pleasure and affection that all young men seek, gay or straight, but also gave him the freedom to not be tied down to a singular relationship. He did end up meeting a young man named Ervin who shared his artistic nature, and the two had a casual, intermittent sexual relationship for three years.

In September 1917, Orre began working on a tramp steamer to raise funds to allow him to study at Pratt. For the next two years, he visited ports throughout the world, including ones in China and Japan. By 1919 he had returned to his home and resumed his teaching career at Tahuya.

In the summer of 1920, Orre's parents purchased a parcel of land from the Pixleys on Hood Canal. A few months later, Orre left the comfort of his family and community and headed east to attend Pratt.

When he arrived in New York, he immediately took full advantage of what the city had to offer. He ravenously explored Brooklyn and its neighboring boroughs, attending live theater, classical concerts, and art exhibitions. He saw the legendary ballerina Anna Pavlova perform and attended a lecture by Robert Henri, one of the leading artists of the period. His instructors at Pratt brought him and his class to the Metropolitan Museum to sketch and to the Fulper Company to receive instruction in pottery production.

In 1921 he became class president and was nicknamed "Claude" by his fellow students. His Pratt yearbook photo bears the inscription, "Claude's ambition is to be a collector—of romantic experiences. He confesses that there is a fascination in what you are afraid of and Claude is afraid of girls. He says he finds safety in numbers, however."

For the past several years, Orre had dreamed of creating an artistic enclave near Hood Canal where visitors could pay a fee and support his and his friends' artistic expressions. Now that his parents owned land that could support such a project, he began making the design plans at Pratt.

When he completed his term at Pratt, he returned to the Northwest, where he taught briefly at the University of Washington. Then, in 1923, he accepted a position at Seattle's Ballard High School, where he would remain employed for the next twenty-nine years as an art instructor.

Simultaneously with his teaching profession, he finally realized his vision for an artistic enclave on Hood Canal. By 1924, Olympus Manor became a haven for local and visiting artists and adventurers.

In February 1927, Orre was wandering along the wharf in Seattle when he met a handsome young man who was reading on the pier. The two struck up a conversation and found that they shared a lot in common. The young man turned out to be the world heavyweight boxing champion, Gene Tunney, who was appearing at the Pantages Theatre in Seattle on February 7. The two men formed an immediate friendship based on their love of art and literature. They spent an exciting time together until Tunney had to return to the East Coast, but they remained in contact through letters. A few months later, Orre was off again on another cruise, this time to Japan, Korea, and China, accompanied by a friend, the writer and scholar Upton Close, whom he had known from the University of Washington. Orre's sketches from this trip appeared as illustrations in Close's 1929 publication *The Lives of Eminent Asians*.

Back in Seattle, Orre continued his teaching position at Ballard High School, while over at Hood Canal he reigned over the magic atmosphere of Olympus Manor. Nobles and Tunney retained their friendship through correspondence until the champion invited his friend to join him in the summer of 1928 at his camp in Spectator, New York, to assist him in his training for his upcoming fight against Tom Heeney. The two men solidified and enhanced their friendship, and Orre reveled in the attention he received from his friend and the circle of celebrated personalities that surrounded him. It has been speculated by several of Nobles's closest friends that the two men had an affair before Tunney's marriage in October 1928. Although there is no evidence to support this, some of Nobles's letters do indicate a romantic love and possessiveness of Tunney. In a letter to his close friend Erna Tilley dated July 26, 1928, he mentioned that his "nose was out of joint" over hearing of Tunney's upcoming trek to Europe with writer Thornton Wilder, whose sexual orientation is still being debated. But with the champion's extraordinary good looks, athletic build, and refined intelligence, it is hard to imagine that Nobles wouldn't have fallen for him. However, Tunney had a successful marriage and became the father of four children. Nobles accepted the unrequited situation and even became friendly with Tunney's wife, Polly. The two men would occasionally see each other over the years and remained close for the remainder of their lives.

Orre Nobles with his class at Ballard High School, circa 1935
Collection of the Mason County Historical Society, Shelton, WA

By 1929, Orre was off to Asia again with an adult former student named John Dean. Extant letters in Thomas Handforth's archive seem to indicate that the two men were a couple. They spent the summer in Japan and then moved on to Korea and Manchuria, finally ending up in Peking. Orre was acquainted with Helen Burton, the American proprietor of the Camel Bell Shop in Peking. A successful entrepreneur, Burton specialized in Asian arts, crafts, and antiquities. It was probably through Burton that Orre met Helen Fette, who asked him to design modern carpets for her business, the Fette-Li rug company in Peking.

Beginning in October 1929, Nobles became the master designer for the "Fette Looms." Besides standard Chinese design elements, the rugs also incorporated striking modernist designs in the Art Deco style, and some reflected imagery based on the Northwest landscape. By spring of 1930, he had designed over 125 rugs for the company to sell to the American, Chinese, and European markets.

A year later, Orre and John were still in China. In a letter to their mutual Seattle friend Walter Fullaway dated March 5, 1931, John wrote, "To go back to Seattle holds no heartthrobs for me. . . . Orre and I are doing well in this old romantic cambulac of a khan. . . . Leisure, culture, and an atmosphere of the yellow house about us tends to make for an enriching of the blood by the addition of a million or so Oriental corpuscles." By June 1931, Orre and John had met up with artist Thomas Handforth, who had just come to China on a Guggenheim Fellowship. The two men stayed with Handforth in his rented home filled with art and antiquities until leaving for Shanghai on their way back to Seattle in August.

It didn't take long for Orre to conceive of a business plan wherein he would lead groups of people on Asian tours during his summer recess from teaching. This lasted until 1937 with great success, bypassing the destructive effects of the Depression that halted the dreams of less fortunate people. John Dean moved to New York to pursue a career in academics but later returned to the Northwest, where he held a position at Boeing, married, and adopted a son.

Olympus Manor continued to thrive, and he purchased three hundred acres nearby to expand its economic and artistic potential, developing additional cottages near the main residence. The income from renting to the nearby Bremerton Navy Yard employees and military personnel, in addition to his income as a teacher, provided Orre with enough money to purchase a lot on Seattle's First Hill that offered a sweeping view of downtown and Elliott Bay. He built a small, fourteen-by-twenty-four-foot home and filled it with treasures he found in local estate auctions and antiques stores and through basic scavenging. He named the house Windy Cliff.

Although Orre was not painting or producing fine art, some of his students began making names for themselves. They included printmaker Art Hansen, illustrators Gus Swanberg and Bill Johnson, and painters James Martin and Richard Gilkey.

In 1952, Orre retired from Ballard High School after the semester ended, and the following month, a fire destroyed Olympus Manor. The caretaker, a troubled thirty-two-year-old former marine named Don Colburn, was killed in the conflagration. After the initial shock of the incident, Orre drew up plans and elevations for Olympus Manor II the same year. Unfortunately, the project was never realized.

Over the next three years, Orre traveled extensively throughout Mexico. After living at Windy Cliff for seven years, he was forced to sell his property to make way for an upcoming freeway in 1962. He rejected the unfair reimbursement offered to him and sought a higher amount, which he was awarded. With his financial demands met, he postponed leaving until the city workers hoisted the tiny house up at 3:00 a.m. and moved it to 1623 South King Street, although it was placed on the new foundation backward. Legend has it that Orre was still inside sleeping during the move. He changed its name from Windy Cliff to its new moniker, Breezy Bluff.

Orre Nobles died in his home of a stroke on December 14, 1967.

SOURCES

Orre Nobles personal journals provided by the Schneider family

1922 Pratt yearbook, *Prattonia*

Martin-Zambito Archive, Seattle

Orre Nobles archive, Mason County Historical Society, Shelton, WA

Erna Tilley, *A Gateway to Friendship*, published by Viola and Don Healy, privately distributed

Irving Petite, "Frances Huson: Sorts Mail, Shucks Oysters," *Seattle Daily Times*, Apr. 13, 1958, 137

E-mail exchanges between David Martin and Jay Tunney, Gene Tunney's son

Michael Fredson, *The Artist Colony on Hood Canal*, Mason County Historical Society, 2011

Don Duncan, "Driftwood Diary," *Seattle Times*, Mar. 26, 1967, 4

Orre Nelson Nobles
(1894–1967)
Untitled (Seattle harbor),
circa 1921
Ink and gouache
14½ x 19½ in.
Collection of the Mason
County Historical Society,
Shelton, WA

Greeting card reproduc-
ing Orre Nobles's 1915
watercolor of the Panama-
Pacific International
Exposition
Collection of Paden and
Norma Prichard

Orre Nelson Nobles
(1894–1967)
Untitled (male nude), circa
1930
Gelatin silver print with
watercolor on painted
mount
14 x 11 in.
Private collection

FROM AN ORIGINAL WATERCOLOR – DONE IN SAN FRANCISCO
IN 1915 – by ORRE NOBLES

Orre Nelson Nobles
(1894–1967)
Olympus Manor II: archi-
tectural rendering, 1952
Ink and watercolor
17¼ x 23¼ in.
Collection of the Mason
County Historical Society,
Shelton, WA

Orre Nelson Nobles
(1894–1967)
Olympus Manor II: archi-
tectural rendering, 1952
Ink and watercolor
17¼ x 23¼ in.
Collection of the Mason
County Historical Society,
Shelton, WA

Entrance to Olympus
Manor
Real photo postcard
Collection of Thomas H.
Wake

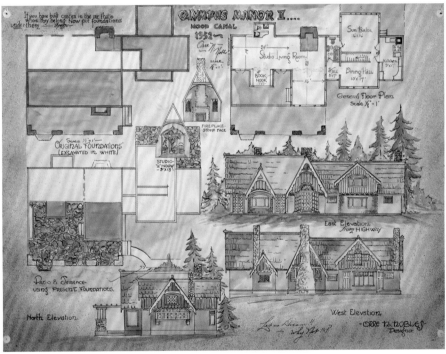

Orre Nelson Nobles
(1894–1967)
Decorated envelope for
Christmas card, 1964
Watercolor and ink
3⅞ x 8⅞ in.
Private collection

Orre Nelson Nobles
(1894–1967)
Decorated envelope for
Christmas card, 1963
Watercolor and ink
3⅞ x 8⅞ in.
Private collection

Orre Nelson Nobles
(1894–1967) with assis-
tance from his students at
Ballard High School
Christmas card created for
Gene Tunney, 1927
Relief print with gouache
and metallic ink
8 x 8½ in.
Private collection

Orre Nobles advertising
card, 1927
Ink, graphite, and gouache
on printed card
Private collection

Western Union telegram
to Orre Nobles from
Gene Tunney, August
1952. Tunney wrote to
express condolences after
a fire destroyed Olympus
Manor.
Private collection

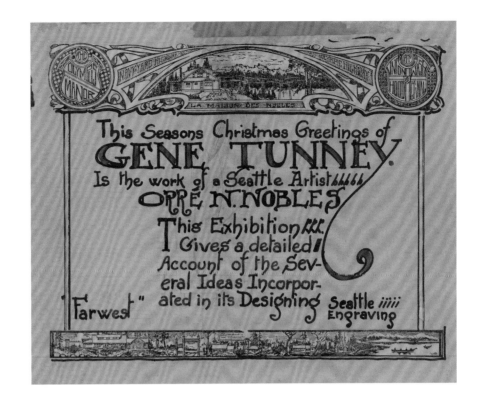

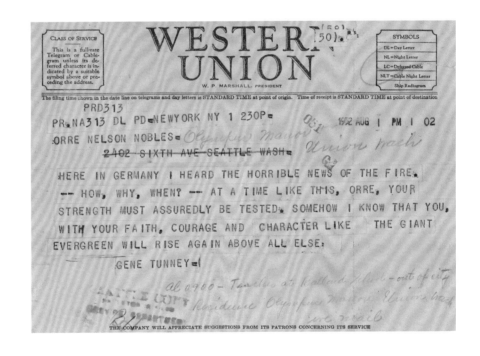

(top)
Orre Nobles at his Seattle
home, Windy Cliff, circa
1960
Private collection

(center left)
Orre Nobles with a broken
parasol, circa 1928
Collection of the Mason
County Historical Society,
Shelton, WA

(center right)
Gene Tunney
Inscribed "After the wash
at the pump"; photo taken
in 1928 at Tunney's training camp at Spectator, NY,
where he was accompa-
nied by Orre Nobles
Collection of the Mason
County Historical Society,
Shelton, WA

(bottom left)
Gene Tunney (left) and
Orre Nobles at Tunney's
training camp at Spectator,
NY, 1928
The photograph is
inscribed to Nobles's
close friend and former
student, Walter Fullaway:
"To Walter, my right hand
man, who guarded the
chateau while I guarded
the 'Big Boy.' September 3,
1928"
Private collection

(bottom right)
Gene Tunney (left) and
Orre Nobles in Seattle,
1959
Private collection

(top)
Orre Nobles (seated) and
John Dean in China circa
1930 (detail)
Collection of the Mason
County Historical Society,
Shelton, WA

(center)
From left: Marig Nobles
(mother), Viola Nobles
(sister), Orre Nobles,
George Nobles (brother),
circa 1912
Collection of the Mason
County Historical Society,
Shelton, WA
Photo restored with
Photoshop

(bottom left)
Orre Nobles playing piano
in his home, circa 1965
Malibu Press photograph
Ivan and Lori Babbitt,
Malibu, CA
Collection of the Mason
County Historical Society,
Shelton, WA

(bottom right)
Orre Nobles reading in his
home, circa 1965; a photo-
graph of Gene Tunney is
displayed on the fireplace
mantel
Malibu Press photograph
Ivan and Lori Babbitt,
Malibu, CA
Collection of the Mason
County Historical Society,
Shelton, WA

Orre Nelson Nobles
(1894–1967)
Rug designed for the
Fette-Li Company, Peking,
circa 1930
Seattle waterfront motif
83 x 49 in.
Private collection

Orre Nobles posed with
his Seattle waterfront
design rug, circa 1935
Collection of the Mason
County Historical Society,
Shelton, WA

Orre Nelson Nobles
(1894–1967)
Rug designed for the
Fette-Li Company, Peking,
circa 1930
Northwest landscape motif
54 x 36 in.
Collection of Paden and
Norma Prichard

Orre Nelson Nobles
(1894–1967)
Rug designed for the
Fette-Li Company, Peking,
circa 1930
Abstract cityscape motif
83 x 50 in.
Private collection

Excerpts from Orre Nobles Diaries

Besides eloquently describing his day-to-day activities and musings about his life and art, Nobles also documented meeting, falling in love with, and finally leaving a young Australian man named Owen Griffiths whom he met on board a ship to Hawaii, where Griffiths worked.

    Nobles used a series of abstract squiggles to indicate sexual and intimate activities. They are represented here by ***. In some cases, he wrote in French and used Morse code as well.

    Throughout his diaries, he mentions two intimate friends named Tommy and William, or Bill, a gay couple whom he refers to as "The Boys." He had multiple sexual experiences with them individually and as a couple. Sometimes Nobles also used the word "chat" to indicate secret sexual experiences. Nobles also writes a fascinating documentation of his aversion to war and potential conscription during World War I.

    These are exceedingly rare personal documents recording the life of a young gay man outside an urban center in the early twentieth century.

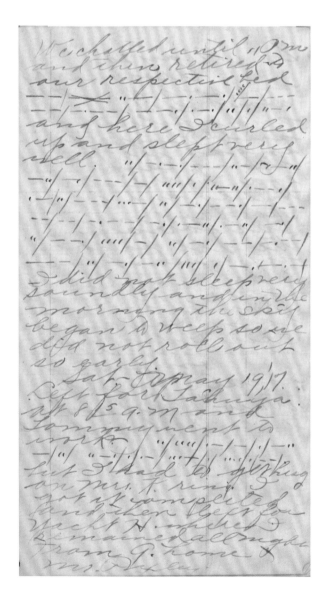
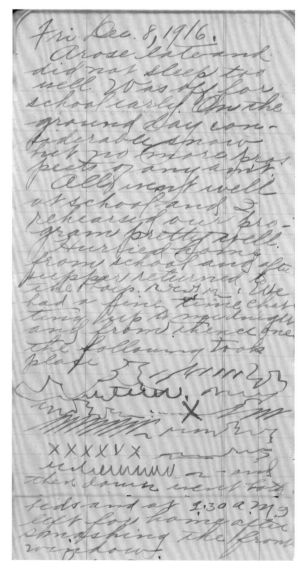

VOLUME III: 8/2/1914 THROUGH 12/31/1914

FRIDAY, OCTOBER 16, 1914

Just 5 years ago today did that great dream-fairyland, the AYP [Alaska-Yukon-Pacific Exposition] close forever its beautiful portals never again to be entered. How sad it did seem to me that those beautiful forms of plaster and clay could not always exist and be a joy to the province and the people.

TUESDAY, NOVEMBER 3, 1914

[First mention of Tommy and William and their new houseboat]

SUNDAY, DECEMBER 13, 1914

Sunday and a beautiful sunrise to greet us though plenty of cold to boot. I left early . . . and paid "The Boys" a visit in their new abode. Somehow I seem to have a great liking for them but why shouldn't I? I think I should be quite satisfied to live as they do and enjoy life as I see fit.

VOLUME IV: 1/1/1916 THROUGH 9/30/1916

FRIDAY, JANUARY 21, 1916

Soon after supper Tim came in on me and then things began & continued on until 1:30 a.m. I thought that I should fall fast asleep then for part of the evening but I finally became warmed up to __ and then the end was inevitable. Retired at 2:00 a.m.

SATURDAY, APRIL 29, 1916 [AT A DANCE AT THE SCHOOL GYMNASIUM]

At 1:30 p.m., the floor was cleared and dancing begun. I was Orrie on the spot immediately and kept it up until 4:00 a.m. Paul left for home at 2:30 a.m. and went through from Ballow to Allyn. I took the Victor up arriving at 6:00 a.m., going immediately to the hotel and to bed. At 8:00 am Paul turned in and it was 10:30 am when we awoke.

SUNDAY, MAY 14, 1916

At noon, the girls and myself went to Pixley's with Big John. We were all decked out in male and female attire. Here we had a big time musically and otherwise.

FRIDAY, MAY 19, 1916

The day being rather leaden at dawn soon day turned into drab and then it tearfully began to cry. . . . Yesterday I purchased a small Skokomish basket, very tiny but a splendid example of their basketry.

SATURDAY, MAY 20, 1916

I returned to Tahuya with Tommy and William. I asked Tom to stay with me overnight. He did so and we had <u>Some</u> time.

SATURDAY, JUNE 10, 1916 [AT SEA ON THE *MAKURA*, OF THE CANADIAN-AUSTRALIAN ROYAL MAIL STEAM SHIP COMPANY, EN ROUTE TO HAWAII]

After dinner I had an appointment with my velvety little waiter Owen Griffiths in the smoking room. I was more than anxious to speak with him as I have taken such a fancy to him. He is the most beautifully spoken of anyone whom I have

met. I was certainly delighted to learn that he knew Hood Canal and we parleyed for some time together.

WEDNESDAY, JUNE 28, 1916 [IN HONOLULU]

At a Chinese joint I procured some pies and watermelons and made out with that and then Captain Marden offered to bunk me for the night in his quarters. We lay on the lawn until 11 p.m. and then made up our cots and retired.

WEDNESDAY, JULY 12, 1916 [IN MAUI]

As I sit here thinking and comparing that where could I find a place like Washington. I want that one little spot that burns and twinkles low & high in my heart. That one place where I can live and be happy. Only dear old Washington can supply it. Not even the moon as it gleams so radiantly through the haunting places of Hawaii can offer me any solace. It must peep through the stately branches of the grand fir before it can stir me. Ah! Washington, my Washington, of all the places in the world give me Washington, my Washington.

WEDNESDAY, JULY 19, 1916 [IN HONOLULU]

Dressed up today really and truly and strutted to town.

FRIDAY, JULY 21, 1916

At 4 p.m. the *Makura* anchored off harbor and at 5 p.m. tied up at Pier 6. I recognized several chaps as she tied up but did not see Owen among any of the boys. I feared that he signed off in Sydney but later he came on deck and I surely was happy to see him. He looked as usual, very pleasant and jolly. Later he came in the wharf and we had one good long handshake. It did seem good to see him again. I went aboard and we had a chat and a half and [in] PM we struck out for the city. We took a run to Waikiki and sat for hours and hours talking over old times by the side of the "Beautiful Sea."

Orre Nelson Nobles
(1894–1967)
Untitled (male nude), circa 1935
Gelatin silver print
3¼ x 2⅛ in.
Collection of the Mason County Historical Society, Shelton, WA

Orre Nelson Nobles
(1894–1967)
Untitled (male nude), circa 1935
Gelatin silver print
3¼ x 2⅛ in.
Collection of the Mason County Historical Society, Shelton, WA

Orre Nelson Nobles
(1894–1967)
Untitled (male nude), circa 1935
Gelatin silver print
3¼ x 2⅛ in.
Collection of the Mason County Historical Society, Shelton, WA

  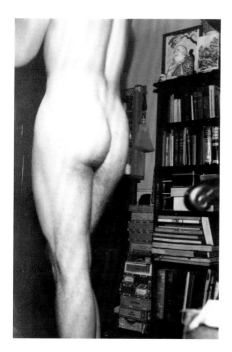

Orre Nelson Nobles
(1894–1967)
Untitled (male nude), circa
1935
Gelatin silver print
3¼ x 2⅛ in.
Collection of the Mason
County Historical Society,
Shelton, WA

Orre Nelson Nobles
(1894–1967)
Untitled (male nude), circa
1935
Gelatin silver print
3¼ x 2⅛ in.
Collection of the Mason
County Historical Society,
Shelton, WA

Orre Nelson Nobles
(1894–1967)
Untitled (male nude), circa
1935
Gelatin silver print
3¼ x 2⅛ in.
Collection of the Mason
County Historical Society,
Shelton, WA

Page from Orre Nobles's
diary, dated Thursday,
July 26, 1916
Coded abstract lines
indicate an intense sexual
encounter with Owen
Griffiths
The page is dated
Thursday, July 26, 1916
which indicates it was
written after midnight
since July 26, 1916 was
on a Wednesday
Courtesy of Steven
Schneider

SUNDAY, JULY 23, 1916 [AT SEA EN ROUTE TO VICTORIA, BC]

In the evening Owen visited me and we certainly had a lovely time visiting. He is the *sweetest* individual I have ever met of the masculine sex.

MONDAY, JULY 24, 1916

Owen was my visitor again this evening. I certainly did enjoy the evening with him. Our conversation ranged from . . . [followed by a series of many pronounced abstract squiggles indicating a sexual encounter, perhaps their first].

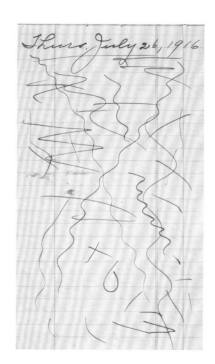

TUESDAY, JULY 25, 1916

I can smell the fragrance of dear old Washington even though she is still 1,000 miles over the horizon.

After luncheon I again resumed work on my sketch completing it in the early afternoon. It created quite a furor on deck. Owen was greatly pleased with the result. In the evening he again visited me and it seems as that I can never weary of him. I don't wonder that he is really loved to death. Seldom will I find one more attached than to him. He possesses a beauty of manner & poise really unusual in its loveliness of quality.

WEDNESDAY, JULY 26, 1916

At an early hour I retired to my room and made a wee sketch of the Olympics for Owen. It is not highly satisfactory yet it will answer the purpose. Owen paid me a slight visit at 10 p.m.

THURSDAY, JULY 27, 1916 [THE SHIP PULLING INTO VICTORIA]

I did not like much to bid Owen adieu as he surely found a snug place a way down in my heart.

WEDNESDAY, AUGUST 2, 1916

From all appearances Owen has forgotten his promise to drop me a line. He has evidently returned on the voyage of one more round trip to Sydney.

MONDAY, AUGUST 14, 1916

My first most delightful surprise this morning was a letter from Owen. Bless his heart, it surely seemed good to know that he was so near at Vancouver. I had pictured him sailing across the broad Pacific toward Australia. I immediately wrote to him and invited him down to spend a holiday.

TUESDAY, AUGUST 22, 1916

I remained in Seattle to pass some time with Ernest [Ernest Leo, a close family friend]. In the PM, Ernest went to keep a date and I went to the city where Ed and I took in the new Crystal Water Palace. I find that I retain my little knowledge in swimming.

WEDNESDAY, AUGUST 23, 1916

Arose early and slept well in Ernest's Louis XIV boudoir.

Ernest, myself, and Mr. Fisher spent some time out on the shady lawn discussing very shaky subjects. Ernest seems jammed and crammed with the masses. Oscar Wilde occupied the stage for some little time.

THURSDAY, AUGUST 24, 1916

Rather tired and a little disappointed not to have received a letter from Owen on my return.

SATURDAY, AUGUST 26, 1916

I had an inspiration to go to town and spend some time in the library. This I did. I read Oscar Wilde principally because I wanted to know something of him. In reading his *De Profundis* written while he was in jail, I was sad to learn that he did not justify his license and lewdness after all as Ernest supposes.

TUESDAY, SEPTEMBER 5, 1916

The first day of school. My! My! My! Nine more months and then! then! then. What then! New York City or bust will be my slogan from now on.

SUNDAY, SEPTEMBER 10, 1916

I took some time today reading Emerson's essay on friendship. Up to the present time, I had never yet quite understood the true meaning of friendship. However, since having been to Honolulu, I can read it and understand it with a delightful degree of beauty. I seemed to have experienced real friendship which I cannot explain. I also have learned to greatly love his essay on "Love." I went in swimming today and had a good time splashing about up at "The Boys."

(top)
Orre Nobles in his dugout canoe, circa 1924
Collection of the Mason County Historical Society, Shelton, WA

(top right)
Orre Nobles on horseback, inscribed "After a mile descent at the water of the Colorado River," circa 1920 (detail)
File repaired with Photoshop
Collection of the Mason County Historical Society, Shelton, WA

(center left)
Orre Nobles in drag with unidentified friend on left and sister Viola on right in front of the Tahuya, Washington, post office, circa 1916
File repaired with Photoshop
Collection of the Mason County Historical Society, Shelton, WA

(center right)
Orre Nobles (right) with unidentified man, circa 1917
PH Coll 586, Orre Nobles Photograph Collection
University of Washington Libraries, Special Collections, UW40157

(bottom)
Orre Nobles (left) with friend Wayne "Willy" Wilhelm at Coney Island, June 5, 1921
PH Coll 586, Orre Nobles Photograph Collection
University of Washington Libraries, Special Collections, UW40156
Wilhelm was a close friend of Nobles's when they attended the Pratt Institute together. Nobles's diary entries indicate that the two men were likely lovers.

WEDNESDAY, SEPTEMBER 13, 1916

Awoke early and thought about someone all day partially in an attitude of sadness and longing. I finally decided to drop the thought knowing that if it were to be it must be.

At about 8:30 p.m., William came into the river and stopped at Goldwin's float. He hollered to me but I did not hear. Little did I know that he had brought the someone whom I had longed for all day [Owen]. It seemed good, too good to really be true. My, I could scarcely believe it. We had tea, chatted, and retired about midnight.

THURSDAY, SEPTEMBER 14, 1916

When I got home in the PM I found the house beautifully clean and a lovely supper awaiting me. It really did seem good. We had a lovely evening together.

SATURDAY, SEPTEMBER 16, 1916

In the evening, Owen and myself took the *Tyee* [Orre's canoe] and set out for Union. The evening was perfectly lovely and on route home we had a delightful moon.

TUESDAY, SEPTEMBER 19, 1916

After school and a delightful supper "Some One" [Owen] and myself set out for Yacht Haven [nearby Yachthaven, Washington]. Here we spent a pleasant evening despite the fact that Mr. Pixley was very glum.

We retired at 11:00 p.m. and slept well.

WEDNESDAY, SEPTEMBER 20, 1916

[At a teachers' convention in Shelton, Washington, Nobles seems to be curious about the sexual orientation of two male teachers.] We had quite a conventional time but met most of the new teachers. Mr. Hitchcock seemed quite strange a married man while Mr. Bennett with his très petit moustache was quite a picture.

SATURDAY, SEPTEMBER 23, 1916

Arose early and began work setting of Owen's beautiful black opal which he procured in Northern Australia. The whole day flitted along until about 4 p.m. when I began setting the stone. Completing it and putting in the final crimp I cracked the lovely gem. It almost sent me into hysterics. I could not forgive myself for doing such a thing. Owen, however, would not hear of me feeling so and he insisted that I forget about it.

SUNDAY, SEPTEMBER 24, 1916

Worked on the ring today all forenoon and succeeded in getting the stone set and looking pretty well. Owen seemed perfectly happy with it.

THURSDAY, SEPTEMBER 28, 1916

After a delicious supper Owen and myself took *Tyee* [Orre's canoe] out and had a sunset row. In the Narrows we kindled up a fine fire and spent the evening lying on the beach talking. On route home we almost got stranded on the oyster beds.

Orre Nobles (left) with
his Australian lover,
Owen Griffiths, holding
a geoduck, Union,
Washington, 1916 (detail)
PH Coll 586, Orre Nobles
Photograph Collection
University of Washington
Libraries, Special
Collections, UW40159

Orre Nobles (standing)
playing with his
Australian lover,
Owen Griffiths, Union,
Washington, 1916
PH Coll 586, Orre Nobles
Photograph Collection
University of Washington
Libraries, Special
Collections, UW40160

Orre Nobles (seated) with
his Australian lover,
Owen Griffiths, Union,
Washington, 1916
PH Coll 586, Orre Nobles
Photograph Collection
University of Washington
Libraries, Special
Collections, UW40161

SATURDAY, SEPTEMBER 30, 1916

The last day of September here and I am not in New York City. Nothing will prevent me from being there a year from today.

At 7:30 p.m. the folks already began to arrive [for a dance in the school's gymnasium where he taught]. At about 9:30 p.m. the Jap[anese] lights were lit and a pretty sight the whole affair surely did make. . . . At 9:45 the 1st Two Step was struck up. Miss Marcia was my partner. Most all of the dancers were on the floor the first dance. From now until after midnight I did not miss a hop. At about 1:00 a.m. eats was served and such a supply and such real quantities of good things. I had only one day spent with Mrs. Pixley. She explained Mr. Pixley's actions to me and I must say that I was surprised to learn that he acted in such a manner to Mr. Griffiths.

VOLUME V: 10/2/1916 THROUGH 5/13/1917

MONDAY, OCTOBER 2, 1916

Arose late this morning and bid Owen a final adieu. I hate to see him go but after all it is perhaps best. We are not exactly of the same realms in spite of our affection for one another. After bidding him goodbye I went to school to return to a cold house and no steaming hot supper awaiting me. It seemed quite dreary after our cozy chats.

WEDNESDAY, OCTOBER 4, 1916

I had a splendid salmon trout supper with green corn and cucumbers. The first real decent meal since Owen left me.

FRIDAY, OCTOBER 13, 1916

At 4:30 a.m. the alarm went off and found me in William's bed. At 5:00 a.m. Tommy arose and found that Fluffy [Nobles's dog] had puked all over everything.

SATURDAY, OCTOBER 14, 1916

Mrs. Pixley and myself had a chat about Mr. Pixley's attitude toward Mr. Griffiths.

THURSDAY, NOVEMBER 2, 1916

My relation to Owen has changed since his return. I am beginning to know that I met him for an extremely beneficial purpose.

SATURDAY, NOVEMBER 4, 1916

When I returned I found Owen in not too good a mood. I worked on his fob but he didn't want to accept it. He spent some little time trying my affection but when he found that I would not be moved he gave up his effort and softened again. I made an opal pin for William out of his opal quartz.

SUNDAY, NOVEMBER 5, 1916

The "Boys" *** came into the river but did not call.

MONDAY, NOVEMBER 6, 1916

I returned home and found Owen a little pouty but all smoothed over. He suggested that he would go tomorrow.

TUESDAY, NOVEMBER 7, 1916

A big day in the history of Orrie and the nation. I went to school early with Owen a bit peeved. I must admit that I haven't been nice to him. I feel that he is out of place or I am too selfish. I know that my affection for him has totally changed. In fact it has been a complete reversal of things.

I only kept school until 2:00 p.m., and then dismissed. I went immediately home and Owen hadn't started to get dinner so I rushed things a bit. He wanted me to ask him to remain until tomorrow. But I would not do so. So he was a bit irritated. We borrowed Carlson's skiff and rowed over to Union. He tried me very much and said several cutting and perhaps very true things to me en route. At Union we took a long walk up the Skokomish Valley and had an understanding and poor Owen how badly he felt after having treated me so. When we returned to Union I never experienced such a chaotic state of mind. It seemed as all the forces of the universe were pulling me. There was Owen and I seeking to dodge the Pixleys. There was Mrs. Pixley pulling tenaciously at me and there stood Tom *** awaiting a chance to talk with me and I with him. Such a chaos. But the steamer came and Owen was away for Seattle. Then the stress was worse than ever.

I hurried down and cast my first vote for President Wilson and at 11:00 am all wrought up and almost exhausted I went home with the "Boys" ***

SATURDAY, NOVEMBER 11, 1916

I took my paints and lunch and we [Orre and his dog Fluffy] prepared for an outing on the Upper Sister Point. We had dinner and leaving our canoe we continued down the beach to "Austin's Point" to the "Boys" *** We found them at home OK and ready to return to the river. So we remained and came back with them with the float in tow. I was then at their place until 10:00 p.m. and we had a most rambunctious "ruff house."

MONDAY, DECEMBER 4, 1916

En route home I stopped at "The Boys" *** and had a chat. Tom insisted I remain for supper which I did with not much coaxing. Of course the usual evening ensued. Tom and I the party. Tom was most affectionate with his teeth and whiskers and we enjoyed a real love tussle.

FRIDAY, DECEMBER 8, 1916

Hurried home from school and after supper returned to "The Boys." *** We had a fine time chatting up to midnight and from thence on the following took place *** and then down went both beds and at 1:30 a.m. I left for home after smashing the front window.

THURSDAY, DECEMBER 14, 1916

"The Boys" *** came up and we had a pleasing evening together. En route to school this morning I stopped in and took some papers to them. I could not resist the temptation of pulling them out of bed so I took Tom by the head and dragged him out into the kitchen pulling both legs off of the bed. I then proceeded to get Bill out and a general ruff house ensued. They got my goat properly tonight. So much so that I did not know just which way to turn.

MONDAY, JANUARY 1, 1917

This new year finds me at home with my head thrust out of the window listening to the chimes, canons, guns, and noises of Tacoma and the neighboring vicinity. . . . I know not where a new year may again find me. Perhaps some thousands of miles from home. I may be in the great city of Gotham among its towering piles and I may be elsewhere.

THURSDAY, JANUARY 4, 1917

We enjoyed a pleasant musical evening and for the first time Jerome and I slept together.

MONDAY, JANUARY 15, 1917

I began hammering on a Mexican dollar which Mr. Pixley gave to me. It is my intention, if possible, to make a ring for William out of it. I have decided that I am expending altogether too much affection uselessly. I must control more closely my strength and ambition.

THURSDAY, JANUARY 25, 1917

En route home I stopped at "The Boys" *** and William and I "went a round" much to both of our satisfactions. He succeeded in getting me most foul.

THURSDAY, FEBRUARY 1, 1917

Enroute home as usual, I stopped at "The Boys" *** and spent an agreeable time. Just as I was leaving "Bill" *** procured my goat and the result was a ruff house. He became boldly bold and I resisted as much as possible. As I was leaving I gave him a whack and he became vexed and for the first time I really saw him provoked. I was sorry but I love him just the same and it still all comes out in the wash.

MONDAY, FEBRUARY 12, 1917

Today finds me in Tahuya!! Oh! Where will years from today find me. I hope happy in little old N.Y. with *William.*

WEDNESDAY, FEBRUARY 14, 1917

It's Valentine's Day and it skipped by unnoticed. I was cross today in school probably because of a most morbid and severe attack of "Wanderlust." It always comes this time of year but never had I experienced such an attack. Samoa seems to be the new feeding ground for my imagination.

SUNDAY, FEBRUARY 18, 1917

I decided to go to "The Boys" *** and then decided again that I would not. I feel that I am coming too much to be dependent upon people and especially "The Boys." ***

SATURDAY, FEBRUARY 24, 1917

At early dawn I began house cleaning and was an extremely busy woman all day long as I cleaned up "for a fair."

WEDNESDAY, MARCH 14, 1917

After an early supper I went up to "The Boys" *** and for a few moments decided that I was not apparently welcome company and as I was preparing to "sell my papers elsewhere" Bill jarred loose but Tom was glum all evening.

THURSDAY, MARCH 15, 1917

I wrote the first draft of my letter of resignation [from school] today. I feel that it is best that I go away. I believe that the purpose for which I was needed has been served and that it will be mutually beneficial for me to leave this year.

SATURDAY, APRIL 7, 1917

Yesterday was William's 25th birthday. Of late I am a trifle concerned as to the outcome of the present situation in the warring countries & the U.S. The selective conscription will take me in the 1st skimming and of course my love for war is not great.

WEDNESDAY, APRIL 18, 1917 [AFTER LEAVING HIS TEACHING POSITION AT TAHUYA]

When I arose this morning I beheld for the 1st time myself at 23 yrs. I had left dear old two-two [the school] behind and many dear things which are now only remembrances.

SUNDAY, APRIL 29, 1917

Rolled out of bed to the music of a tearful sky and we decided to work in oil today as we have threatened for the past year to do. Early the dining room was in shape for study work and for the first time I applied my hand to real oil paints. We decided that our study should be a photo showing "The Tree" and the mountain. We labored away all day and by 4:30 had completed "some thing." It was my first endeavor so minor imperfections could be excused. . . . After dinner I set out for Tahuya and there went up to see "The Boys." *** Tommy was there and so was Adam. Here I learned for the 1st time that conscription had carried in the U.S. Houses so I must prepare.

MONDAY, APRIL 30, 1917

For the first time I have thought of Tahiti as a possible refuge if I can leave the dear U.S.A. I believe that it could be made an interesting place.

WEDNESDAY, MAY 2, 1917

I called upon Tommy and found him "alone" *** and we enjoyed a chat together. He gave me some of his Alaska views. Slept on a piece of *wedding cake* and dreamed of him last night.

SUNDAY, MAY 13, 1917

Arose late and enjoyed my usual making chat with Mr. Pixley. I surely do enjoy to talk with him more than with any one I have yet met.

VOLUME VI: 5/14/1917 THROUGH 8/2/1917

MONDAY, MAY 14, 1917

I open a new book this morning in a rather disappointed and hopeless frame of mind. The future of this book is uncertain and its fate is in no way evident. It is with a different aspect that things appear to me now. When last I opened a new book all looked bright and happy & my distant horizon of hope appeared not far off. It is different today. I am asked to sacrifice a year, maybe two, aye maybe a life for a cause which I deem wholly unjust and inexcusable.

TUESDAY, MAY 15, 1917

I was greatly pleased to read of Allan Clark's success in his studies at the [Chicago] Art Institute and also his remarkable success in modeling the form of Ted Shawn. I read an Art Institute catalogue and it set me all agog. [Allan Clark (1896–1950) was a prominent American sculptor originally from Tacoma.]

SUNDAY, MAY 20, 1917 [TEXT INCLUDES MORSE CODE]

I had numerous bad dreams the fore-part of the night. I saw Tommy tonight .. .-..
--- ...- . ... -- [I love him] and he said that he would not be leaving until Wed.

TUESDAY, MAY 22, 1917 [TEXT INCLUDES MORSE CODE]

I have almost desired to hurry home + spend time in trying to decide just what
course to pursue prior to June 5 "The Great Day" -.. .- -- .. - -.-- .... . .-.. .-.. [Damn
it to hell]

If I could but face it with an attitude of righteousness I should feel better: but as
conditions now appear I am working against a clear conscience. [June 5 was the first
draft registration day in the 48 states and Washington, DC.]

FRIDAY, MAY 25, 1917

At 7:00 p.m. I jumped into my canoe and paddled for the *last time.*

Up the river to my school house. When I entered the school room it haunted me
like a tomb in its barrenness. It was more than I could stand. As a final goodbye I
went to each seat + there placed each dear occupant and thinking of them as I have
always known them. I bid each goodbye. I believe tho I feign and not confess it
that I lost a quart of tears in that room in five minutes.

MONDAY, MAY 28, 1917 [TEXT INCLUDES MORSE CODE]

Arose at 6 am and puttered about until 9 am when I left for Tahuya. I then went to
Union . . . and here I met Tommy and bid him a final au revoir .. .-.. --- ...- . ...
-- .-.-.-.. .... --- .-.-. . .. .- .-.. .-.. ... . -- .- --.- .- .. -. [I love him and hope I
shall see him again]

TUESDAY, MAY 29, 1917 [TEXT INCLUDES MORSE CODE]

I arose early and bid Mr. Pixley good-bye for the last time. He threw his arms about
my neck and rather hugged me and bid me a last good bye. . . . At about 5 p.m. we
left and the Pixleys remained on the dock until I was out of sight. I could see -.. . .- .-
[dear] Tom pulling the Bagley scrapper and bid him a ... .. .-.. . -. - =[silent] goodbye.

TUESDAY, JUNE 5, 1917

Today is that most glorious of glorious days when the youth [of] *free* America shall
each one individually be given the privilege of contributing all he possesses to his
Democratic Republic.

SATURDAY, JUNE 9, 1917

We [he and William] meet "Bunnie" down town [Seattle] and carted her about with
us. We ate a bite at the Public Market and laughed ourselves ill. Ernest came tod-
dling in at 2 a.m. and seemed a bit burned. After smoking a couple of cigarettes he
retired and insisting that the lady whose picture hung on the wall take her hands
off her hips at once. She had them on when we left however.

MONDAY, JUNE 11, 1917

We [he and Ernest] then returned to town [Seattle] and went to the artist [Yasushi]
Tanaka's studio where I met the most famous Miss Cann [Tanaka's wife, Louise
Gebhard Cann, who was a writer]. I was not carried away by the artist's genius and
especially not by his nudes.

Don Jefferson Sheets (left) and Wayne "Willy" Wilhelm, Orre Nobles's close friends and fellow Pratt students at Coney Island, June 5, 1921 (detail); PH Coll 586, Orre Nobles Photograph Collection University of Washington Libraries, Special Collections, UW40168

WEDNESDAY, JULY 4, 1917

A famous day in American history but it finds me with little or no interest in a single thing alive or dead. It just seems as tho the old world has been turned completely over.

FRIDAY, JULY 20, 1917

Today at last the great bubble came to a head and has burst. It has been festering for a long time. The fat men in Washington, DC, has pulled the key and Orrie is one of the 500,000 unfortunates. 1282 being the great number. . . . I have decided to get my money out of the bank and get things arranged so that if it be necessary for me to go to jail I shall have nothing to confiscate by the state. I shall never have the name soldier leveled on my name and I sincerely hope and pray that William is not drawn.

TUESDAY, AUGUST 7, 1917 [GOING TO HIS MILITARY PHYSICAL EXAMINATION]

Alas that most famous day is here when I go before the famous triad scheme the Hon. Major Dean, Dr. <u>Shitsa,</u> and Mr. Galbraith. Early I made ready the clunk of clay for which the gov't of this "*Great*"?? democracy asks in order that it be stacked atop the rotting and festering decay of carrion European fields so that "*Democracy*" might live. Glorious world I must say, that one can not possess the clay that encompasses his soul. 10,000,000 decaying, grim skeletons are gazing skyward tonight on some rent fields of Europe. Thousands of bodies are the haunt of ghastly, uncanny crabs which creep and crawl amid the ribs and pelvic bones. Those whom are slumbering in the covering deep. Cannot Democracy live without this sacrifice: if not well then the hell with Democracy. Give me the Stone Age. No Democracy on the face of God's green earth would I give for my two precious hands. I have spent years in the education of them and I expect to possess them. When I entered the room for examination I saw the young men in their nude forms standing awaiting the time for the appraisal of their precious clay my heart leapt and bounded. When I saw them the cream of the nation dance a jig sung by a pussy gutted M.D. the ire of my very soul embroiled my sensitiveness. I said that if I ever get a whack at such a proposition I shall give it some blow that shall send it staggering to the gutter from whence it sprung. When a fat-headed, red faced vulgar filthy-mouthed brute can handle my body to his own liking without my consent I believe it time for a change. He reported that my right foot was somewhat flat and my heart seemed a bit off. When I left I felt that I should be exempt and I feel that I should be so.

TUESDAY, AUGUST 21, 1917

At Yacht Haven I found the summer guests breakfasting. I hustled in and received a note stating that a long distance call awaited me at Union from Tacoma. I was quite startled and much surprised when mother told me that I had received my exemption bronze and paper.

Malcolm Roberts
1913–1990

"I am as gay as pink ink!" —Malcolm Roberts

Malcolm McNair Roberts was Seattle's first Surrealist painter as well as one of the region's finest theater and dance performance designers.

He was born to Chester Roberts and Edith Day McNair Roberts, who had moved to Seattle from Kansas and became partners in a very successful business called the Imperial Candy Company. The couple had three children; the eldest was named Virginia, followed by twins Malcolm and Elizabeth. Mrs. Roberts passed away in 1916, and the three children were raised by their father.

Malcolm Roberts began art instruction in 1928 at the classes of the Seattle Fine Arts Society under Mark Tobey. He attended Broadway High School where, in 1931, during his junior year, he assisted art instructor Hannah Jones in creating stage and costume designs for the school's production of *The Royal Family of Broadway*. This would mark the beginning of Roberts's successful, multi-decade career in theatrical design.

That summer, he made his first trip to Europe. His father had established yet another successful candy business called Société Candies that provided a good income for the family.

After graduating from Broadway High in 1932, he studied at the Art Institute of Chicago for one year before returning to Seattle. He next enrolled at the University of Washington, where he studied with Viola Patterson, whose expertise in printmaking would serve him well in the coming years. That same year, one of his paintings was accepted in the 18th Annual Exhibition of Northwest Artists, the region's most prestigious venue since 1914. Sponsored by the Art Institute of Seattle, the annuals continued the following year at the Seattle Art Museum, which had just opened to the public in 1933. For the next ten years, his paintings were accepted in the annuals and often won prizes. Four of his paintings entered into the museum's permanent collection.

Roberts's interest in stage and costume designs led to his association with the Dance Department at the Cornish School (now Cornish College of the Arts). In 1934 he designed the stage sets and costumes for the Cornish Dancers production of Welland Lathrop's *Circus Harlequinade*. He also tried his hand at acting, receiving a minor role in a production of the Century Club Theatre's *The Drunkard*.

One of the featured performers in this cast was Chet Huntley (1911–1974), whom Roberts knew through Cornish and the UW. Huntley, who also designed the costumes and stage sets for this production with local designer Elida Miller, would later become well known as a television news anchor on *The Huntley-Brinkley Report*.

Malcolm Roberts
(1913–1990)
Costume design for
the Cornish Dancers
production of Welland
Lathrop's *Circus
Harlequinade*, 1934
Watercolor and gouache
12 x 9 in.
University of Washington
Libraries, Special
Collections, Karen Irvin
Papers
UW40138

Malcolm Roberts
(1913–1990)
Costume design for
the Cornish Dancers
production of Welland
Lathrop's *Circus
Harlequinade*, 1934
Watercolor and gouache
12 x 9 in.
University of Washington
Libraries, Special
Collections, Karen Irvin
Papers
UW40139

In 1935, President Roosevelt's WPA art projects were initiated in Seattle. Roberts became part of the local roster of artists, producing paintings as well as lithographs that he hand-colored. He explored modernist and Surrealist elements, focusing on local subject matter and natural forms found in shells, driftwood, and beach detritus. Roberts would sometimes use gay subtexts in his subject matter that usually went over the heads of his straight contemporaries.

In late 1936, Roberts was honored with a solo exhibition at SAM.

Kenneth Callahan, the museum's curator as well as the principal local art critic, reviewed the show in the *Seattle Sunday Times*, commenting, "A one-man exhibition of paintings which has attracted as much attention as any held in the Seattle Art Museum by local painters, is the work of Malcolm Roberts, now on view. Most visitors are surprised, some pleased and many frankly bewildered. Seattle has had little opportunity of seeing Surrealist paintings; no other local artist has attempted to enter this particular field of painting."

Another writer for the newspaper was society columnist Virginia Boren, who took advantage of the public's naïve reaction to Surrealism, writing, "Said a woman more frank than informed, to Artist Malcolm Roberts: 'How do you get that way . . . so you can paint such pictures?' Answered Surrealist Malcolm Roberts: 'I eat Mince Pie every night.'

"They called it 'painting jibberish that reminded them of the writings of Gertrude Stein' . . . they were mystified by the abundance of feathers in the paintings . . . they label the paintings 'queer.'

"'Why, Mr. Roberts, please explain those paintings of yours to me.' 'Oh no, you explain them to me . . .'

Setting aside his acerbic wit, he attempted to explain. . . . 'The Surrealist paints from his subconscious mind. . . . He really accents realism. Sometimes I feel that I am more a new realist than a Surrealist for I just take unrelated objects that attract my eye and use them in a varied arrangement. Or, I take unrelated objects and put them together to express a thought. I like to make them very decorative. I enjoy using color in the decorative sense. I feel that the Surrealist, or as I say, the new realist, can produce paintings around which one could build a very interesting room or even home.'"

The year 1937 proved to be one of creative stimulation with impressive results. In April he attended a dance performance by Martha Graham at Seattle's Moore Theatre. He likely knew Graham from her teaching at Cornish four years earlier and through her friendship with Mark Tobey. Roberts went on to create several dance-themed prints for the WPA obviously inspired by Graham. That summer, Roberts was also included in a very successful exhibition of WPA art held at the Frederick & Nelson department store's gallery. Besides Roberts and other local talents including Z. Vanessa Helder, artists from thirteen states were represented.

Contrary to his production, he felt that his WPA obligations and commissions were holding back his personal creativity. In a letter to Kenneth and Margaret Callahan dated July 1937, he wrote, "I haven't painted a stroke except at the WPA where I am doing cartoons for 6 panels in mosaic. Each 12 feet high and 6 feet wide—I'm using an enormous figure in each one—It has to be about fishing—why I don't know. So behind the figures I'm using nets—lobster pots in wave designs—ropes—piles of fish—rather fun, really. . . . Spent last week at Eagle Harbor—the Yacht Club had their regatta there with the Royal Canadian Yacht Club from Victoria and Vancouver—marvelous fun—the English lads are irresistible and kept me hopping from flattie to flattie—and I only fell *twice.* I think yachting people are swell on the water—hate them on the land."

During his time on the WPA projects, he continued to pursue his interest in theatrical design. In 1938 he designed the costumes and stage sets for Lee Foley's production of *Giselle* for the University of Washington's dance program held at the federally funded Seattle Repertory Playhouse. Foley was a renowned dancer and instructor who had worked and taught in New York as well as being a major force in Seattle at Cornish's Dance Department. He had relationships with men and women but eventually married a woman and had one son.

At that time, Roberts was in a romantic but open relationship with painter Morris Graves. In 1939 they moved into a home on Melrose Avenue East, on Seattle's Capitol Hill, with composer John Cage and his beard wife, Xenia. Roberts achieved a significant honor when, later that year, his painting *Games of Ribbons & Bones* was shown in the exhibition *American Art Today* at the 1939 New York World's Fair, although it is not included in the official catalog. Graves and Tobey were also included in the exhibition. Meanwhile, Cage had just developed his famous prepared piano to score dancer Syvilla Fort's *Bacchanale* at Cornish.

Roberts's high-strung personality was at odds with that of the mischievous Graves, so their living arrangement soon came to an end.

Robert Bruce Inverarity (1909–99)
Morris Graves and Malcolm Roberts, circa 1936
Robert Bruce Inverarity Papers, 1940s–97, Archives of American Art, Smithsonian Institution
Digital ID: 6469

Malcolm Roberts with his
portrait of Ann Erickson,
1936
Newspaper clipping,
stamped December 14, 1936
International news photo
by *Post-Intelligencer* staff
photographer
Courtesy of The Seattle
Public Library

In 1940, Roberts collaborated with Jane Givan and Robert Iglehart to produce stage and costume designs for Bonnie Bird's newly formed American Dance Theatre at Cornish. The dances utilized diverse music selections, including Bach's Third English Suite, John Cage's "America Was Promises" (set to Archibald MacLeish's poem), and "Any Man's Saga" by George McKay. The soloists included Bonnie Bird, then head of Cornish's dance department, as well as Syvilla Fort and Dorothy Herrman.

For the next two years, Roberts pursued painting, theater designs, and interior decorating. In 1942 he joined the army, working in the camouflage division of the antiaircraft coast artillery brigade.

In a letter dated November 11, 1942, writing to Margaret and Kenneth Callahan from Ojai, California, he said, "I've been painting up here—very loose, wet sort of things. I can't seem to settle down to the old tightness—it's a good thing though as yet nothing really interesting has resulted."

By this time, his father had died, leaving Malcolm with a trust fund that would enable him to live comfortably and indulge his artistic pursuits. The following year, he married a lesbian friend named Ann Erickson in Pasadena, where she had moved the previous year from Seattle. Ann was part of the cultural circle Roberts traveled in, and the two had been very close friends for several years. Although they gave birth to a child, the marriage soon ended.

He returned to Seattle and resumed working with dancers Lee Foley and Karen Irvin until 1947, when he moved to Los Angeles to seek a career as an interior decorator. His production of fine art was now limited to design work and he essentially ceased exhibiting paintings. He developed a fine reputation in Southern California, even designing a large home for mobster Mickey Cohen. According to Roberts's friend Ivar Haglund, Cohen ordered Roberts to "furnish the home entirely with antiques, but they had to be new antiques." He complied and, drawing on his Surrealist past, created a bust of Queen Victoria with a state-of-the-art FM radio hidden inside.

His time in Los Angeles was brief, and he soon returned to Seattle. He spent the remainder of his professional life creating outstanding designs for the Cornish Ballet with Karen Irvin and her life partner, Mea Hartman. His interior design business continued to flourish, and he traveled as often as he was able, living for part of 1963 in Italy.

In the early 1970s he formed a design business with Seattle decorators Barbara Thomas and Jean Anderson. He lived the remainder of his life in a small, elegant apartment and never returned to painting again.

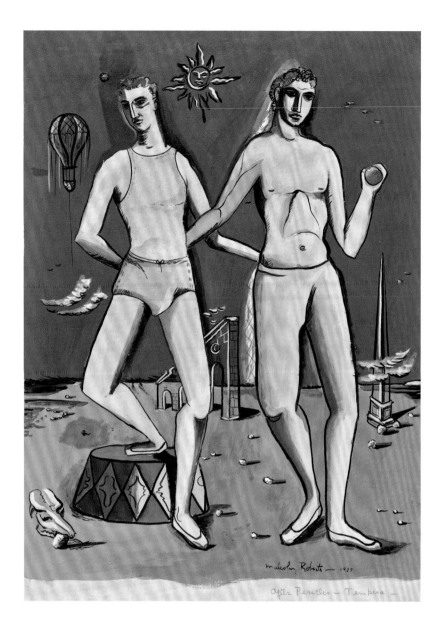

SOURCES

Interview with Sheila Farr, writer and personal friend of Malcolm Roberts and his sister Virginia, July 6, 2019

Interview with designer Michael McQuiston, a close personal friend of Malcolm Roberts, Oct. 28, 2019

Kenneth Callahan, "Seattle Art Museum," *Seattle Sunday Times*, Dec. 20, 1936, 4

"Society Folk See Graham in Recital at Moore," *Seattle Daily Times*, Apr. 5, 1937, 13

Virginia Boren, "Malcolm Roberts One-Man Show Is at Museum," *Seattle Daily Times*, Dec. 10, 1936, 27

Betty Cornelius, "Lee Foley Soon to Organize Repertory Ballet Group Here," *Seattle Daily Times*, July 11, 1946, 8

"Much Originality Noted in Federal Art Exhibition," *Seattle Daily Times*, June 28, 1937, 10

Ivar Haglund, "Ivar's Decorator: Seeks Antiques in Spooky Nooks for Ivar's on 5th," *Seattle Daily Times*, Nov. 3, 1956, 2

Personal letters from Malcolm Roberts to Kenneth and Margaret Callahan, Martin-Zambito Archive, Seattle

Malcolm Roberts
(1913–1990)
After Pericles, 1937
Tempera
22 x 16 in.
Private collection

Malcolm Roberts working
on *Fisherman no. I*, 1937
Miscellaneous
Photographs Collection,
Archives of American Art,
Smithsonian Institution
Digital ID: 2348

Malcolm Roberts
(1913–1990)
Fisherman no. I, 1937
Linoleum mosaic on
plywood
72½ x 36½ in.
Smithsonian American
Art Museum, transfer
from the General Services
Administration

Hans Bok (1914–1964)
In the Project Studio, 1939
Pen and ink on paper
20 x 25½ in. (framed)
Museum of History &
Industry, Seattle

Malcolm Roberts's
Fisherman no. I is depicted
on the wall.

Malcolm Roberts
(1913–1990)
Acrobats, circa 1935
Color stencil on cream
paper
14 x 12 in.
Allocated by the US
government, 1943;
commissioned through the
New Deal art projects
Collection of the Newark
Museum 43.668

Malcolm Roberts
(1913–1990)
Ballet Movement, 1937
Lithograph with
watercolor on ivory paper
15⅝ x 11⅜ in.
Allocated by the US
government, 1943;
commissioned through the
New Deal art projects
Collection of the Newark
Museum 43.669

Malcolm Roberts
(1913–1990)
The Beach, 1935
Tempera on canvas
24⅛ x 20⅛ in.
Seattle Art Museum,
Eugene Fuller Memorial
Collection
36.79

Malcolm Roberts
(1913–1990)
View of Aurora Bridge,
circa 1936
Tempera
17¾ x 22½ in.
Seattle Art Museum,
Eugene Fuller Memorial
Collection
37.104

Mother bird - 3 little ones - *pink tights & shoes*

Shocking lion - *pink tights - pink raffia - gold crown*

Malcolm Roberts
(1913–1990)
Costume design for the
Mother Bird character
in the Cornish Ballet
production of *West of the
Moon*, 1958
Graphite and crayon
12 x 6¼ in.
University of Washington
Libraries, Special
Collections, Karen Irvin
Papers
UW40143

Malcolm Roberts
(1913–1990)
Costume design for the
Shocking Lion character
in the Cornish Ballet
production of *West of the
Moon*, 1958
Graphite and crayon
12 x 6¼ in.
University of Washington
Libraries, Special
Collections, Karen Irvin
Papers UW40144

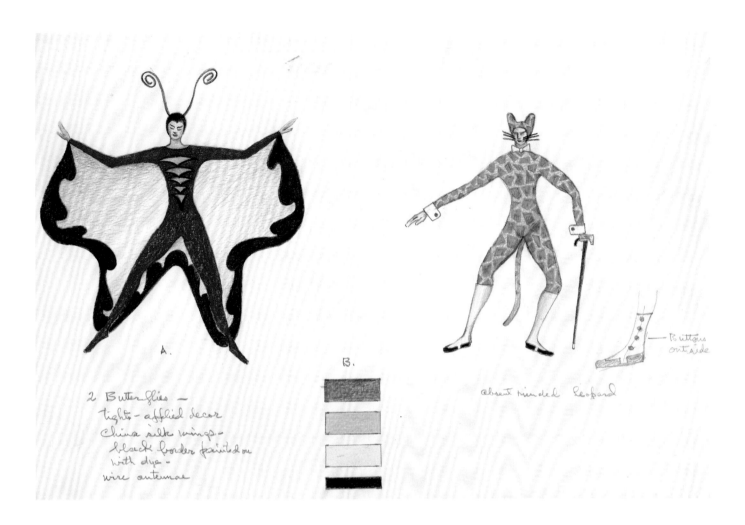

Malcolm Roberts
(1913–1990)
Costume studies for
the Butterflies and
Absent-Minded Leopard
characters in the Cornish
Ballet production of *West
of the Moon*, 1958
Graphite and crayon
12 x 16 in.
University of Washington
Libraries, Special
Collections, Karen Irvin
Papers
UW40145

Malcolm Roberts
(1913–1990)
Stage set design for the
Cornish Ballet production
of *West of the Moon*, 1958
Tempera with applied
metal foil
14¾ x 15¾ in.
University of Washington
Libraries, Special
Collections, Karen Irvin
Papers
UW40146

"I was inspired to become a potter by Bernard Leach when he visited the University of Washington and lectured about his years in Japan as a potter. A few years later, more encouragement came when Shoji Hamada visited our studio [in 1963]. He purchased three of my drawings for himself and a piece of our pottery for his museum. I believe art is created by a force outside myself that I am the tool used to produce a work. I strive to be as skilled as possible so if a piece of art does happen through me, it has been crafted to the best of my ability." —Lorene Spencer

Lorene Rhua Flower Spencer was born in Wallace, Idaho, and had moved with her family to Spokane by the age of seven. As a teenager, she attended art classes at the Spokane Art Center, a public cultural educational institution established in 1938 under President Roosevelt's New Deal programs. Her interest in art was part of her family heritage. Her maternal grandparents were both artistically oriented; her grandfather had an architectural firm in London and her grandmother was a painter.

Lorene attended the University of Oregon, where she studied sculpture, ceramics, and architecture. She served in the US Navy during World War II at the Anacostia Naval Air Station in Washington, DC, working as a specialist photographer concentrating on coded materials, secret documents, and experimental equipment.

She met Ralph E. Spencer (1914–1973), while he was serving in the Coast Guard at Astoria, Oregon, and they soon married. Ralph was born in Spirit Lake, Idaho, and lived there until 1935, when he moved to Seattle to attend the University of Washington. He studied chemical engineering at the UW until he enlisted in the Coast Guard in 1942, serving as a motor machinist's mate in Depoe Bay, Oregon.

In her later years, Lorene explained that both she and Ralph were aware of their homosexual orientations but, like many gay people of their generation, they had innocently thought that if they married and had children, these feelings would resolve and change to heterosexual orientation—which, naturally, did not happen. However, they decided not to act on their same-sex attractions and remained a couple.

After their marriage, Ralph and Lorene worked in a family business running a fishing resort on the Umpqua River in Oregon, where they built boats and manufactured docks. After a few years, in 1948, they sold their share of the business and moved to Newberg, Oregon, where they made their first ceramic works. Ralph designed and made their own pottery wheel and would later custom-build them

Ralph and Lorene
Spencer, circa 1950
Martin-Zambito Archive

for other artists, schools, and teachers. Their routine started with Ralph mixing the clay and making the glazes while Lorene designed and executed the forms. After some initial success, they started marketing their work through the Meier & Frank department store in Portland.

In Newberg the first of their four children was born. But Newberg's largely conservative political leanings became too stressful and so the family headed for Seattle in 1951, there establishing the Spencer Pottery business. Around this time, Lorene took a correspondence course from the New York School of Interior Design and shortly afterward won a national Young Designers Award.

The Spencers felt a close connection to their region and decided to use three individual Washington State native clays for producing their wares: one retrieved from the Spokane area, one from near Monroe, and one from the Auburn area. These were mostly composed of a common blue clay compound. In 1952 their work was included in the Ceramic National competition, sponsored by the Syracuse Museum of Fine Arts (now the Everson Museum), in Syracuse, New York.

In April 1953, Lorene was selected for a national exhibition at the Akron Art Institute called *Young Designers, a National Survey*. Her work was featured in the April 1953 issue of *Living for Young Homemakers* magazine.

These validations fueled the couple's determination to expand their business. Lorene developed her skills by taking painting courses with prominent local artists Fay Chong and Kenneth Callahan. The Spencers became very close to the Callahan family for several years, but when Kenneth Callahan began making cruel remarks about homosexuals in social situations, they slowly diminished their friendship.

By 1955, Spencer Pottery was located in the Seattle suburb of Tukwila. The Spencers were now recognized as being among the leading ceramic artists in the region. They participated in the highly regarded Northwest Craftsmen exhibitions at the University of Washington's Henry Art Gallery from 1955 to 1964, winning several awards.

They were also active members of the Clay Club, founded in 1948 in Seattle. The club's exhibitions, also held at the Henry Art Gallery, were extremely successful. The organization brought accomplished ceramic artists like Peter Voulkos to the Northwest to do demonstrations, lectures, and workshops. Other Clay Club members included Virginia Weisel and architect Robert Shields.

As advocates for the medium, Lorene taught pottery at Edison Technical School for four years beginning in 1952 and Ralph taught pottery in several Seattle schools from 1960 to 1963.

The Spencers received a number of commercial commissions, including ceramic works for the Washington State Library in Olympia as well as several for regional schools and churches. When they expanded their studio to include mail-order business, it increased sales and commissions from national and international customers. When the renowned Japanese ceramic artist Shoji Hamada (1894–1978) taught a summer course at UW in 1963, the Spencers attended. They invited him to their studio, where he purchased some of their work. The Spencers followed the example of Hamada, whose utilitarian production ware created at Mashiko, Japan, reflected their own interest in making utilitarian objects in an artistic manner. This was reinforced by Hamada's friend and colleague Bernard Leach, the other major influence on the Spencers; his interest in Mingei, the Japanese folk-art movement, was the model for their own business plan rather than a more exclusive focus on fine art.

Lorene Spencer (left) and life partner Ruth Henry, 2008
David Martin, photographer

"We like to have people pick up our pieces; to turn them over in their hands and feel the finish and weight and balance," Lorene wrote in 1956. "When we sell our ware at the Bellevue Arts & Crafts Fair for instance, we try to avoid giving our booth a museum-like, do-not-touch atmosphere. We want people to handle our things. They are for use, everyday use."

Lorene, who never lost interest in drawing and painting, joined the Northwest Watercolor Society in the 1950s. She exhibited her paintings with them from 1958 through 1971, winning several awards along the way. She also participated as a painter in the Northwest Annuals at the Seattle Art Museum. Her subject matter in the 1960s and '70s began to reflect her interest in social issues as well as the anti-war and women's movements.

During the summer months, the Spencers would sometimes set up small annexes of their pottery studio on Washington's Bainbridge and Whidbey Islands.

Lorene had solo exhibitions of her work at the Frye Art Museum and the Northwest Craft Center in Seattle, as well as the Museum of Contemporary Craft in Portland. She also exhibited at numerous small venues throughout the state.

After Ralph passed away in 1973, Lorene continued her own work in ceramics and created gift accessories out of her studio. She began a long-term relationship with Ruth Henry (1937–2012), living first in Olympia, and moving in 2008 to Apache Junction, Arizona, where they remained until their respective deaths.

SOURCES

Byron Fish, "Mud on Shoes? You Could Mold Pottery as Do Others Here," *Seattle Times*, Dec. 22, 1952, 8

Laurie Fish, "Couple's Pottery Hobby Turns into Thriving Business," *Seattle Times*, Nov. 11, 1956, 23

Elaine Fleming, "Creativity Cages Tukwila Family," *Auburn Globe-News*, Sept. 25, 1968, 9

Catherine B. Fisher, "Spencer Pottery—Tribute to Yank Ingenuity," *Highline Times*, Oct. 4, 1956, 10

The Ralph & Lorene Spencer Papers, Seattle Public Library

Personal friendship with Lorene Spencer

Lorene Spencer (1923–2016)
Untitled, circa 1966
Acrylic on panel
30 x 30 in.
Collection of the Museum
of History & Industry,
Seattle
2010.43.1

Lorene Spencer (1923–2016)
Pike Place Market series
Untitled (brothel), 1969–70
Ceramic, enamel, and
collage
6 x 9 x 8¾ in.
Collection of the Museum
of History & Industry,
Seattle
2010.43.4

Lorene Spencer (1923–2016)
Pike Place Market series
Paul's Wall, 1969–70
Ceramic, enamel, and
collage
6½ x 11 x 9½ in.
Collection of the Museum
of History & Industry,
Seattle
2010.43.10

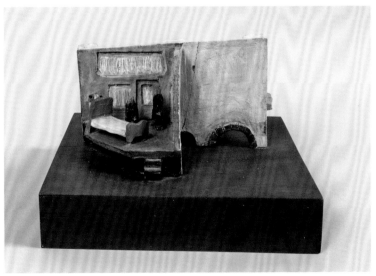

Lorene Spencer at the
pottery wheel, circa 1955
Courtesy of the Seattle
Public Library

Lorene Spencer (1923–2016)
Pitcher, circa 1955
9¾ x 6 in.
Private collection

Lorene Spencer (1923–2016)
Weed pot, circa 1960
7½ x 7 in.
Private Collection

Lorene Spencer (1923–2016)
Weed pot, circa 1955
5½ x 6 in.
Private Collection

Lorene Spencer (1923–2016)
Weed pot, circa 1960
6 x 6½ in.
Private collection

Lorene Spencer (1923–2016)
Bottle, 1971
11 x 8 in.
Private collection

Lorene Spencer (1923–2016)
and Ralph Spencer
(1914–1973)
Branch Bottle, 1959
15½ x 10 in.
Private Collection

Lorene Spencer (1923–2016)
Bottle, 1977
9½ x 7½ in.
Private collection

Ralph Spencer, circa 1955
Scan from slide
Martin-Zambito Archive

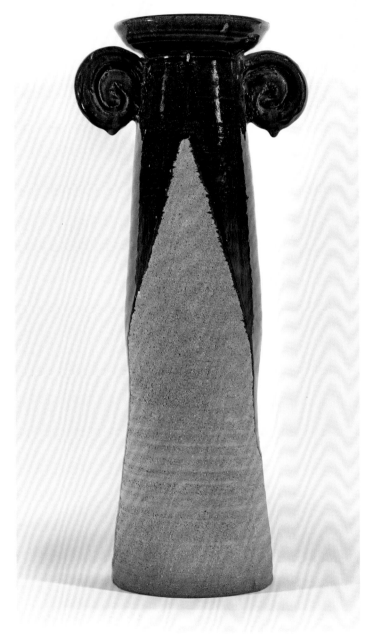

Lorene Spencer (1923–2016)
Vase, 1971
19 x 6 in.
Private collection

Lorene Spencer, circa 1955
Photo-booth photographs
Martin-Zambito Archive

Sarah Spurgeon
1903–1985

Edna May "Sarah" Spurgeon was born in Harlan, Iowa, where her father was a successful businessman and partner in the Trans-Mississippi Grain Elevator in Galva, Iowa. She graduated from Galva High School and then attended the University of Iowa, where she received her bachelor of arts degree and certificate of education in 1927 and, in 1931, a master of arts degree in the combined fields of graphic and plastic arts and in art history. Her thesis was titled "Decorative Figure Arrangement (a painted thesis)."

At the university, all four of her primary instructors were women: Ellen Thornberg, Irma Bratton, Catherine McCartney, and Alma Held.

Spurgeon continued her education at Harvard University under a Carnegie Fellowship for two summers in 1929 and 1930. At Harvard she attended one of the country's earliest museum studies programs under Paul J. Sachs (1878–1965). Around this time she also attended the Grand Central School of Art in New York, studying with George Oberteuffer (1878–1940) and with George Bridgman (1865–1943), known for his expertise in life drawing.

She then went on to teach at the University of Iowa for four years. During her time there she exhibited her oil paintings in national and regional exhibitions including the Corcoran Gallery, the Kansas City Art Institute, and the Joslyn Museum in Omaha, Nebraska, as well as winning several regional awards. In 1933, Spurgeon attended the Chicago World's Fair, A Century of Progress International Exposition. It was there that she first saw the paintings of Thomas Hart Benton (1889–1975), whose work she admired and was later influenced by, especially in the use of tempera as an artistic medium.

Her work was noticed by famed Iowa artist Grant Wood (1891–1942), and he hired her to assist him, along with other talented young artists, to create a series of murals for the Iowa State University library in Ames, Iowa, in 1934. The murals were commissioned under the Civil Works Administration as part of President Roosevelt's emergency employment New Deal programs. She also modeled for a few of the female figures in the murals. As she recalled, "All the boys put on jeans and I had an apron made out of old-fashioned dark blue calico. . . . Most of the people on the project were men. In fact I don't recall another woman besides myself being there in Iowa City."

In a 1964 interview recalling her time with Grant Wood she stated, "He was sort of chubby and colorless in appearance and a very quiet, very gentle person. His suggestions I'm sure were almost always well received because he was not aggressive in his promotion or criticism." Many of the techniques that she learned from the senior gay artist she continued to use in her own work and imparted to

Sarah Spurgeon outside the home that she designed and decorated with her life partner, Amanda Hebeler, circa 1960
Former collection of Robert Purser, scan provided by Martin-Zambito Archive

her students. One of the visiting artists invited by Wood to view the progress of the murals was Jean Charlot (1898–1979), an extremely talented muralist, who had worked primarily in Mexico and was admired and encouraged by Diego Rivera. Charlot's interaction with Spurgeon and the other young artists also made a lasting impression on her.

She told her interviewer, "I've lost Grant's recipe for priming and I wish I hadn't, because it was brilliantly white. I've never found anything to equal it. It was composed of zinc white in a powder form. Then it involved ammonia, and it was USP ammonia; it wasn't household ammonia, it was the pure quill. This was all put together hot. . . . So, that was one thing I learned—the mechanics of preparing a canvas. And that stayed with me. I have my students do that now. I don't have them buy a ready-prepared canvas. I have them build their own stretchers and put the canvas on, and then prime it. I feel that that [mural] experience was a very valuable introduction to the technology of painting. It meant a lot to my teaching, to my students. They get a lot out of that actual physical contact with the dimension and the size. Long before they paint on it; and I find that's one of the best routes into composition. It's a more natural route into composition than the design route." Following her experience with Wood, she produced her own mural, a map of Iowa City for the University Demonstration School that covered two walls measuring approximately twenty-two by eight feet.

In 1935, Spurgeon was hired to teach English at Buena Vista College in Storm Lake, Iowa. The school was only eighteen miles from her parents' home and both were suffering from serious health problems that concerned her. At the time, the school had no art department and she endeavored to start one. She became the only faculty member of the department and struggled to establish it, even doing some of the construction work for making the gallery into a space for exhibiting art. Since there were no funds available from the school, she used her own money to purchase basic art supplies for the students.

In 1939, Spurgeon moved to Ellensburg, Washington, to accept a position in the Art Department of Central Washington College of Education (now University). Around this time she began using Sarah as her given name, although she never legally changed it. In 1942 she took a two-and-a-half-year leave of absence to work for the Boeing Company as a production illustrator on the B-17 and B-29 aircrafts. She had attempted to join the military to serve in the war but was rejected. In Seattle she joined Women Painters of Washington and became involved in their exhibitions and lectures.

After the war, she returned to Ellensburg and resumed her position at the college. Sometime in the 1940s Spurgeon met fellow CWCE professor Amanda K. Hebeler (1890–1969), who had joined the faculty in 1924. Hebeler had earned her

BS and MS degrees from Columbia University, with graduate study at Yale and the University of Southern California. Director of the College Elementary School from 1929 until 1956, she was actively involved in numerous educational and cultural organizations in the region. She was professor of education from 1935 until her retirement as professor emeritus in 1960. In 1963 the school was renamed the Amanda Hebeler Elementary School (later named the Washington Center for Early Childhood Education). The school was closed in the spring of 1981. Today, Hebeler Hall at the university is named in her honor.

In 1954, Spurgeon painted a large modernist mural for the Ginkgo Petrified Forest Museum—now known as Ginkgo Petrified Forest Interpretive Center—near Vantage, on the Columbia River. She designed and executed the twenty-foot-wide interior mural, while architect Lionel Pries designed the exterior decorations at the entrance to the building. The petrified forest was discovered in 1931 by a fellow CWCE faculty member, geologist George F. Beck, whom she later memorialized in a portrait now in the university's collection.

After the mural was completed, she and Amanda spent three summer months in 1955 touring various cities in Italy.

Spurgeon went on to be a major force in the university's art department, and was a beloved teacher even though some of her students whimsically referred to her as "the general" for her strict professionalism. Her influence was acknowledged by her students in 1959, when the staff of the university's yearbook, the *Hyakem*, dedicated the book to her, stating, "Even more than a teacher is probably the best description that could be written of Miss Sarah Spurgeon, associate professor of art on Central's faculty. Even more than a teacher—a true inspiration to her present and her former students in this artist and art educator. . . . And, too, we want to dedicate our 1959 annual to this teacher who, no matter how busy she is, always makes it a point to have plenty of time, ample time, to listen with real under-standing and sympathetic interest to a student's problems, troubles, joys, sorrows, successes . . . dreams."

Her life partner, Amanda, passed away in 1969, and Spurgeon retired in 1971. A final tribute came in 1978 when Central Washington University celebrated the dedication of the Sarah Spurgeon Gallery with an exhibit featuring fifty-five of her former students.

Her last years were plagued with poor health, and she relied on former students and friends to assist her, especially the prominent regional artists Jane Orleman and her husband, Richard C. Elliott. Spurgeon passed away in October 1985, surrounded by loved ones and in the arms of her intimate friend, jewelry artist Ramona Solberg (1921–2005).

Spurgeon's mural for the University of Iowa as well as her mural and decora-tive work for the Ginkgo Petrified Forest Museum have been destroyed.

Neither Sarah's nor Amanda's obituary contained any mention of the other's name.

Jean-Antoine Watteau
(1684–1721)
Pierrot, formerly titled
Gilles, 1719
Oil on canvas
Musée du Louvre, Paris
Bequest of Dr. Louis
La Caze, 1869
Wikipedia, source: The
Yorck Project (2002), *10.000
Meisterwerke der Malerei*

Sarah Spurgeon
(1903–1985)
Untitled, circa 1935
Oil on canvas
25 x 20 in.
Yakima Valley Museum,
Yakima, WA, gift of Jane
Orleman
2012-099-001

Spurgeon based her
untitled painting on
Watteau's *Pierrot*, setting
herself in an Iowa
landscape around the
time she was working with
artist Grant Wood.

SOURCES

Spurgeon, Sarah, "Sarah Spurgeon interview" (1964), *CWU Retirement Association Interviews*, 85, http://digitalcommons.cwu.edu/cwura_interviews/85

Sarah Spurgeon Papers, Central Washington University Libraries, Special Collections

Interview with Jane Orleman, May 31, 2019

Peter Hastings Falk, *Who Was Who in American Art, 1564–1975: 400 Years of Artists in America*, vol. 3, (Madison, CT: Sound View Press, 1999)

E-mail correspondence with David McCartney, University Archivist, Dept. of Special Collections and University Archives, University of Iowa Libraries

Sarah Spurgeon, circa 1950
Former collection of
Robert Purser, scan
provided by Martin-
Zambito Archive

Amanda Hebeler (left) and
Sarah Spurgeon, circa 1960
(detail)
Courtesy of the Ellensburg
Public Library, Edna
May "Sarah" Spurgeon
Collection

Sarah Spurgeon and
Amanda Hebeler in the
kitchen of their Ellensburg
home, 1962
Courtesy of the Ellensburg
Public Library, Edna
May "Sarah" Spurgeon
Collection

Sarah Spurgeon
(1903–1985)
Untitled (Galva, Iowa),
circa 1934
Oil on canvas
18 x 20 in.
Yakima Valley Museum,
Yakima, WA, gift of Brian
and Sandra Bach
2014-090-003

Sarah Spurgeon
(1903–1985)
Storm Lake, Iowa, 1937
Oil on canvas
25⅛ x 29½ in.
Central Washington
University Permanent
Collection,
Ellensburg, WA

Sarah Spurgeon
(1903–1985)
In Extremis, 1970–80
Collage
8½ x 12 in.
Collection of Jane
Orleman and Richard C.
Elliott

Sarah Spurgeon, circa 1960
Courtesy of the Ellensburg
Public Library, Edna
May "Sarah" Spurgeon
Collection

Sarah Spurgeon in 1954,
working on her mural
for the Gingko Petrified
Forest Museum,
Vantage, Washington
Adding Rocks
Photograph, 1955
Courtesy of Archives
and Special Collections,
Central Washington
University, Ellensburg, WA

Postcard showing
the interior mural by
Sarah Spurgeon for the
Gingko Petrified Forest
Museum, Vantage, WA,
in 1954
Published by Ellis Postcard
Co., Arlington, WA
Original Ektachrome
photo by J. Boyd Ellis
Courtesy of the Ellensburg
Public Library, Edna
May "Sarah" Spurgeon
Collection

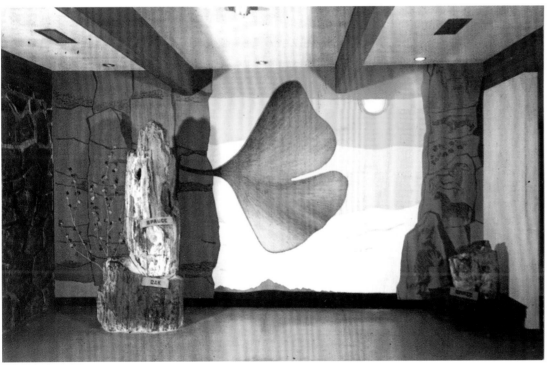

Sarah Spurgeon
(1903–1985)
*Portrait of Dr. George F.
Beck*, 1968
Oil on canvas
48 x 59⅞ in.
Central Washington
University Permanent
Collection,
Ellensburg, WA

George F. Beck was a
professor of geology at
Central Washington
University known for
establishing the Ginkgo
Petrified Forest State Park
in Vantage, Washington.

Sarah Spurgeon
(1903–1985)
Self-portrait, circa 1942
Pastel
19 x 24¾ in.
Collection of Jane
Orleman and Richard C.
Elliott

Virginia Van Winkle Weisel was born in Seattle, the youngest of three children. After graduating from Roosevelt High School, she attended the University of Washington from 1942 through 1944, but then interrupted her education to serve in the Women's Army Corps during World War II. After her military service, Virginia returned to the UW, working for several years at the University Book Store to assist with her tuition. She received her BA in painting in 1950, and in 1951 won the university's first School of Art Award for Outstanding Work.

At the UW, Virginia had studied under the acclaimed Swiss ceramic artist Paul Bonifas, and she became his teaching assistant from 1952 to 1954. In the latter year, she won Honorable Mention for a ceramic wine set exhibited in the *Northwest Craftsmen's Exhibition* at the Henry Art Gallery.

After moving briefly to New York City to pursue a career as a painter, she returned to the West Coast and received a teaching fellowship in ceramics at Mills College in Oakland, California, studying with Elena Netherby and assisting her instructor, Antonio Prieto, before receiving her MFA in 1956.

She then reentered the military and served as an area crafts supervisor, Special Services, in Ascom City, South Korea. During this time, she began a relationship with another service member whom she met through the Red Cross, Aurilla Marie Doerner (1932–1996), who was originally from San Francisco.

While in Korea, Virginia studied that country's extraordinary ceramic history, which became a substantial influence on her work, especially in her earlier years of production. After serving for one year, she traveled with "Rilla" throughout Asia and Europe, studying art for six months, before settling back in the Northwest. They originated a pottery studio called the Kiln that operated in Bellevue, Washington, from 1958 until 1962. The studio gave classes and produced utilitarian and artistic pottery aimed at the general public.

During this period Weisel exhibited at the University of Washington's Henry Art Gallery and through various crafts-oriented organizations, becoming one of the region's most prominent ceramic artists. She did not rely solely on regional support, stating, "I'll load up my car every once in a while and head for other cities, contacting other sales possibilities."

The two women moved to Oakland in 1963, but returned to the Seattle area in 1967. While Virginia pursued her ceramic production, Rilla created a sound financial base for the couple by working for Nordstrom's department store and becoming a successful insurance professional with Mutual of Omaha. This allowed Virginia to work unencumbered and promote her art. One of her unique lead-glazed stoneware bottles even appeared in the December 1966 issue of *House*

Beautiful magazine's annual holiday "Boutique for the Home" section, giving her national exposure.

In 1971, Virginia ceased her ceramic production to concentrate on sculpture in wood, stone, and bronze. She began by studying with and assisting Oregon sculptor Leroy Setziol (1915–2005). Highly influenced by British sculptors Henry Moore and Barbara Hepworth, Weisel's organic, biomorphic shapes integrated well into the Northwest design aesthetic. As with her ceramics, she became very successful in her new medium, selling briskly through Seattle's Foster/White Gallery and Gump's department store in San Francisco.

Virginia Weisel (left) and Rilla Doerner in Italy, 1957–58
Courtesy of the family of Virginia Weisel

In October 1973, Virginia met one of her longtime artistic inspirations, Dame Barbara Hepworth. She visited the eminent sculptor at her studio in St. Ives, Cornwall, for a brief meeting and conversation. Upon her return to Seattle, Virginia sent Hepworth one of her ceramic bird feeders made during the previous decade, as well as a silk Japanese coat. Hepworth responded, "I cannot thank you enough as nothing could have been found for me which could give more pleasure and hope for the New Year." Tragically, Hepworth would die in an accidental fire in her studio on May 20, 1975, less than two years after Weisel's visit.

Because of Rilla's sound financial investments, the two women were able to move in 1982 to Sonoma, California, where they built a house with a studio large enough to accommodate Virginia's sculpting.

Rilla assisted other professional women in the area with business and financial decisions, and she and Virginia became active with local cultural organizations, indulging Virginia's love of opera and volunteering with the Quarryhill Botanical Garden in the Sonoma Valley.

In 1996, after suffering from health problems, Rilla shockingly ended her own life, resulting in Virginia falling into a deep depression that put an end to her artistic output. Her health declined as well, and after a home accident, she was hospitalized in 2005. With assistance from friends and family, Virginia was able to remain in her home until 2015, when she was moved to a residential care facility in Sonoma. She died on June 28, 2017, at the age of ninety-four.

At Virginia's request, she was cremated, with half her ashes buried along with her family at Lakeview Cemetery in Seattle. The remaining ashes were scattered on Puget Sound, where Rilla's ashes had been released after her death. Her friends and family released her remains at Three Tree Point on August 3, 2018, with a vodka toast to a life well lived.

SOURCES

Interviews with Weisel's niece Patsy Snyder and cousin Thula Weisel, Nov. 20, 2018

Interview with Virginia Weisel by Polly Rawn, *Puget Soundings*, Art Issue, Apr. 1959, 17

Virginia Weisel's personal archive held by her family

Virginia Weisel
(1923–2017)
Vase with floral motif,
circa 1955
5 x 5 in.
Collection of Thula
Weisel

Virginia Weisel
(1923–2017)
Vase with dogwood
motif, circa 1955
8¾ x 4 in.
Collection of Thula
Weisel

Virginia Weisel
(1923–2017)
Bottle, circa 1958
10 x 6½ in.
Collection of Thula
Weisel

Virginia Weisel
(1923–2017)
Covered casserole, circa
1958
7 x 14¾ in.
Commissioned by
LaMar Harrington
Private collection

Virginia Weisel
(1923–2017)
Bottle, circa 1960
6 x 5 in.
Private collection

Virginia Weisel forming
a vessel, circa 1958
Courtesy of the family of
Virginia Weisel

Virginia Weisel
(1923–2017)
Bottle, circa 1960
6 x 5 in.
Private collection

Virginia Weisel
(1923–2017)
Bottle, circa 1968
5¾ x 5 in.
Private collection

Virginia Weisel at Ascom
City, South Korea, 1957
Courtesy of the family of
Virginia Weisel

From left: Henry Lin,
Virginia Weisel wearing
her handwoven vest,
Robert Sperry, and Hazel
Koenig, 1958
Courtesy of the family of
Virginia Weisel

Virginia Weisel
at Williams Field,
Chandler, Arizona, 1946
Courtesy of the family of
Virginia Weisel

Virginia Weisel incising a
large bowl, 1956
Courtesy of the family of
Virginia Weisel

Various bottles made by
Virginia Weisel at Mills
College, 1956
Courtesy of the family of
Virginia Weisel

Virginia Weisel
(1923–2017)
Bottle, circa 1968
7 x 5 in.
Collection of Ashford
Creek Pottery and
Museum

Virginia Weisel
(1923–2017)
Bottle, circa 1968
4 x 4½ in.
Private collection

Virginia Weisel
(1923–2017)
Bottle, circa 1968
4 x 4 in.
Private collection

Virginia Weisel
(1923–2017)
The Embrace, 1973
Elm
16 in.
Collection of Mel and
Leena Sturman

Virginia Weisel
(1923–2017)
Opus 1, 1972
Chinese elm
11¼ x 9¼ in.
Collection of Lindsey
and Carolyn Echelbarger

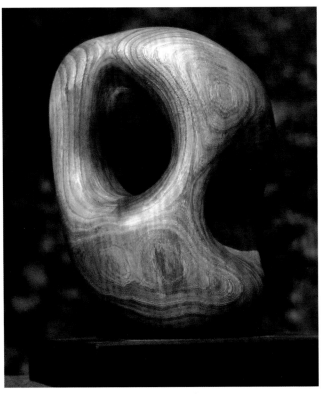

Virginia Weisel
(1923–2017)
Contortion #2, 1986
Alabaster
13 x 6 in.
Collection of Lindsey
and Carolyn Echelbarger

Virginia Weisel
(1923–2017)
Magnetic Moment, 1986
Black walnut
13 x 7 x 6 in.
Collection of Thula
Weisel

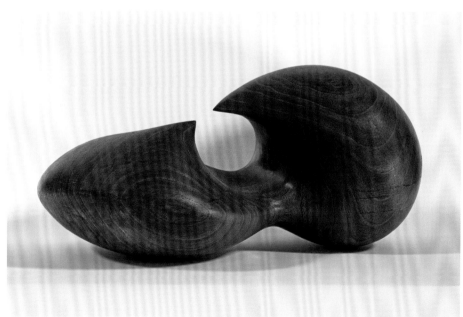

Clifford Wright

1919–1999

"I would soon learn that this versatile fellow named Clifford Wright, with whom I instantly became friends, saw his job not only as making guests comfortable and listening to their problems, as he did mine, but making love to everyone who seemed to need it, both men and women. He also claimed to masturbate four times a day, often on his paintings, which lay scattered over the floor of his studio and which he would pick up from time to time and daub at, paint mixing in with semen, something of which Clifford, a rather juicy-looking fellow, had plenty!" —Edward Field

Charles Clifford Wright was born in Seattle to Finnish immigrants Arvid Kallunki and Edith Pekkanen. His birth name was Oswald Kallunki.

According to one of Wright's friends, the writer Edward Field, Wright located his birth parents through the Red Cross and found that his biological father had given him and his siblings up for adoption, unable to care for them as a single father after the early death of his biological mother. Young Clifford was soon adopted by a Seattle couple, Charles P. and Bertha May Wright.

His early art training was at the Cornish School (now Cornish College of the Arts), where he studied with Mark Tobey and Walter O. Reese.

After befriending several of the prominent gay artists in Seattle, including Tobey and Morris Graves, he was given a position as an assistant at the Seattle Art Museum in the early 1940s.

In 1945, Wright's painting *Growth & Disintegration of Plants* was accepted into the Seattle Art Museum's Northwest Annual, the most prestigious regional art exhibition at the time. With other concerned artists, he donated one of his paintings to an anti-fascist fundraising art auction held on May 22, 1945, to benefit Spanish refugees living in France. This event was sponsored by the Frederick & Nelson department store in downtown Seattle. By the end of the year, he was given a solo exhibition at SAM that ran from December 5, 1945, through January 6, 1946.

In July 1946, Frederick & Nelson's Little Gallery of Northwest Art assembled a traveling exhibition of prominent Washington State artists to be displayed at the Chicago gallery of Marshall Field & Company, the parent company of F&N. Besides Wright's work, the exhibit featured other celebrated local figures such as Graves, Tobey, Peggy Strong, Kenneth Callahan, and Ebba Rapp.

In the fall of that year, Wright headed for New York to pursue his dream of becoming a successful artist. Being an outgoing and charismatic person and with some connections from his friendships with Tobey and Graves, he made important social and artistic connections, especially in gay circles.

In 1947 he was awarded his first residency at Yaddo, an artists' community in Sarasota Springs, New York, just 160 miles north of Manhattan. His stay was so successful that he returned the following year to be the assistant to Elizabeth Ames (1885–1977), who was executive director of Yaddo from 1924 until 1969.

Within this creative environment and with financial assistance for materials, Wright continued to work and to expand his social and professional contacts. Back in Seattle, his work was included in a successful group exhibition in February 1947 at F&N's Little Gallery, whose influential director, Theodora Lawrenson Harrison (1890–1969), was a champion of talented young artists. He also received his first important national exposure in the December 1947 issue of *Magazine of Art*, in an article entitled "Clifford Wright: A Painter of the Grotesque," by Anita Moore.

Clifford Wright, circa 1945
Photograph by Frank Murphy
Martin-Zambito Archive

"In the Northwest, from which an ever-widening stream of talent seems to spring," she wrote, "there is a young Surrealist painter, Charles Clifford Wright, who at the ripe age of twenty-six is represented in a number of private collections, has had two one-man shows in his native Seattle, is now preparing for another in San Francisco and Salt Lake City.

"His paintings are full of vitriolic satire which comes as a distinct shock to the average observer, a disturbing menace to peace of mind. His pointed remarks, made through scathing line and color, relentlessly pierce one's complacence."

Wright's paintings are likely the result of post–World War II angst, although his work, grotesque as it may have appeared, had influences ranging from the Belgian painter James Ensor (1860–1949) to Japanese shunga to the erotic frescoes in Pompeii and Herculaneum, whose decaying surfaces are not unlike Wright's scraped and layered textures.

Edward Field described thus Wright's early years at Yaddo: "Arriving at the back door of the Yaddo mansion, I was met by Clifford Wright, a large, fair-haired, Scandinavian American painter who served as the host, greeting new guests and making them comfortable, in return for which he got room and board plus a tiny stipend for his art supplies. . . . The ritual of the Yaddo day was much like that on an ocean liner. And as on a sea voyage there were sudden love affairs that often ended in broken hearts before the arrival in port. Clifford Wright, resident stud, helped to console these unfortunates by listening to their miseries or, if possible, with his fat prick."

Wright's career was poised for success when in 1948 his painting *Man with Blue Dog* was included in the Whitney Museum's Annual Exhibition of Contemporary American Sculpture, Watercolors and Drawings. This was followed by two solo exhibitions in New York at the prestigious Weyhe Gallery in 1949 and the Delius Gallery in 1950. He was beginning to be collected by distinguished art professionals, such as Arthur Everett "Chick" Austin Jr. (1900–1957), the prescient director of the Wadsworth Atheneum, as well as by fellow artists, including Seattle friends Tobey and Graves, each of whom was at the height of his national career.

In 1949, Wright became an unwitting target in a political battle at Yaddo instigated by poet Robert Lowell.

Edward Field recalled, "Things had hardly settled down at the time of my arrival from a scandal that had erupted the year before. Poet Robert Lowell, who was subject to mental breakdowns, had telephoned the FBI that Yaddo was a nest of Communist subversives, and in the paranoia of the time, the Feds had swooped down in a raid, carting Clifford Wright off to jail and confiscating his address book, which left him terrified, since it was full of his gay friends, most of them in the closet in those dark days when being a homosexual was as risky as being a commie. Clifford's background check revealed, not that he was a Communist, but that he had deserted the army—he explained to me later that he didn't see any reason to stay in the army once the war was over and just took off. It demanded all of Elizabeth Ames's considerable powers to get him out of jail."

Wright's open attitude about sex, perhaps informed by his Seattle artist friends—like Morris Graves, whose polyamorous nonconformity is well documented —led him to physical intimacy with both men and women. Some of his conquests, like poet Ralph Pomeroy (1926–1999), formed an emotional and sexual attachment to Wright, while others, like the British writer Marc Brandel (1919–1994), had kinky leanings that were not to Wright's tastes. Wright's undated diary entry about Brandel stated, "My red headed novelist colleague has flown his colors and it was discovered that he was the favorite tart in his English boy's school, that he was brought to America by the secretary to Neville Chamberlain (from whom he swiped one thousand bucks and whipped off to Mexico), that he is sadistic with women (he brought his jointed whipping cane with him), that he offers to make me do until a suitable female arrives. Though he is a jolly companion, I gently rejected his kind proposal."

In the summer of 1952, Wright met the Danish essayist Elsa Gress (1918–1988), who was at Yaddo on a fellowship. The two formed a close bond and became good friends.

With his painting career going strong, his offbeat subject matter was an improbable choice for inclusion in the Second International Hallmark Art Award traveling exhibition for his painting *A Christmas Picture*, which won him a hundred-dollar award. The exhibition began in 1952 and traveled to large venues including the Carnegie Institute in Pittsburg, the Institute of Contemporary Art in Boston, and the California Palace of the Legion of Honor in San Francisco, ending up in his hometown of Seattle in June 1954 at the University of Washington's Henry Art Gallery.

By 1955, Wright's time at Yaddo had ended and he was beginning to attempt to connect with his birth family. He returned to the West Coast at the behest of his biological father, who gave him enough money to travel to Finland to meet family members and become acquainted with his cultural heritage. In a lapse of judgment, he embarked on his journey with a hunky male lover, who unfortunately abandoned him and stole most of his money, leaving Wright stranded in Scandinavia.

He contacted his friend Elsa Gress, who was then living in a small apartment on Teglgårdsstræde in central Copenhagen. Within weeks, the two were married.

In 1957 the couple rented an apartment on the Amagerbrogade on Copenhagen's island of Amager.

It was here that they had two children and Clifford also adopted Elsa's son from a previous relationship. In 1962 he published a book on his perceptions of American art titled *The Hero of the New World*, issued in Danish by Borgens Forlag. He augmented his income by working as a commercial illustrator and designer of book jackets.

After a few years, the family moved to an abandoned village schoolhouse in Åsø. Inspired by their time at Yaddo, they developed an artist residency that they named "De-center," which was self-funded but soon ran out of money.

In 1972, Count Peter Moltke offered them the use of a house at his estate Marienborg on the island of Moen, where they remained until 1981, when they moved to another donated space.

In 1985, Wright's work was presented once again in the US in a three-person exhibition at New York's Fischbach Gallery titled *A New Romanticism: The Unworldly, the Unknowable, the Unspeakable*. Three years later, he exhibited at the House of Denmark on the Champs-Élysées in Paris.

Along with his fine art, Wright's commercial output included theater designs as well as creating posters for the Danish State Railways. In 1989 he completed his final project, decorating the railroad station in Sønderborg.

Clifford Wright died on September 30, 1999, in Damsholte on the island of Moen, Denmark.

SOURCES

Numerous e-mail exchanges with the artist's son, Jonathan Wright

Anita Moore, "Clifford Wright: A Painter of the Grotesque," *Magazine of Art*, Dec. 1947

Edward Field, *The Man Who Would Marry Susan Sontag and Other Intimate Literary Portraits of the Bohemian Era* (Madison, WI: University of Wisconsin Press, 2005)

E-mail correspondence with Edward Field, Nov. 9, 2019, and January 21, 2020

Copy of a diary excerpt from Wright's woodpecker painting dated May 3, 1948, and affixed to the back of the painting's frame

http://arslonga.dk/Clifford_Wright.htm

Seattle Daily Times, May 6, 1945, 27

Clifford Wright (1919–1999)
Merry Christmas, 1953
Mixed media
24 x 20 in.
Collection of Jonathan
Wright

Clifford Wright (1919–1999)
Untitled, verso of *Merry
Christmas*, 1950–60
Collage
24 x 20 in.
Collection of Jonathan
Wright

Clifford Wright (1919–1999)
Merry Christmas, circa 1952
Mixed media
24 x 20 in.
Collection of Jonathan
Wright

Clifford Wright (1919–1999)
Untitled, verso of *Merry
Christmas*, 1950–60
Collage
24 x 20 in.
Collection of Jonathan
Wright

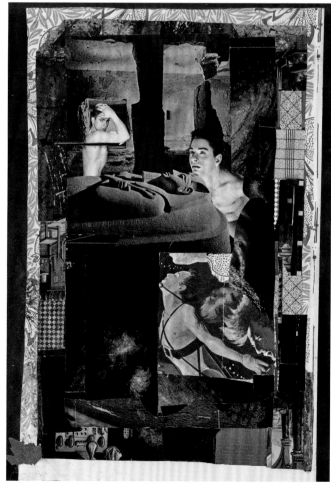

Clifford Wright (1919–1999)
Bob Crabshaw, 1945–50
Tempera
24 x 20 in.
Collection of Jonathan
Wright

Clifford Wright (1919–1999)
Self-Portrait, 1945–50
Tempera
24 x 20 in.
Collection of Jonathan
Wright

Clifford Wright (1919–1999)
The Bye By By Camel, 1948
Tempera and ink
12 x 16 in.
Collection of Jonathan
Wright

Clifford Wright (1919–1999)
Untitled, 1984
Mixed media
24½ x 32⅞ in.
Collection of Jonathan
Wright

Clifford Wright (1919–1999)
Untitled, 1945–50
Ink
20¼ x 23⅞ in.
Collection of Jonathan
Wright

Clifford Wright (1919–1999)
Untitled, 1945–50
Mixed media
24 x 20 in.
Collection of Jonathan
Wright

Clifford Wright (1919–1999)
Untitled, 1945–50
Mixed media
24 x 18 in.
Collection of Jonathan
Wright

Clifford Wright (1919–1999)
Untitled, 1945–50
Mixed media
20¼ x 23⅞ in.
Collection of Jonathan
Wright

Clifford Wright (1919–1999)
Untitled, 1945–50
Tempera
35 x 24 in.
Collection of Jonathan
Wright

Clifford Wright (1919–1999)
Untitled (eight figures),
1945–50
Mixed media
36¼ x 27½ in
Collection of Jonathan
Wright

This catalog was produced in conjunction with the exhibition *The Lavender Palette: Gay Culture and the Art of Washington State*, Cascadia Art Museum, October 24, 2019–January 26, 2020.

Front cover: Delbert J. McBride (1920–1998), untitled, circa 1930, watercolor and gouache, 15¼ x 11 in., private collection

Back cover: Howard Harsch Studio, silhouette portrait of Jule and Orlena, circa 1930, photograph courtesy of Gretchen Harsch

Frontispiece: Orre Nelson Nobles (1894–1967), rug designed for the Fette-Li Company, Peking (detail), circa 1930, 83 x 49 in., private collection

Page 4: Thomas Handforth (1897–1948), untitled, circa 1940, watercolor, 24 x 18 in., collection of the Tacoma Public Library

Page 10: Jon Arnt (1906–1982), *Portrait of Robert Joffrey*, circa 1952, gelatin silver print with texture screen, 9½ x 7½ in., private collection

Note on photo captions: if no photographer is listed, the photographer is unknown.

Designed by Phil Kovacevich
Copyedited by Nick Allison
Proofread by Carrie Wicks

Printed in Italy

ISBN: 978-0-9989112-2-9

Cascadia Art Museum
190 Sunset Ave. #E
Edmonds, WA 98020
425.336.4809
CascadiaArtMuseum.org